Management – Culture – Interpretation

Edited by
Andreas P. Müller
Stephan Sonnenburg

The book series of the Karlshochschule International University explores new ideas and approaches to management, organizations and economy from a cultural and interpretive point of view. The series intends to integrate different perspectives towards economy, culture and society. Therefore, management and organizational activities are not seen as being isolated from their context, but rather as context-bound and dependent on their surrounding cultures, societies and economies. Within these contexts, activities make sense through the allocation, the interpretation and the negotiation of meanings. Sense-making can be found in performative processes as well as the way social meaning is constructed through interactions. The series seeks innovative approaches, both in formulating new research questions and in developing adequate methodological research designs. We welcome contributions from different interdisciplinary and collective ways of thinking and seeking knowledge which focus on the integration of "Management – Culture – Interpretation".

Edited by
Prof. Dr. Andreas P. Müller
Prof. Dr. Stephan Sonnenburg

Karlsruhe, Germany

Andreas P. Müller • Lutz Becker (Eds.)

Narrative and Innovation

New Ideas for Business
Administration, Strategic
Management and Entrepreneurship

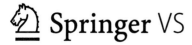
Springer VS

Editors
Prof. Dr. Andreas P. Müller
Prof. Dr. Lutz Becker

Karlsruhe, Germany

ISBN 978-3-658-01374-5   ISBN 978-3-658-01375-2 (eBook)
DOI 10.1007/978-3-658-01375-2

The Deutsche Nationalbibliothek lists this publication in the Deutsche Nationalbibliografie; detailed bibliographic data are available in the Internet at http://dnb.d-nb.de.

Library of Congress Control Number: 2013931202

Springer VS
© Springer Fachmedien Wiesbaden 2013

Printed on acid-free paper

Springer VS is a brand of Springer DE.
Springer DE is part of Springer Science+Business Media.
www.springer-vs.de

Contents

Outlook

Foreword

Every revolution was first a thought in one man's mind.
Ralph Waldo Emerson (1803-1882)

The whole thing began when Lutz Becker and Andreas Müller intensively started discussing Bruce Sterling's constructivist ideas and motifs expressed in his novel "Zeitgeist". A key concept in the novel is the major consensus narrative, a converging discursive construction of social reality.

Is reality a narrative construction? Would it possible to extract trends in society and economy from these narratives? Which narratives are really relevant? The ones spoken in the media, the chats in the supermarket or the narratives in industrial assembly lines? Would it be possible to extract trends from these narratives? Could it be a new approach to early recognition in business and society? Could innovation be derived from these narratives?

While reflecting on research approaches and opportunities as well as methods and applications for the real business world, the discussion between us both – Andreas has a background in linguistics and cultural anthropology and Lutz a background in economics and a professional career in the IT and media business – produced an overwhelming stream of ideas, questions, and perspectives. Indeed, Lutz had conducted research on early recognition in the 1980s and 1990s and Andreas has a long track record in analyzing the discourses in industrial organizations. It felt like we were opening Pandora's box.

We tried to share our Pandora's box by writing a first article on the topic (Becker and Müller 2010). Nevertheless we had the feeling (and still have) that we were only scratching the surface. That's why we decided to organize a scientific conference at Karlshochschule International University: Narrative and Innovation. Our question was: "How can innovation be derived from societal narratives and how can these narratives contribute to industrial and social innovation?"

Contributors and participants from all over the world reflected on the broad (and also ambiguous) topic. The faculty met the business community; experts in linguistics met experts in organizational theory. The topics and outcomes of the conference were really surprising and exciting for us. The contributors addressed issues we had not even thought of when planning the conference. Deep-diving research met truly hands-on business.

Our book on "Narrative and Innovation" firstly gives an overview of the discussion during the conference. Secondly, Mihai Nadin, who contributed with an additional article, completes the reflections on the current state of research. Last but not least, the narrative itself was included in the book; therefore, we agreed with three keynote speakers, Florian Menz, and Alfred Kieser together with Suleika Bort, to publish their contributions in the form of a post-conference interview.

The book gives both academia and the business community a first overview of a newly emerging and, we believe, pathbreaking and trendsetting research topic. In a next step we will perform research on the development, application and improvement of suitable methods, both in research and industry.

Karlsruhe, December 2012   Lutz Becker & Andreas P. Müller

Becker, Lutz/Müller, Andreas P. (2010): Über Narrative und Diskurse Innovationschancen aufspüren. In: Gundlach, Carsten/Gutsche, Jens/Glanz, Axel (eds.) (2010): Die frühe Innovationsphase – Methoden und Strategien für die Vorentwicklung. Düsseldorf: Symposion, pp. 211-245.

Theoretical Approach

Narrative & Innovation

Lutz Becker and Andreas P. Müller

Mid-December 2008 – it is the height of the "mortgage crisis" and the German Government's leading economist, Bert Rürup, confesses that the economic prediction models have failed. Another economist, Peter Bofinger, expresses much the same opinion in the media at the time. Thomas Straubhaar, also an expert, puts it in a nutshell: "We have all failed. None of us anticipated the magnitude of the recession. On the other hand, the crisis started in a unique way and at such a speed that it would have been impossible to predict it with our traditional research approaches. Our current models fail for crises of this magnitude" (Straubhaar 2009).

When searching for the first warnings of the economic crisis, a number of signals could already be observed in 2003/2004, accompanied by discussions about a looming crisis in relevant internet forums, for example. Indeed, Guido Hülsmann, a professor in Anger, France, and the Karlsruhe-based lawyer, Harald Wozniewski, had been expressing concerns about structural problems in the world economy and an eventual breakdown for several years, albeit justifying their opinions with different arguments (Hülsmann 2007; Wozniewski 2007).

Stories of this kind raise interesting questions. Is there such a thing as emergent narratives that anticipate social, political or economic upheavals? Can these be operationalized and how can they be operationalized? Would it have been possible to deter the 2008 crash and its aftermath or, at least, to prepare the economy in good time, if the words of warning had been taken seriously? If failures of models, inaccuracies of predictions, collapses in plans are the norm in a complex and dynamic world, and if narratives and discourses move faster than facts and models, this has interesting consequences. We will take it a step further: What if the knowledge embedded in these narratives could be exploited for economic purposes? And to continue a step even further: Can these stories be operationalized in order to develop technical and social innovations and be put to use within innovation systems? These are the questions that we will explore in the following.

Early detection and "weak signals" as a basis for decisions

In 1976, against the backdrop of the 1970s oil crisis, an article is published by H. Igor Ansoff (1918-2002), an American of Russian descent, focuses on the issue of strategic surprises as well as on the weak signals that possibly precede these surprises, and as a result advances the hypothesis that strategic early detection may be possible (Ansoff 1976). According to Ansoff, "strategic preparedness" is the key – avoiding strategic surprises "before the fact", that is before the discontinuities penetrate the organizations and their environment. "If we can succeed in recognizing and processing weak signals, it will shorten the time it takes to identify the problem, gaining time for targeted action, as opposed to reaction under high time pressure" (Bea and Haas 2005: 302, our translation).

There are two basic prerequisites for this: *First,* the perception or recognition of weak signals (scanning) and, *second,* the processing and in-depth relevant analysis (monitoring) (Bea and Haas 2005). The real challenge, however, is that the information necessary for early detection – information about emerging dis-continuities and upheavals – is not located in the core of the information. It can be found in the "weak signals" located on the periphery; these signals rarely reach the receiver via formal information channels, such as monthly reports, SWOT analyses or balanced scorecards (Becker 1993).

And this is exactly the crux of weak signals: It has not been possible to date to predict with a reasonable degree of certainty what or what not can be considered a weak signal. This is because information of this kind is poorly structured, and the receiver is in an extreme state of ignorance (Müller 1987).

This fundamental problem cannot be solved by increasingly efficient information processing systems and methods, as algorithmization or consolidation of data is often performed at the expense of weak, peripheral or implicit information. In this way, the same Cartesian reductionist mechanisms take effect: "However, while reductionism involves concentrating on parts of the information in order to understand the big picture – i.e., in order to establish the rationality of things – it overlooks the connections between the parts and their importance. In the final analysis, complexity is sacrificed at the expense of the rationality of reductionism and deterministic causality, which is expressed in the sequence of cause and effect" (Nadin 2002: 22, our translation). Instead of focusing on superficial cause/effect relations, we deal with phenomena such as the parallelism of causes and the reverse effects in socio-technical and socio-economic systems (Becker 2008). The term created by Frank Schätzing "Kausalitätenfilz" or "interwoven causalities" (Schätzing 2006) best reflects the problem: In complex dynamic worlds, the answers are not always so simple that they can be presented in a spreadsheet.

Once changes in data start appearing in IT systems, we can no longer calmly talk about "weak signals" or even early detection. The argument that the current data of a corporate IT system always provides a retrospective overview clearly demonstrates the dimension of the problem. The available stock of knowledge is often a hermetic and non-convertible mass. The majority of forecasting and planning procedures are grounded on an interpretation of the past and its more or less linear continuation into the future – and, thus, based on the hope that our experience and interpretation are also valid with regard to the future. We project what we have seen in our rear view mirror onto the road in front of us. However, provisions are not made for instability, discontinuities, fluctuations, crises, knock-on effects and upheavals such as tsunamis, exploding space shuttles, manipulated Iraq files, the Lehmann bankruptcy and security leaks at Wikileaks. The declarations of capitulation made by Bert Rürup, Thomas Straubhaar [and other 15 economists] (Heuser 2008) speak volumes. Yet even if we disregard extreme discontinuities of this kind, the typical quantitative methods only provide a superficial and, hence, potentially dangerous certainty. As economist Joachim Starbatty puts it, "Economists notice increasingly little of what is going on around them. They reduce economic reality to statistical time series. These can help us to explain what happened in the past, but do not help us recognize what is brewing. Things that are not dealt with in fashionable mathematically formulated models no longer exist" (Starbatty 2008, our translation).

In order to avoid misunderstandings: In spite of our somewhat provocative statements, we do not wish to criticize the exceptional, useful and important work of colleagues. On the contrary, we urgently need these models; their findings provide us – as entrepreneurs, scientists, politicians and citizens – with some orientation in a complex world. However, there is no doubt that they merely present certain perspectives that bring us closer to a possible reality. In the words of Alfred Korzybski (1958), "The map is not the territory". The models and their results interpret events from specific and, as a result, limited perspectives, thus enabling additional constructions and interpretations of reality. No more and no less. And this is exactly what we hope to provide with our model – additional understanding and orientation.

The central question here is: How can we improve and better instrumentalize perception? We are primarily interested in what H. Igor Ansoff refers to as first-level information or "common knowledge" – information obtained by word-of-mouth or from publications (Ansoff 1976). We assume that information of this kind gradually diffuses its way into the in-system of the organization from "contextual" or "transactional environments" (Ramirez and van der Heyden 2007), hereby losing "weakness" (diffusivity and ambiguity) and, at the same time, becoming stronger, more precise, concrete and critical – but also more worthless.

When information has already become common knowledge, the strategic benefit and the resulting innovation potential derived from it are marginal at best. Indeed, as formulated in Rumelt's proposition, "The more public the information, the longer the information has existed, the more stable the trends, and the more analysis done on the information, the less the opportunity for profit from the information" (Rumelt 1996: 552, orig. in italics).

In the light of this dilemma, we are above all interested in myths, shared world views and subjective realities manifested in these communication processes, as well as in what Bruce Sterling (Sterling 2000) refers to as a change in the "consensus narrative". How can we identify shifts in the "consensus narrative" at an early stage in order to develop innovation systems and, more importantly, options for success?

Strategy and innovation

Innovation is not an end in itself, but should always be measured against its viability, or against the organization's success and rationalization criteria in a given situation (Becker 2008).

Consequently, we are not primarily concerned with innovation in an engineering sense, i.e., new products and processes, or even a singular invention by a singular inventor. Indeed, in recent years another concept of innovation has taken centre stage. Innovation has left its core area – the laboratories and research and development departments. Today we talk about open innovation, supra-company innovation and marketing innovation, organizational innovation, social innovation, and management innovation. In a complex and dynamic society such as ours, innovation has moved away from being merely technical breakthroughs and towards being a strategically planned business venture (Müller-Kirschbaum and Wuhrmann 2008). Thus, innovations are no longer only the product of the corporate inventors: the "brains" and "eggheads" in the laboratories. Innovations traverse the entire organization, also encompassing suppliers, clients and stakeholders – the entire corporate environment. (Becker 2008) In consequence, we see strategy and innovation as two sides of the same coin. Strategies are inconceivable without innovation. On the other hand, innovation can only function if it is integrated in a strategic context; exceptions may confirm the rule.

Innovation is therefore part of a complex strategic constellation with a multitude of feedback processes and the goal of preparing the organization for a possible future and continuing to develop business (business development management).

Richard P. Rumelt from the Anderson School of Management says, that business strategy operates on the very edge of what can be understood (Rumelt 1996). Thus, completely new innovation and strategy constellations emerge as cultural offers for society: "Strategic programmes of companies are communication offers for society, of how things should be seen and how society should continue to develop" (Pfriem 2004: 400, our translation). Developing and implementing an offer of this kind requires knowledge and understanding of the concrete mechanisms that make up culture in general and also, more specifically, of cultural conditions and paths. This is based on the hypothesis that the business venture (or any other form of organization in society) is devoid of intentions or an own awareness. Cognitive performance is produced in the process of communicative collaboration of actors within the organization and its environment (stakeholders) (Rusch 2006).

Furthermore, we assume that there is an intrinsic tension between the necessity to innovate and the innovation aspirations of the actors within the organization, on the one hand, and the maintenance of the status quo by (possibly the same) actors, on the other hand: the state of being torn "between *transformation and stabilization*" (Becker 2008). Innovations can only be achieved if one can be connected to the other: "It has to be sufficiently radical for it to be considered an innovation. The degree of radicality must be sufficiently low for it to receive the necessary acceptance and to be implemented" (Pfriem 2006: 212, our translation). Reality is not simply what it is, but the way we communicate it. Heinz von Foerster (von Foerster 2008: 59) summarizes this in a formula:

$$\text{"reality} = \text{community"}$$

If, for example, we regard markets, fashions, moods or values as collective behaviour, this collective behaviour is only possible because communication takes place between the parties concerned.

The narrative construction of reality

As we have seen, strategy development and innovation are not isolated events. They are integrated into collectives and, in turn, they give rise to changes within these collectives. At the same time, they are reactions to these collectives and the structures of meaning nested within them.

The knowledge in these collectives is necessarily presented in linguistically or numerically codified systems. If the systemic conditions change, the contents also change. According to an ancient linguistic hypothesis, knowledge is relativized by language and vice versa. What implication does this have with regard to innovations, if they are perceived as changes in the inventory of knowledge?

In this context, the term "narrative" is particularly useful. Narratives are a basic form of communication as well as even a basic form of human thought processes. When considering the simplest meaning of the term, however, narratives are stories or discourses, which feature characteristics of stories, such as:

- a reconstructed presentation of the facts, i.e., the description of something that happened previously, whereby a meaningful order emerges as the story is told; thus, narratives present a selection and an interpretation and generate a consensus;
- use of fixed topoi, i.e., pre-shaped "places" from everyday life, which evoke relatively fixed meanings and place our actions in a context; as a rule, case studies or best practice observations are, for example, narratives that present a topos of this kind and thus provide us with orientations;
- the creation of a climax, i.e., stringing together elements with growing importance that reach a peak;
- an explanatory function, in particular if it is important that the listener understands the meaning of a narrative or a story (for example, the concluding sentence of a fable: "and the moral of the story").

The act of story-telling is an action that is directly linked to thought processes and language. We take thought process and language for granted to such an extent that we hardly reflect on their mechanisms. As a result, we systematically limit our perception possibilities, and this is a crucial factor here. It is therefore worth taking a look at the possibilities that arise from removing these limitations. Narratives make it possible to do this.

Narratives are based on archetypal, chronological strings of action that are relatively fixed in sequence, but can generate a useful enrichment of knowledge in their respective forms. They are, as it were, the building blocks of reality. They constitute the basis for passing on knowledge within cultures; they represent the culturally shaped building principles for the organization of knowledge in cultures and they are varied by people in order to identify new ways of acting in a changing world.

A well-known example of an archetype of this kind is the ancient Faust myth, which has been the basis of countless literary works since the 16th Century; its probably best-known version is by Goethe – a drama cast in hexameters about the scholar Dr. Faust. The myth is basically about the confrontation of man with his contradictory deep inner forces, which culminates in him surrendering his soul – a struggle that was already described in the Bible and resulted in expulsion from the Garden of Eden.

As a rule, the story – a narrative consisting of a string of actions or arguments – has a relatively simple structure. Only the actors, the ways of implementing it and the ideologies change depending on the horizons of meaning and answers provided by the intrinsic mechanisms in the text. For example, a story can provide answers to the questions: What do people consider worthwhile, ethically acceptable, politically correct, vulnerable or in need of protection in a society at a given point in time? And, on the other hand, what do they consider to be harmful? The central question is which elements of social practice constitute the "sayable" (Plato) in society and which elements make up matters that are taboo, irrelevant, esoteric, even possibly unthinkable or wonderful. A "Wirtschaftswunder", for example, cannot be repeated at will; rather it is part of a collective overall development, which turns the edges of social identity into central collective orientations. These areas on the edges can shift into the main current of collective interest and then very rapidly promote aspects of social identity that were previously considered radical. Narrative, a term that can simply mean story, can thus be understood more comprehensively. Narratives reflect the profound value sets of a society and a culture. The story is thus a container of culturally entrenched knowledge.

Innovations, it is said, have to suit the times. But what does this mean? Let us, for example, take a look at the hybrid Audi 100, which was launched at the Internationale Automobil-Ausstellung (IAA – the automotive industry's leading trade show in Germany) in Frankfurt in 1989. The concept introduced at that time did not make its breakthrough until 20 years later with the Toyota Prius. Is an innovation only crowned with success, if it is followed by a reversal of trends within society (for example, a new environmental awareness), if it is therefore no longer perceived as radical and the acceptance threshold drops? Were these eco-automobiles ahead of their time, or were they on the periphery – without a way of connecting with mainstream society? How do we know when the time has come?

Organizations are at the mercy of the uncertainty of having to adapt to changes that are either difficult or impossible to forecast. In fact, this state is also a chance to optimize business processes and maintain fundamental adaptability on an ongoing basis (Menz 2008). However, the degree to which changes can be expected in society varies – ranging from the inevitable, generally legitimate modernization and renewal through to the occurrence of unpredictable shifts in the state of affairs. The management of organizations is thus forced to tolerate ambiguities and, in addition, take part in shaping future trends. Indeed, innovations and their positioning are elements that contribute to the interactive advancement of reality in society. We understand interactive advancement as creative collaboration between the actors in a company and its stakeholders within a complex environment, which provides the narrative slides described above for the representation of the collective. The debate about possibilities of action is not conducted in a dialogue, but rather in a "trialogue". Qualitative, interpretative instruments are necessary in order to understand how to gain access as well as to identify and produce successful entrance scenarios.

Alfred Kieser has suggested utilizing "stories" for organizational development on several occasions, as these meaningfully correspond with the "common beliefs" of employees and their organization of knowledge, on the one hand, and identify new ways of introducing management concepts as "meta-stories", on the other hand (Kieser and Muley 2003). Of course stories cannot be directly imposed upon employees like concepts from the drawing board; however, they can be legitimized in the context of interactive implementation and developed in appropriate arenas: "Thus, the strengths and weaknesses, chances and risks of the company are not simply facts that are evaluated, but the result of an interpretation process, within which suppliers and clients are interviewed, and opinions of shareholders and the public are drawn from the economic press, etc." (Kieser and Muley 2003: 127). We suggest taking this a step further and using social narratives as a resource, thus enabling us to identify useful additional possibilities for action for business in areas of interest.

Owing to the vast number of options, areas monitored, interdependencies and indicators with which management is confronted, we do not consider it useful to focus on early detection in terms of extensive "scanning" and "monitoring" for emerging potential dangers and hazards. Risk orientation of this kind will always be deficient: Although it may succeed in avoiding risks, it fails to identify creative potential. True entrepreneurship is more strongly "characterized by the ability to turn a problem into a business opportunity and possibility" (Pfriem 2006: 209). We therefore want to focus on the anticipation of opportunities and innovation potential as a starting point for a "creative response" as described by Schumpeter (Schumpeter 1947). Thus, narratives can also be found in the foundation of innovations, for example.

How can upcoming socio-economic transformations or shifts in paradigms that challenge established rules and regularities be detected at an early stage? "There's a big transformation coming, a change in the story line. There aren't many ways to go through it" (Sterling 2000: 151). This is what Bruce Sterling's protagonist, Leggy Starlitz, says in his novel "Zeitgeist". Yet how can changes, upheavals and deviations in the "storyline" lived by our society be predicted? Can knowledge about upcoming transformations be operationalized?

Nevertheless, a "prerequisite for exploiting opportunities of this kind is (...) the ability of management to identify information at an early stage, to assess its potential effects and to develop the necessary willingness and ability to take action" (Becker 1993).

Narratives are the repositories of knowledge of society

Narratives are communicative constructs, which, on the one hand, reflect the shared construction of reality within a community (Bruce Sterling's "consensus narrative", 2000) and, on the other hand, represent only one of many social realities – including the possibilities for action that are available to persons in this reality. As a rule, the contents of narratives represent a successful experiment of people having mastered one of the challenges of life. The major consensus narrative is the (quantitatively) prevailing story within a community concerning a specific situation, based on and defined by the culture (Rieger and Ron 2007). Narratives are therefore a kind of memory of society.

We suggest applying discourse analyses for the strategic and innovative development of the organization. Discourse analyses explore the change in social structures in conjunction with discourse practice. In simple terms, this consists of all the linguistic utterances produced by a society, which help to shape its collective social orientations. Changes in society are announced, accompanied, supported and also initiated by changes in discourse practice. The triggers for this can be economic, cultural, and political or originate from a different area, whereby it is primarily of interest to us to identify these triggers. In principle, these are weak signals that can become catalysts and trigger momentous processes. As a rule, these triggers emerge on the periphery of discourse practice, namely as a result of minimal changes of a component of communicative processes:

- the speakers may have changed the modalities (choice of means of expression), new topic areas may have moved into focus, whilst others may have slipped into the background;
- socio-cultural values or evaluations may have changed;
- new actors and interest groups, who are changing the market, may have emerged.

In all cases, these are small-scale changes that can set off bigger processes. According to our working hypothesis, these triggers can be identified as elements of narratives by performing qualitative discourse analyses.

Investigations integrating this kind of discourse analysis are based on linguistic and textual principles and methods, which draw on the instruments of conversation analysis, micro-sociology and other social sciences to analyse and interpret the materials (texts, conversations, interviews, etc. from authentic contexts). This type of language analysis is inspired by the social sciences, aiming to propose "rich interpretations" of individual phenomena. This involves developing an understanding of terms in their broadest sense, allowing semantic ambiguities and meanings located in both the core and the fringes of semantics with a methodologically-based approach, thus enabling "inconspicuous information" to access thinking processes. In principle, the analyses are therefore located between the micro-structures of communicative action and the macro-phenomena of social change, whereby they focus in particular on the ideological components of communicative action. Ideologies can be seen as the "sayable" and "thinkable" within a society – the things we frequently take completely for granted. However, our own rationality often acts as an obstacle, as described above. In particular, an evaluative interpretation of previous contents (generally) pushes new lines of thought into the background. Our interpretations are grounded in the known.

Example
A textual analysis can provide clarification here. Let us take a look at an example, in which we will limit ourselves to a rather rough outline. The testimonial of the HR Director of Volkswagen AG Italia, Paolo Lombardi, is featured in the prospectus of language-learning software (Digital Publishing 2009); it ends with the following sentence:

- with sophisticated learning software products (1st line)
- our employees can move with fun towards a learning culture, (2nd line)
- which we, as e-driven company, need for the future. (3rd line)

The author places the company in a specific context by using the term *learning culture* (line 2) as a goal and the term *e-driven company* (line 3) as a cause. The term is placed after references to *learning software* (line 1) and *learning culture* (line 2), which can also be read as a chronological sequence with a point of culmination (*move ... towards*, line 2) – evidence of narrative structures. We would like to begin by exploring the starting point - the term *e-driven company* – and then take a look at the goal formulated with the term *learning culture.*

The term *e-driven company* is formulated as a cause and is placed very close to the word *future* (line 3) at the end of the sentence and, thus, in an exposed position. On the one hand, it is introduced as if self-evident and, on the other hand, it can be understood metaphorically. Indeed, the *"e-"prefix* is found in terms such as e-commerce or e-business, where it prototypically denotes a digital and Internet-based corporate culture – a reference which has been borrowed here. In addition, the participle *driven* has a double meaning: first, it stands for the technical operations of the automobile manufacturer and, second, for the concept of "being driven" in the fast-moving automobile industry.

The term *e-driven company* is comparatively new; research into the term has provided little evidence. It comes over as modern and possibly visionary and innovative. However, we would like to examine it more closely and critically. The *e*-prefix emerged in the 90s, gaining a new meaning with the boom and the rapid downturn of the new economy at the end of the 90s, associating it with the negative results of irrational start-ups. In the (task-oriented) field of operations, on the other hand, its meaning has consolidated more positively (for example, with terms such as e-procurement, e-teaching); in this context it has a factual basis (computer-aided working). The trend towards computer-aided automation and standardization is and always has been expected among automobile producers. It does not represent anything new, but rather a central line of their development. In this respect, *e-driven* is a kind of flash photograph of today, but nothing particularly innovative. The term itself has less abstract semantic properties than, for example, the term *learning culture*, and in this respect its function in the text is factual.

It is noticeable that the term *e-driven* tends to mask out the company's cultural tradition in this example. There is no connection made to mass production at Volkswagen, personnel integration and customer response in all levels of society. Yet traditional values are particularly important for automobile manufacturers, because automobiles are high-involvement products. At the Daimler AG plant in Wörth, for example, the truck cabins are still largely welded by hand in order to maintain not only quality, but also to uphold the "traditional values of the era of industrial expansion" (Neuberger and Kompa 1987). Successful corporate change must take into take into account these cultural components alongside the systemic components.

In this context, the semantic of *learning culture* (line 2) is only partly connected. Naturally "learning culture" stands for an innovative concept of business development, providing that the change is part of the company's programme, and it sets out a useful way forward in the automobile industry – an industry, which is rapidly changing and shaped by technological developments. Learning cultures can also take into account systems of consciousness of learners, patterns of action and preferences of the persons involved and adapt systematically (Kösel 2007). This involves taking stock of the communicatively developed standards of every-day conduct of employees and, in turn, implementing appropriate initiatives.

Potentially, the concept "learning culture" therefore promises to deliver tailor-made innovations in a dynamic environment. In order to do this, however, there has to be a consensus with regard to the starting point. In this context, we believe the term *e-driven* is relatively meaningless in relation to the speaker's intention to present learning culture as the goal of a development. He is almost certainly following the trend towards "*e*-labelling" - a fashionable way of designating work and processes. However, the term has semantically ambivalent connotations and leaves gaps.

The conclusion of this very brief analysis is that the causal link suggested in the text is not clear, resulting in ambiguity and raising questions with regard to two aspects: first, the connection between the statement and the core values of the corporate culture; second, the competence of a management that adopts trends unquestioningly. In brief, the manager is clearly following a fashion with this statement, which is represented by two terms.

In order to continue this work, it is necessary and useful to systematically compare micro-textual analysis and social-cultural semantics and to derive operational tasks from the findings. This requires a format in dialogue form, enabling the analysis to be performed in situ, which provides a maximum degree of authenticity by optimally integrating the corporate system and culture. We suggest the PTAP method for this – an innovation system, which we will focus according to the considerations of text-oriented research.

Digression: The PTAP method

The *PTAP method* (Prospecting-Targeting-Alignment-Programs) was developed in order to prepare and implement strategic and organizational changes in a targeted manner, enabling rapid and target-oriented reactions to developments within the market or business environment. Originally intended for the development of marketing concepts, the method is chiefly applied in change management, innovation or business development projects, starting with the problem analysis and generation of ideas through to systematic implementation in projects and, finally, the monitoring of performance. The PTAP method synchronizes the approach in the organization, thus improving the prospects of success of complex innovative projects.

The PTAP method combines a system-oriented approach and communication theory with a project-based leadership concept. The objective is to find suitable ways of dealing with complexity and dynamism and to guide organizations towards innovation and change. The focus is on practical feasibility in day-to-day operations. We have formulated three hypotheses, which constitute the foundation for the practicability of innovative projects:

The first PTAP hypothesis is that an organization, such as a company, department or administrative unit, can be seen as a succession of stages or episodes. Organizations that are capable of surviving do not remain static, but also do not simply go with the flow. They always work towards a specific goal, although this goal can never be seen as a fixed final state. Indeed, goals change parallel to general conditions as time progresses. The image is therefore more of a journey; after having reached each destination of the journey, the next destination is fixed depending on the prevailing conditions or the experience acquired to date.

Second, the PTAP method is based on the hypothesis that each person looks at "things" with an individual perspective. This perspective can be compared to a kind of map or navigation system: one person sets his navigation system to the shortest route, whereas the other sets his to the quickest route. A tourist might select a route out of a guide book, and the commuter takes the same route day in day out. Yet which route is the right one? Each person has his own map, which he also shares with other people, and this map determines his path. The images, routes and rules of the navigation systems in our minds and hearts are shaped by our origins, childhood, emotions, knowledge, experience, social context and communication. This map helps us to make our way through the jungle of life; however, it also makes it extremely difficult for us to leave the path that has been laid out for us. It is particularly difficult when two differently shaped maps have to be synchronized, for example, the maps of engineers and of designers. In this case, two worlds collide.

A further fundamental hypothesis of the PTAP method is that a manager can only be as good as his employees. People often forget that it always takes two parties to result in a communication or leadership problem. If a culture shaped by communication blockages or confidence gaps slowly spreads below the surface of an organization, it can lead to a variety of repercussions and consequences. Thus, the triad of leadership, strategy and organization has to function in harmony. If an organization is not capable of reacting to changes on the market or in the business environment, even after applying its expertise and good intentions, then it is a very good reason to look for underlying causes.

We call these transitions between different mental maps and representation systems internal "thresholds". On the one hand, these are potential causes for disruptions in the leadership process or the capacity for innovation or for weaknesses in goal achievement. They can also, however, offer potential for changes and improvements that have not yet been identified. The synchronization of organization therefore involves identifying, levelling out and – if necessary – overcoming these thresholds.

The innovation process is based on measuring different positions ("prospects"), on assessing both one's own abilities and the business environment as well as on defining a reasonable goal with different dimensions ("targeting"). Following various preparatory steps ("alignment") projects ("program") are launched in order to meet the goal. However, a consensus must be reached on the destination and the route, as well as on the appropriate "means of transport" (set of measures). Finally, the outcome is measured on the basis of pre-determined criteria, in order to determine a new location (see "prospect").

Phase 1: Prospect – identify potential

The first phase plays the role of a radar: This phase involves understanding what makes the organization "tick" and where it is currently located ("crossroads"). It entails analysing the complex networks of relationships within an organization as well as how they "interlock" with the environment and markets in order to identify the different "problem zones" of an organization (the „thresholds"). This is performed by carrying out methodologically based interviews and brain storming sessions to record the inventory of narratives in the organization and compile the relevant collective orientations ("how do we work", "how are we successful", "what portfolio do we offer", "what do our customers talk about", "what are our weaknesses").

The prospect phase can be split into several sub-phases in order to draw up a multidimensional picture of the situation.

Phase 2: Targeting – develop alternative goal systems

The second major phase is about specifically defining goals. The collective inventory of narratives recorded in the previous phase is analysed with regard to the basic values, the actors involved and the existing modalities. This involves prototypically identifying the core values of the organization on the basis of the narrative structures. Substantial target images ("blueprints") are derived from this and these constitute the conceptual basis for all further activities. Parallel to this, analyses of the environment and the markets emerge that are subject to the same analysis criteria. It is crucial that this phase is carried out in a value-free and non-biased manner and that the target images are presented as alternatives before even considering their feasibility or the ways in which they can be implemented.

Phase 3: Alignment – synchronize goals and approaches

This phase involves testing the viability of the target images. In repeated analyses, the internal company narratives are put in a relationship with discursive data in the immediate environment of the company (for example, business divisions, portfolios, key accounts). As all of the criteria are developed on the basis of the material itself, the goals of all parties involved can be synchronized and a consensus can be reached on the goal. The priorities, alternatives for implementation and ways of implementation are jointly developed in order to activate "organizational energies" and generate a common will to implement the project. In this phase, it is possible and acceptable to raise questions of principle regarding the optimization of processes and functions as well as regarding radical changes of paradigms.

The phase of aligning the activities in the direction of the identified innovation potential is almost certainly the most challenging step in the entire process, as not only the environment but also the so-called "thresholds" have to be considered at this stage. Nevertheless, with a high degree of authenticity of analysis data and the systematic involvement of all parties involved, it is possible to successfully develop a common "organizational will". Agreements and respective responsibilities and commitments should be set out in writing (principle that everything can be manifested).

Phase 4: Program – guarantee structured implementation

This phase is about defining specific intentions and projects, setting out responsibilities and competencies, as well as awarding contracts. Specifically adapted methods of project management are applied, which involve determining and monitoring milestones, quality gates, results and measurement criteria.

The PTAP method – with its focus on textual analysis to develop the entrepreneurial power of innovation as presented in this article – is a methodologically sound approach, working in repeated analysis loops and generating the criteria for development from within the organization. As a result, the development of entrepreneurial concepts is authentic and does not involve imposing an external system on the organization, which as a rule produces new thresholds. This has a dual benefit for the organization: on the one hand, it enables a personal stance with regard to the conflict between maintenance of the status quo and flexibility and, on the other hand, it shows the possibilities for action both in the core and at the fringes of the relevant markets. It thus makes it possible to identify starting points for innovation initiatives with relatively little effort.

Conclusion

"You see: The deeper reality is made out of language. (...) It means there is no such thing as 'truth'. There's *only* language. There is no such thing as a 'fact'. There is no truth or falsehood, just dominant processes by which reality is socially constructed. In a world of language nothing else is even possible" (Sterling 2000: 151).

Narratives present an additional perspective in a planned innovation process. Analysing narratives makes it possible to recognize and interpret certain weak signals. The method can be applied pragmatically in different "stages" in the context of innovation systems with relatively little effort. Narratives are not to be confused with "stories" in this context. The latter are frequently named when discussing the possibilities of business development and organizational adaptation. Narratives include stories, but not vice versa.

The findings from work with narratives should be integrated into the conceptual deliberations of company management in two ways.

Firstly, a gap identified by Ansoff can be closed. This gap is located between the supply and use of early detection information by the decision-maker(s) and is – without doubt - a huge gap: "Again, it is the familiar, surprise-threatening information, that is typically rejected by managers (until the moment of crisis), as 'too abstract' unreliable, unrelated to past experience and therefore irrelevant to the problems of the firm" (Ansoff 1976: 132). Or, in other words, information is only too often blended out if it does not fit into one's world view, unless it is believed to be useful for what Dirk Baecker calls "clever decisions": "We talk about decisions when the communication of innovation and routine succeeds in also determining the reversibility chances of these decisions with a view to the expectations for the future and in the light of both technological uncertainties and evaluative uncertainties. We can talk about clever decisions, if these predetermined reversibility chances are able to react to weak signals at an early stage, and one's attention does not block signals of this kind" (Baecker n.d.). This will only be successful if the approach to narratives described here is integrated and implemented as part of a systematic innovation and strategy process.

Secondly, effective early detection and sound decisions derived from it must be followed by effective implementation. Early detection and responsiveness management, or what the Düsseldorf-based Henkel group calls "sense and response", are two sides of the same coin. Indeed, leadership skills and strategic and organizational competences must go hand in hand with early detection capabilities. It is fatal to not recognize opportunities. It is equally fatal to see them and not be able to react appropriately.

References

Ansoff, H. I. (1976): Managing Surprise and Discontinuity – Strategic Response to Weak Signals. In: ZfbF, 28. Jg., pp. 129-152.

Baecker, D. (2003): Organisation und Management. Frankfurt/Main: Suhrkamp.

Baecker, D. (n.d.): Organisation als temporale Form: Ein Ausblick. In: Meissner, J. O./Wimmer, R./Wolf, P. (eds.): Praktische Organisationswissenschaft: Eine systemtheoretische Einführung, Heideberg: Carl-Auer Verlag. Online: http://homepage.mac.com/baecker/papers/OrganisationalstemporaleForm.pdf

Bea, F. X./Haas, J. (2005): Strategisches Management. Stuttgart: Lucius & Lucius.

Becker, L. (1993): Früherkennungs- und Reagibilitätsmanagement: Silberstreifen am Horizont. In: Gablers Magazin Nr. 8/93.

Becker, L. (2008): Führung, Innovation und Wandel. In: Becker, L./Ehrhardt, J./Gora, W. (eds.) (2008): Führung, Innovation und Wandel. Düsseldorf: Symposion, pp. 15-48.

Digital publishing (2009): Corporate Language Training. Brochure (16 pages). München.

Flohr, U. (2008): Zu viel Vorsprung. Online: http://www.spiegel.de/auto/aktuell/0,1518,546187,00.html (09.01.2009).

Gundlach, C./Nähler, H. (2008): Innovation mit Triz. Düsseldorf: Symposion.

Heuser, J. (ed.) (2008): Turbulente Krise: Wirtschaftsweiser Rürup zweifelt an Prognosen. Online: http://www.spiegel.de/wirtschaft/0,1518,596909,00.html.

Hülsmann, J. G. (2007): Die Ethik der Geldproduktion. Translated by: Robert Grözinger. Waltrop/Leipzig: Manuscriptum Verlag.

Huntington, S. P. (1996): Kampf der Kulturen – Die Neugestaltung der Weltpolitik im 21. Jahrhundert. Hamburg: Goldmann.

Kieser, A./Muley, A. (2003): The Importance of the Storyline. In: Müller, A. P./Kieser, A. (eds.) (2003): Communication in Organizations. Frankfurt/Main: Lang, pp. 119-134.

Korzybski, A. (1958): Science and Sanity. The International Non-Aristotelian Society. Lakeville.

Kösel, E. (2007): Die Modellierung von Lernwelten. Bd. 2. Die Konstruktion von Wissen. Bahlingen: SD-Verlag.

Menz, F. (2008): Postbürokratische Organisationen und Ungewissheit: Zum Verhältnis von Identitätsmanagement und Selbstorganisation. In: Menz, F./Müller, A. (eds.) (2008): Organisationskommunikation. München/Mering: Hampp, pp. 141-166.

Müller, G. (1987): Probleme im Umgang mit „schwachen Signalen" – Erfahrungen aus der Verwirklichung einer strategischen Frühaufklärung. In: Blick durch die Wirtschaft; Nr. 21/30.01.1987.

Müller-Kirschbaum, Th./Wuhrmann, J.-C. (2008): Innovationskultur bei Henkel. In: Becker, L./Ehrhardt, J./Gora, W. (eds.): Führung, Innovation und Wandel. Düsseldorf: Symposion, pp. 335-351.

Nadin, M. (2002): Anticipation. Die Ursache liegt in der Zukunft. Baden: Lars Müller Publishers.

Neuberger, O./Kompa, A. (1987): Wir, die Firma. Der Kult um die Unternehmenskultur. München: Beltz.

Pfriem, R. (2004): Unternehmensstrategien sind kulturelle Angebote an die Gesellschaft. In: Forschungsgruppe Unternehmen und gesellschaftliche Organisation (FUGO) (ed.) (2004): Perspektiven einer kulturalistischen Theorie der Unternehmung. Marburg: Metropolis, pp. 375.

Pfriem, R. (2006): Unternehmensstrategien – Ein kulturalistischer Zugang zum strategischen Management. Marburg: Metropolis.

Ramirez, R./ Van der Heyden, K. (2007): Interactive Role for Scenarios in Strategy. In: Shape, B./ Van der Heyden, K. (eds.) (2007): Scenarios for Success: Turning Insights into Action. John Wiley & Sons.

Rieger, F./Ron (2007): Die Wahrheit und was wirklich passierte. In: chaos computer club: 24C3 2334.

Rumelt, R. P. (1996): Comment on 'Forecasting: Its Role and Value for Planning and Strategy'. In: International Journal of Forecasting, Vol. 12, pp. 439-574.

Rusch, G. (2006): Konturen konstruktivistischer Ökonomik. In: Rusch, G. (ed.) (2006): Konstruktivistische Ökonomik. Marburg: Metropolis.

Schätzing, F. (2006): Nachrichten aus einem unbekannten Universum – Eine Zeitreise durch die Meere. Köln: Kiepenheuer & Witsch.

Schumpeter, J. A. (1947): The Creative Response in Economic History. In: Journal of Economic History, Vol. 7 (1947), pp. 149-159.

Starbatty, J. (2008): Warum die Ökonomen versagt haben. In: FAZ, 03.11.2008. Online:
http://www.faz.net/s/RubB8DFB31915A443D98590B0D538FC0BEC/Doc~ EBDB1A14571A54DDB8BC4DEBB5CA46930~ATpl~Ecommon~Scontent .html, 06.01.2009.

Sterling, B. (2000): Zeitgeist. New York: Bantam Books.

Straubhaar, T. (2009): Kranz, B. : Sieben Gründe für Optimismus. In: Hamburger Abendblatt. Online: 03.01.2009.
http://www.hwwi.org/Einzelansicht.5045.0.html?&no_cache=1&tx_wilmedi encen-
ter_pi1%5Bid%5D=996&tx_wilmediencenter_pi1%5Bback%5D=2881&cHa sh=04d40d0402.

Von Foerster, H. (2008): Das Konstruieren einer Wirklichkeit. In: Watzlawick, P. (ed) (2008): Die erfundene Wirklichkeit – Wie wissen wir, was wir zu wissen glauben? Beiträge zum Konstruktivismus. 4. Aufl. München/Zürich: Piper.

Wozniewski, H. (2007): Wie der Nil in der Wüste. Norderstedt: Books On Demand.

Wozniewski, H. (2009): Finanzkrise verstehen und Konsequenzen ziehen. In: Becker, L./Gora, W./Ehrhardt, J. (eds.) (2009).: Führen in der Krise. Düsseldorf: Symposion, pp. 359-286.

Organizational Perception and Cultural Orientation: A Context-Based Approach to Corporate Foresight

Roland Hergert

Introduction

Uncertainty about market developments, customers' behavior and societal developments is rising. Against this background, the resource knowledge – in this case knowledge about the future – is becoming crucial and one of the most significant competitive factors. But this specific knowledge is not objective. It is the output of cognitive interpretations, social interaction and, therefore, it has to be invented rather than found. This subjective interpretation process imparts the innovative potential to environmental stimuli. Thus, the organization's cognition, its mental models and their development potential are of particular interest. In this case the following questions are relevant:

- How can corporations generate modes and forums in which different options are mentioned?
- How could complexity and ambiguity be minimized?
- What are the cognitive conditions for covering contingencies?
- How can cognitions and culture be dealt with within innovation processes?

Thus, the identification and the reflection of the organizational relevance filter that shapes the perception processes are fundamental for the early recognition of societal change, trends and market niches. To perceive organizational reality, for instance, through the constricted perspective of strategic business areas limits the organization's focus on competitors and bears the risk of copying instead of creating innovative products.

- What kinds of categories are being used by organizations to structure their environment and represent their cognitive reality?
- How are they connected or how do they interact in organizational schemata and codes? Are there possibilities to manage this process?

From a cognitive perspective, innovations are generated by placing cognitive categories in different contexts or using them in a different way. Connecting categories in interactive schemata is the role of culture: Cultural programs process the correlation between semantic categories in a moral, sensual or affective way (Schmidt 2004: 77).

Thus, organizations have to be aware of their cultural codes and reflect them in open interactions. In this case organizations are able to influence the interaction between their identity and societal issues. Creating and incorporating new contexts in organization processes – carrying surprising strategic orientations – is the challenge for strategic management activities.

Early recognition concepts – interrelation between strategy and recognition

The discussion about early recognition concepts goes back to Aguilar (Aguilar 1967). He invented the concepts of scanning and monitoring processes. In Germany the discussion took place in the context of conventional controlling processes, such as key data/performance indicators. But these instruments are not adequate for strategic management because of their ex-post character, the extrapolation of data and their short-term perspective. Indeed, the fact that they all ignore the observer's subjective point of view is much more relevant than all early recognition instruments – including scanning and monitoring. To give you an understanding of what the author means, let's take a look at a very common model of early recognition.

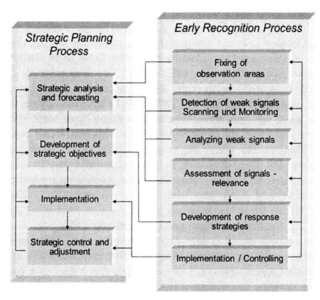

Figure 1: Interrelations between strategic planning and early recognition processes (own, modified on the basis of Hammer 1998: 266; Krystek et al. 1999: 181)

In this concept, the early recognition process is linked or integrated into the strategic planning process. However, if you look at it more closely you will miss feedback effects: signals being perceived and processed. In addition, if there are discontinuities, strategy is adapted, disregarding the fact that the organization's strategy influences the observation of the environment. In fact, strategy structures the environment, provides relevance criteria and steers the focus of intention. Ansoff uses the typical SBA approach for the segmentation of the company's environment. In this case, the focus is given by the current strategy and the filtering of data is processed by the forecasting techniques used by the firm, which Ansoff called the surveillance filter (Ansoff, McDonnell and Edward 1990: 66). Thus, an organization's action modifies the environment and vice versa. And internal data-processing mechanisms attach relevance to stimuli. But what kind of criteria is being used by companies to structure the environment into observation areas and give relevance to stimuli?

In reality, companies use the logic of strategic business units and product portfolio techniques, and the PIMS concept to analyze threats and opportunities, strengths and weaknesses. Thus, the relevance of stimuli is measured by the factors of success. However, this is not the only way to do it according to Mintzberg and others. He criticizes the assumptions of the PIMS concept as follows: "finding a correlation between variables (such as market share and profit, not 'profitability'!) is one thing; assuming causation, and turning that into an imperative, is quite another. Data is not dicta. Does high market share bring profit, or does high profit bring market share ... or does something else (such as serving customers well) bring both? Market share is a reward, not a strategy!" (Mintzberg, Ahlstrand and Lampel 2005: 99). In addition to that, the PIMS data base is not even representative. The data is taken from established firms; the young firms that build up emerging markets with innovative products are not included: "Perhaps the young, aggressive firms, which were pursuing rather different strategies of rapid growth, may have been too busy to fill out the PIMS forms, while those in the emerging industries, with a messy collection of new products coming and going, may have been unable to tell BCG [Boston Consulting Group] which firms had which market shares, or even what their 'business' really were" (Mintzberg, Ahlstrand and Lampel 2005: 99).

Another concept which is used very often is the competitive model by Porter, which goes beyond competitors, adding suppliers and consumers as categories of the organization's environment. Liebl describes this model as a cognitive representation of strategic interlinkages (Liebl 1996: 44). But again, this model also disregards the possibility that the company has an impact on its environment. The environment is not static. Smircich and Stubbart interpret this understanding of strategic management as follows: "This view emphasizes recognition of what already exists. Environmental analysis thus entails discovery, or finding things that are already somewhere waiting to be found"(Smircich and Stubbart 1985: 725).

If you pursue the idea of finding something, you won't obtain anything really new. It is creative interaction within the environment and the need to change categories that lead to innovations: "Companies can be drawn toward behaviors that are generic in their detail as well as their orientation. One need only look at the copycatting and 'benchmarking' going on in business these days. [...] managers and researchers alike are tempted to become codifiers of the past rather than inventors of the future. [...] Some of the most famous battles in business and war have been won, not by doing things correctly, following the accepted wisdom, but by breaking the established patterns – by *creating* the categories in the first place [...] Burger King might have joined the 'fast-food hamburger group', but it was Mc-Donald`s that created the initial vision and wrote the rules for the group. Some firms stay home and do 'competitive analysis'; others go out and create their own niches (leaving them with no competition to analyze!)" (Mintzberg, Ahlstrand and Lampel 2005: 117).

So, companies have to act very carefully when they choose categories to segment their environment. Maybe non-competitors – referring to Porter's model – are more interesting because their categories used for data interpretation lead to completely new trends. So, again, be aware of your mindset with regard to categories used for trend exploration and interpretation. Plans, strategies and visions – understood as a collective representation and expectation of changing environments – deceive perception by creating "blind spots" and, hence, lead to weak points (Weick and Sutcliffe 2001: 82).

Thus, if categories – often evolved from historic experiences – have such a huge influence on data interpretation processes, it might be useful to take a look at how cognitive information processing works.

Insight into human perception processes – how we represent our environment

If we take a look at modern theories of human perception (Goldstein 1989: 22-23; Sternberg 2011: 29; Anderson 2001: 21-58) and the latest results of brain research (Roth 1997: 107-108; Roth 2001: 453; Singer 2000: 10), perception is not a passive process of copying or reproducing reality. It is an active process of selecting data out of the environment, which permanently offers an infinite amount of stimuli, of which we pick up only a few. But what kind of instruments do we use to reduce complexity, to select the data we need to survive and to make decisions? Three different approaches to perception will be introduced to provide a brief overview of the major laws of perception.

The cognitive approach to perception

In the cognitive perspective of perception, schemata or mental models direct our information selection processes and give us a structure to interpret stimuli (Neisser 1996: 26). These structures are the output of learning processes taking place in social exchanges, communication and within cultural contexts and norms. The cognitive approach to perception focuses on how perception is affected by the meaning of a stimulus and by the subject's expectations (of the meaning) (Goldstein 1989: 26). Thus, the meaning of a stimulus is strongly affected by experiences and expectations – we see what we want to see or are able to see.

Thus, we use cognitive patterns, schemata or scripts to orientate ourselves in a complex world. We have schema representations for various categories and we

use scripts to behave consistently in a social or cultural context: We have a specified schedule of how to act in a restaurant and we learn how to do it in foreign
countries (Schank and Abelson 1977: 36). A schema can be described as a representative general knowledge structure that incorporates typical facts about a
category. The most important aspect of this structure is that it stores knowledge
in a flexible way that allows variation and may have different levels of abstraction (Sternberg and Ben-Zeev 2001: 66). It contains several slots to hold specific
information and values about a category. Thus, categories may have various
distinctive characteristics and can differ a lot between people or have different
meanings in different social contexts or cultures.

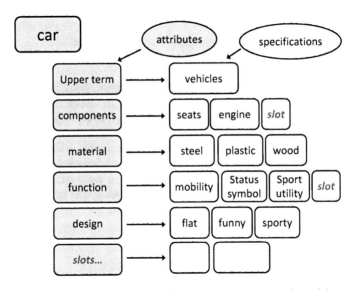

Figure 2: Knowledge representation with schemata – representation of the category "car"
(own, based on Anderson 2001: 156)

As can be seen in Figure 2, there could be different ways of describing the
category car. For instance, if it is described as a thing to get from place A to B, it
is totally different to a sports utility function car – in particular, regarding values
or topics such as strategic traffic planning or environmental conservation.

According to a research project, conducted by Mitroff in 1988, the US auto
executives, especially those of GM, entertain the long standing and unquestioned
assumption about the car world – as a necessary condition for success – that cars
are primarily status symbols. This led to a strategy in which styling is more

important than quality (Senge 2001: 214). The consequence was that Toyota emerged very successfully with high-quality products.

Context dependency of perception – the Gestalt approach

How companies deal with unfamiliar stimuli and events causing strategic discontinuities is a classical question (Ansoff 1976). The Gestalt approach - founded by Wertheimer, Köhler and other German psychologists – has proven to be particularly useful for understanding how we perceive unfamiliar, contradictory or ambiguous stimuli. Their research focuses on how we perceive groups or even parts of objects to form integral wholes. According to the principle of *proximity*, we tend to organize elements close together into units (Andersen 1980: 53). Figure 3 illustrates that principle: We perceive four pairs of lines rather than eight separate lines.

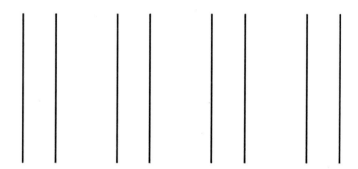

Figure 3: Principle of proximity
(Anderson 1980: 53)

Another major principle of the Gestalt approach is the law of *similarity*. According to this principle, we perceive Figure 4 as columns of circles alternating with columns of squares, because the similar shapes appear to be grouped together: Objects that look alike tend to be grouped together (Goldstein 1989: 23).

Figure 4: Principle of similarity
(Goldstein 1989: 23)

To summarize the mayor ideas of the Gestalt approach, we refer to the overall principle of "Prägnanz". According to that, we tend to perceive any given visual array (whatever we are seeing) in a way that most simply organizes the disparate elements into a stable and coherent form. Thus, the meaning of data has to be consistent; there is a need to process the great load of information in such a way that the environment makes sense (Stadler et al. 1995: 81). This means also that stimuli are ignored when they interfere with the consistency and stability of a mental representation.

It is well known that the same given visual information can hold different possibilities of interpretation, but ambiguity is perceived as a threat and therefore suppressed Figure 5 gives an illustration of this phenomenon.

Figure 5: Figure-ground segregation – Rubin's reversible face-vase figure
(Goldstein 1989: 204)

We perceive objects when they form figures against their background. This separation of figure and background is called figure-ground segregation. This pattern can be perceived either as two black faces in front of a white background, or as a white vase on a black background. The difficulty in real life is that you have to decide what you want to see – a cash cow or a poor dog? Köhler goes further. "In his view, the most important condition for seeing a thing, or Gestalten of any kind, is *being set off against* relatively homogeneous surroundings. Thus for him, figure and ground are not products of habit, but "two very concrete and phenomenologically real modes of existence of the optical" (Ash 1995: 180).

It was mentioned before that perception is dependent on knowledge organized in any kind of mental structure. Thus, the way data is interpreted depends on the context information as you can see in Figure 6.

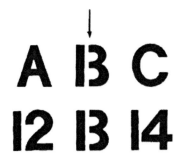

Figure 6: Context/knowledge-dependency of perception
(Goldstein 1989: 102)

Thus, the principles of Gestalt psychology tell us that we should pay attention to the overall stimulus pattern (Goldstein 1989: 206). Maybe the context is more important than the given stimulus.

The social constructionism view of perception

It was mentioned that perception is directed from schemata that form categories by putting attributes and categorical knowledge in relation to one another. This idea of knowledge representation in terms of categories is taken up by the constructionism approach; however, it criticizes the fact that the process of generating categories has not been discussed. Thus, constructionism emphasizes the aspect of human communication processes. Human reality is constructed by human communication; it is the output of societal discussion and takes place in a historical context (Gergen 2002: 156). Communication and language are very important in this approach because meanings are generated by social exchange imparted by language. Thus, categories and their meanings are socially constructed. The reciprocal process of putting knowledge into other social contexts creates new understandings and new meanings. Categories or words obtain their status as facts by being used within a community (Gergen 2002: 87). Thus, innovation often occurs when terms are used in another context.

Cognitive and cultural perception within organizations – how companies structure their environment

To connect these results with management issues or to transfer them into a management *context,* the corporate culture model of Schmidt is very suitable. This model is very similar to the schema model function. According to Schmidt, companies use a categorical knowledge structure to describe their environment. In his model these categories interact with emotions, morals and passions and create a reciprocal structure, which companies use to perceive stimuli and give meaning to them. This interrelation between knowledge and emotion – categories and specifications–is called corporate culture (Schmidt 2004: 77).

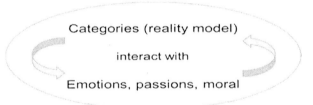

Figure 7: Culture – interaction of knowledge and emotions
(own, modified based on Schmidt 2004)

But what kinds of categories are used by mangers or what are the elements of a corporate reality model? In an empirical study, the author has identified four relevant categories or, in other words, four questions managers ask themselves when labeling an issue or interpreting data (Hergert 2007: 299-330):

- How do *competitors* behave?
- What do *politics* call for?
- How does this affect our *product*?
- How will our *customers* react?

Thus, to give a stimuli or an issue organizational relevance, it has to deal with one or more of these categories. But, beware of the categories you are using: If you look at competitors, you will imitate and not invent; if you follow what laws force you to do, you will adapt to a structure instead of creating a new one.

To bring an issue to a company's top agenda you have to use categories that are legitimated by internal processes – relevant issues are legitimated interpretations (Dutton 1986: 3-7; Dutton 1987: 80; Dutton 2002: 96).

This legitimation process also includes the use of emotions and moral aspects that are consensus within the company. The moral or emotional interpretation of data makes the difference between your interpretation and that of your competitors: The same categories will be connected in another way. Thus, the question of creating innovation is also a question of what kind of passions guides your categories.

Playing with categories – cognitions and innovation

In management theory the discussion about early recognition systems starts with Ansoff's model of weak signals. He presumes that weak signals are evoked by so-called strategic discontinuities. In a cognitive way of thinking you can call these phenomena strategic dissonances. Cognitive psychology uses the term "cognitive dissonance" to describe a discomfort caused by holding conflicting ideas or inconsistent cognitive elements ("elements which do not fit together") simultaneously (Festinger 1957: 11-13). The theory of cognitive dissonance proposes that people have a motivational drive to reduce that dissonance. There are three strategies to achieve that (Festinger 1957: 18-27):

- change behavior,
- justify behavior by changing the conflicting cognition or elements (not always possible),
- justify behavior by adding new cognitions acting as a buffer.

Thus, if you perceive strategic dissonance, you can deny it by looking out for good arguments to do so, fooling yourself – or invent new cognitions/strategy. Often people choose the third strategy – the easiest. A closely related term, cognitive disequilibrium, was coined by Jean Piaget to refer to the experience of a discrepancy between something new and something already known or believed.

According to the question of early recognition, it could be a good idea to use strategic dissonance as an "innovation trigger". In this case, early recognition systems have to create dissonances – as much as possible. In a cognitive way of interpreting organizations´ recognition processes, it has to be mentioned that early recognition of stimuli and changing environments is not a process of searching and finding. It is more a process of generating stimuli, a creative process of interaction of environmental stimuli with organization cognition and culture. This is the organization's real unique selling point.

It is a challenge for companies to apply changing categories and attributes used and interpret the creative output for inventing. Some do this by testing prototypes in a very early stage of development, others by participating in open societal discussions.

Often it is not really obvious what makes a product successful. Some good examples are provided by Nike and Mercedes – taken from Liebl: Betsy Parker from Nike said that 80% of Nike's products are used by their customers in different ways and the Mercedes A-class was developed for young families, but was bought by older pensioners (Liebl 2000: 63). So, how can this be dealt with? Liebl said that trends are societal innovations, surprising new interpretations and meanings rather than developments that go in a specific direction – as issue lifecycle assessments assume (Liebl 2000: 66). Referring to the Nike and Mercedes example, Liebl states that – according to the results of cultural sciences – the practical and symbolic interpretation of a product occurs with the start of its usage (Liebl 2000: 65-66).

Different cultures, different innovations – the challenge of integrating different cultures into strategic processes

To summarize the fundamental findings and to give a brief guide for implementing early recognition systems, the following principles have to be considered:

- The environment is not an objective reality. It is always constructed through the social interchange of a group, etc. Perception and meaning are the outcome of interaction: Meanings have to have social validity – company wide.
- Knowledge organized in schemata, scripts or routines guides our perception. The cognitive system constantly produces anticipations.
- Signals or data are always linked to interpretation patterns. Without them there is no meaning. Thus, to find new trends you have to create new patterns.
- For instance, portfolio and SWOT analyses are concentrated expressions of these patterns. The underlying criteria and assumptions of these analyses should be in the focus of early recognition processes.
- There exist numbers of different cultural and functional affected semantic codes – not all of them are shared by the members of the organization.

These principles lead us to a concept of early recognition that emphasizes and appreciates the existence of different cultural coding systems. The objective of such a model is to create new contexts, translate and legitimate them. It sounds easy, but in reality we often present our findings as something real and objective. The translation of trends to the corporate management is one of the most difficult challenges. For instance, environmental issues are very relevant to many managers and corporate strategies, but how can they be translated into business opportunities? What kind of "label" do these issues need to obtain a place on the strategic agenda?

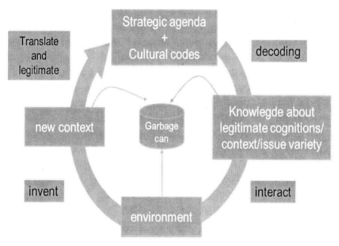

Figure 8: Context-based model of corporate foresight
(Hergert 2007: 342)

The first step of trend exploration in this model is to acquire knowledge about what really is discussed at top management level. Pierre Wack, one of the inventors of scenario-analysis at Shell, said that, "[i]t is impossible to develop scenarios without knowing the worries of the management. […] You need a well-defined perspective of the intended identity and the strategic objectives of the company". This sounds very easy, but in fact the strategy is often not known. Thus, in reality this is a kind of decoding process. The next step is the interaction of the strategy items with the environment, followed or accompanied by inventing new environments and contexts. Finally, there is the need to translate the issue, turning it into a legitimate item on the top management agenda. But again, this is very challenging: Strategy planning is a process of reducing the complexity of the company's environment and early recognition is the process to open the system to cover contingencies – as much as possible. Thus, to put these two together seems to be impossible, but essential: a paradox. To reflect organizations' cognitions and codes, there is a need for "niches", where narratives can take place – temporarily objectless and open. But how can they be integrated into the "formal" strategic process of the company? An old yet exciting idea is to implement what Cohen et al. called a "garbage can" (Cohen, March and Olsen 1972: 12). In this theory, there are not only problems that require solutions, but also solutions that require problems. Thus, the idea of putting newly created contexts – with currently no visible linkage to strategy – in a can and picking it up later when meaning occurs seems to be a good solution for covering complexity and contingency. There seems to be one question left: What could be an adequate institutional form for implementing a garbage can? Kirsch labels garbage cans as "decision arenas", where strategic discourse happens. According to this approach, Kruse develops a map of how "strategic discourse arenas" are structured (Kruse 2011: 199). She also gives some good examples of how issues, opportunities or cognitions that are currently labeled as "not strategy relevant" can be stored. Often these cognitions are linked to people or departments that have been put out of focus or "parked", but gain access to strategic arenas again when the issue/problem arises anew (Kruse 2011: 196). This requires what Weick calls "mindful management and culture" (Weick and Sutcliffe 2001: 159). Weick calls for a management that exposes itself to strategic dissonances in a proactive way. He proposes "to encourage alternative frames of reference", "to reward groups that preserve divergent analytical perspectives" and to "restate the companies' goals in the form of mistakes that must not occur". Doing so, he said, will focus more attention directly on the unexpected, on disconfirmed expectations, and on issues of reliability (Weick and Sutcliffe 2001: 160-162). Summing up, he strongly recommends: "But more important, we urge that you carry your labels for what is going on right now *lightly*. Be prepared to replace them with labels and verbs that pry loose some qualities of your situation that almost everyone else missed. That's challenging. That's diagnosis. That's detective work. That's fun. That's mindfulness" (Weick and Sutcliffe 2001: 158).

References

Aguilar, F. J. (1967): Scanning the business environment. New York: Macmillan.

Andersen, J. R. (1980): Cognitive Psychology and its implications. San Francisco: Freeman and Company.

Anderson, J. R. (2001): Kognitive Psychologie. 3. ed. Heidelberg/Berlin: Spektrum Akademischer Verlag.

Ash, M. G. (1995): Gestalt psychology in German culture, 1890-1967. Holism and the quest for objectivity. Cambridge: Cambridge University Press.

Ansoff, I. H. (1976): Managing Surprise and Discontinuity – Strategic Response of Weak Signals. In: Zeitung für betriebswirtschaftliche Forschung, 28. Jg., pp. 129-152.

Ansoff, I.H./McDonnell, E. J. (1990): Implanting Strategic Management. 2nd ed., Cambridge: Prentice Hall.

Cohen, M. D./March J. G./Olsen J. P. (1972): A garbage can model of organizational choice. In: Administrative Sciences Quarterly 17, pp. 1-25.

Dutton, J. E. (1986): Understanding Strategic Agenda Building and its Implications for Managing Change. In: Scandinavian Journal of Management Studies. August, pp. 3-24.

Dutton, J. E./Jackson, S. E. (1987): Categorizing Strategic Issues: Links to Organizational Action. In: Academy of Management Review. Vol. 12, No. 1, pp. 76-90.

Dutton, J. E. (2002): Strategic Agenda Building in Organizations. In: The Importance of Organizational Identity for Strategic Agenda Building. In: Shapira, Zur (ed.) (2002): Organizational Decision Making. First paperback edition. Cambridge: Cambridge University Press, pp. 81-107.

Festinger, L. (1957): A theory of cognitive dissonance. Stanford: Stanford University Press.

Gergen, K. J. (2002): Eine Hinführung zum sozialen Konstruktionismus. Stuttgart: Kohlhammer.

Goldstein, B. E. (1989): Sensation and Perception. 3rd edition. Pacific Grove: Brooks/Cole.

Hergert, R. (2007): Strategische Früherkennung. Wahrnehmung relevanter Umweltreize oder wie ticken Unternehmen? Marburg: Metropolis.

Kruse, B. (2011): Strategic Discourse: Actors – Issues – Arenas. Berlin: Logos Verlag.

Liebl, F. (1996): Strategische Früherkennung. Trends – Issues – Stakeholders. München/Wien: Oldenbourg.

Liebl, F. (2000): Der Schock des Neuen. Entstehung und Management von Issues und Trends. München: Gerling Akademie Verlag.

Mintzberg, H./Ahlstrand, B./Lampel, J. (2005): Strategy Safari. A guided tour through the wilds of Strategic Management. New York: Free Press.

Neisser, U. (1996): Kognition und Wirklichkeit. Prinzipien und Implikationen der kognitiven Psychologie. 2. Aufl. Stuttgart: Klett-Cotta.

Roth, G. (1997): Das Gehirn und seine Wirklichkeit. Kognitive Neuro-biologie und ihre philosophischen Konsequenzen. 1. Aufl. Frankfurt am Main: Suhrkamp.

Roth, G. (2001): Fühlen, Denken, Handeln. Wie das Gehirn unser Verhalten steuert. Frankfurt am Main: Suhrkamp.

Schank, R. C./Abelson, R. P. (1977): Scripts, Plans, Goals and Understanding. An Inquiry into Human Knowledge Structures. Hillsdale: L. Erlbaum.

Schmidt, S. J. (2004): Unternehmenskultur. Die Grundlage für den wirtschaftlichen Erfolg von Unternehmen. 1. Aufl. Weilerswist: Velbrück Wissenschaft.

Senge, P. (2001): Die fünfte Disziplin. Die Kunst und Praxis der lernenden Organisation. 8. Aufl. Stuttgart: Klett-Cotta.

Singer, W. (2000): Wahrnehmen, Erinnern, Vergessen. In: Frankfurter Allgemeine Zeitung, Nr. 226 (28.09.2000), p. 10.

Smircich, L./Stubbart, C. (1985): Strategic Management in an Enacted World. In: Academy of Management Review, Vol. 10, No. 4, pp. 724-736.

Stadler, M./Kruse, P./Strüber, D. (1995): Die Entstehung von Bedeutungen in kognitiven Systemen: In: Kebeck, Günther (ed.) (1995): Gestalttheorie als Forschungsperspektive. Festschrift zur Emeritierung von Manfred Sader. Münster/Hamburg: Lit, pp. 75-115.

Sternberg, R. J./Ben-Zeev, T. (2001): Complex cognition: the psychology of human thought. New York: Oxford University Press.

Weick, K. E./Sutcliffe K. M. (2001): Managing the unexpected: assuring high performance in an age of complexity. San Francisco: Jossey-Bass.

Interview: Fashion, Innovation and Science

Alfred Kieser and Suleika Bort

Andreas Müller: We are sitting here together with Alfred Kieser and Suleika Bort for an interview about their participation in the conference "Narrative and Innovation". Alfred Kieser is a former Professor of the University of Mannheim, Holder of the Chair of Business Administration and Organizational Behavior and Suleika Bort was formerly his assistant and has now finished her Ph.D. thesis on the role of concepts in organizational studies and organizational theory. They have recently published a research paper together about the role of fashion in organizational theory. We are going to speak about this paper in a minute, but first we are going to speak about our conference "Narrative and Innovation". Alfred, how did you feel when we invited you? Did you have any idea of what was meant by narrative and innovation?

Alfred Kieser: Narrative is always very important in theory. It's important in the discourse between scientists because each theory has to have a narrative, or you have to present your ideas and findings in the form of narratives. So, implicitly, we all tell stories to our colleagues and, of course, also to practitioners. For practitioners in particular, success stories are very important in the discourse with scientists.

AM: Do you make a difference between a narrative and a story?

AK: Not really. I'm not a linguist or a language researcher. I'm not so exact in my terminology.

AM: But it has been said that all of the sciences form part of a narrative because, as you said, all researchers need language and a narrative to tell their stories. Those who are focused on chemistry of physics or whatever – in the end, they are kind of telling stories.

AK: Of course.

AM: Is there something in the topic narrative and innovation that you can identify as important for your own research?

AK: Oh yes, last week I gave a speech to historians. It was about entrepreneurs and, of course, Schumpeter told stories, narratives about entrepreneurs. And nowadays, there is a tendency to tell stories about successful entrepreneurs. These narratives are not really exact; they do not reflect the practice in detail. These are narratives that are told by the entrepreneurs themselves – like Jack Welch, for example. He told stories about his success, his active life as top manager of General Electric, and these stories are retold by journalists and scientists. So, it's very difficult to find something like a real story or a true story, because we all read about successful entrepreneurs in the newspapers, scientific articles and books. So, our impression is always influenced by narratives.

AM: Or the narrative is a representation of what we think it was like. When Jack Welch or an entrepreneur tells his story about his company, it is like a reconstruction of what happened, but not the truth.

AK: Yes, the essence of my talk was that Schumpeter made a forecast that in the long run entrepreneurs would be superfluous because in big companies innovation would be routinized. So, if we look at big companies like Telekom, they have many departments for scouting or finding out about new ideas in the telecom business and developing new ideas in the form of new companies, which are subsidized by Telekom, spin-offs and so on. So all of the entrepreneurial functions are now really routinized, as Schumpeter predicted. My thesis was that the public needs the ideology of the successful entrepreneur as a person; so, we all have a tendency to personalize success in the form of a charismatic entrepreneur. And this is a reaction to the fact that you really can't teach entrepreneurship and really can't explain success. And so narratives, stories about charismatic, successful entrepreneurs are highly popular.

AM: If you can't teach entrepreneurship, isn't it because companies try to institutionalize innovation in a certain way – in departmental structures or whatever – so they get disconnected from the discourse of society and disconnected from the world? Because they concentrate on the bureaucratic or institutional structures? And they lose the entrepreneurial spirit of being able to innovate or create things, which has to be sought outside of the bureaucracy and the institution.

Suleika Bort: You also see that when you look at young start-up firms. Sometimes they are really successful if they have a successful founder – for example, in biotechnology. And then, after a while they are bought by a big pharmaceutical company and they source in the knowledge and the scientists. Then the entrepreneurial spirit of the former founder vanishes, because he can't get along with the structure of that large company. I think, it's hard to teach entrepreneurship because it's a kind of spirit, it's a kind of an attitude you can't really teach. In addition, I think that in large companies the structures don't facilitate innovation and entrepreneurship.

AM: So, the process of organizing somehow inhibits the possibility to be innovative.

AK: It's controlled innovation.

SB: Exactly.

AK: You have to be innovative as an intrapreneur as it is called – an internal entrepreneur – but of course within limits. Innovation is constrained, limited to match the philosophy or strategy of the company.

AM: How does an entrepreneur act when he finds a new idea, identifies market potential, a niche or business model that could operate? How does he identify it? You said that you can't teach entrepreneurship and you used to say that we can't teach storytelling. Why is this? What happens? Is it something very personal? Is it part of a social competence that can't be trained in a university? Is it a characteristic of practitioners, which has no link to organizational theory or study?

AK: All the theorists who deal with entrepreneurship agree on the fact that entrepreneurs have the talent of identifying special chances. So, they are capable of evaluating possibilities for innovation.

SB: The weak signals.

AK: And this you can't teach.

AM: Maybe fashion could be linked to this point, because a lot of business is done with trends. Everybody knows that, for example, social networking in the Internet is a big deal. So, a lot of people are thinking about how to make business out of this trend. Of course not everybody will be a Facebook founder, but still you can make good business by marketing or copying networking. Let's get closer to the work you have done on fashion and look at how concepts are integrated in organizational studies. What is fashion, and how would you define fashion when you think about organizational studies?

SB: I think it's short-termed and it's about hype. It doesn't matter if it's in science, in lifestyle, life in general or in companies. Many people do it because they want to be different, but actually they go with the mainstream. Fashion is always about wanting to be something special, but in the essence you go with the mainstream. Even if you say you don't do it because it's fashion, it's a rejection of fashion. But you live with fashion and you deal with fashion. For example, think about social media - for me, it's an upcoming hype that every company now needs to be engaged in Facebook or Twitter. Companies don't really anticipate what the benefit could be. They just want to be there because everyone is.

AM: It is also big potential when a company works with Facebook and knows that the customers are already there. And parts of the market happen in Facebook; so, it's maybe good advice for companies to be there and participate even if it's mainstream.

SB: Yes, that's right for some industries, but not for all. What can a large chemical company gain from being engaged in Facebook? For example, with regard to their innovation output? They have to be very specific while, developing some special kind of molecule. The process differs from what companies like Procter & Gamble are doing, where everyone can deliver some input to foster innovation.

AM: Something that I perceived in your paper is that organizational study is very susceptible to fashion. How did you reach this conviction?

AK: Researchers are also on a kind of market. They try to create something new and find colleagues who buy their new concepts. So, it's the same as when a company brings out a new car or garment, for example. We are entrepreneurs who are trying to convince potential customers of the virtue of our invention.

AM: Do you have an example? I was wondering, for example, about the big success of system theory – as founded initially by Luhmann, a certain sociologist, and then by certain actors from Witten and other places. They founded a big school or stream of system theory for organizational study. Is this the kind of fashion you are speaking about?

AK: No, we aren't speaking about theories, essentially, because there are so few theories around. We wouldn't have a lot of material. We look at concepts, new concepts within a theory. For example, the garbage can concept of J. March is a concept within behavioral theory.

SB: Concepts are more flexible. They are broader than theories and, therefore, you can change them or explore them from different sides.

AM: Would this mean that a concept, which is very open from a semantic point-of-view, like a metaphor - garbage can is a metaphor that is really open to all kind of users - is more appropriate for forming or constituting a fashion?

AK: The theories are too, but, as I said, there are only few theories around, and you have more material to study when you concentrate on concepts. An example is exploration and exploitation by J. March. There is a difference between exploiting the knowledge you have and exploring new knowledge fields. They are more than metaphors; they are metaphors and of course theoretical content. You can't simply say that everybody speaks about garbage cans; you have to study March and co and studies with garbage cans. And then you have more than just the color of a metaphor to interest your colleagues.

AM: You did research with a sample of 44 concepts. Do you have some more examples of the concepts you used?

SB: Yes, for example, absorptive capacity or institutional logics. Actually, we used a very pragmatic way to identify our concepts. We first identified the relevant organization theories. We then searched for concepts within these theories. As soon as at least three other researchers labeled the identified term a concept, we decided to add them to our sample.

AM: So, it was a very pragmatic approach.

SB: Yes, in the end it was a very pragmatic approach.

AM: The research process counted how often these concepts were used in the pertinent articles in the most quoted journals.

AK: To identify, on the basis of the number of followers, a kind of fashion curve with a slow beginning, then a peak and a drop, like clothes fashion. It's the same. You have few followers in the beginning, then you have a peak and, finally, it tapers off.

AM: It's like a lifecycle.

SB: I think that scientists do not like the idea that there is fashion in science, because it's irrational and does not fit in with the typical meaning of science as such.

AK: Of course, there is no area without fashion. We have the fashion of clothes; we have fashion in the area of health, for example. We have sicknesses that become fashionable and then disappear again from the scene.

AM: So, maybe researchers would not really want to hear your ideas because you are questioning the validity of their imperialism.

SB: But we do not like the fact that fashion has such a negative connotation. It can be something refreshing; it can lead to change; it can have a long-lasting impact and it does not necessarily have to be something bad.

AM: I think, seen from this point-of-view, fashion gives birth to leaders because you create them with fashion; lifecycle comes with hype. You create heroes – people that stand for a mythology concept or stood for it once upon a time. And the leader is now narrating his story of a concept that has somehow been successful. Of course everybody knows that only a few articles have been cited and, of course, these are the founders of theory.

AK: A Nobel laureate is also a kind of a hero, isn't he?

AM: It's an added value that is given to him by society or the community. The number of times you have been cited and the number of Ph.D. titles. You can collect attributes in order to become a hero.

SB: It is one aspect to study the diffusion of fashion, and it is another to look at the origin of fashion. It's really interesting to have a look at how fashion develops and who are the ones that create a fashion.

AM: To open up the last round of the interview: What would your recommendations for young researchers be? What are the implications for management sciences? Management sciences have to be renewed as well. Some scientists say that management sciences are also part of the social or cultural sciences, and that they are not critical enough, too confident about their concepts, and so on. Maybe this is a historical myth and, especially from the European and German perspective of business administration, it is very positivistic and bureaucratic. Maybe this is Max Weber's heritage still. But what are the implications for management sciences if we now find out that narrative and fashion – all these approaches – really work? You can show and prove that organizational sciences, up to certain level, obey these trends and discourses.

AK: As Suleika said before, there are fashions in science, like we have fashion in every aspect of life. We have to point out that fashion is a source of differentiation. That sounds paradoxical but it is true. We differentiate on the basis of fashion. Some are better at applying fashion, and others are not so good at applying fashion. So, fashion is a possibility of differentiating yourself from others and, of course, it is also a possibility to position yourself as a scientist in the area of science. For example, you as a young scientist choose a theory and you choose a methodology which appeals to you, and you follow that. That's positive. Without fashion, you would be lost; nobody would understand you or could categorize what you are doing in the wide field of science. We see fashion positively: It's not a restriction of science or a turn for the bad. It is positive. The point is that, nowadays, with the impact factors and rankings, you have a narrowing down of fashion. So, rankings are triggering a trend towards mainstream. So, for example, mainstream in organization studies is positivistic, empirical and quantitative, and it applies economic theories. This is a very narrow field of science, but the young scientists tend to follow this fashion because it promises a career, and this is dangerous because it means a reduction of innovation and creativity.

SB: The movement towards quantification and economic reasoning in science is more a long-term trend and it leaves no room for being a scientific entrepreneur.

AM: Is it also the consequence of an overall development? Because of the mass of publications nowadays, even mainstream is being pushed towards narrowing its own limits. To be more focused, to be more precise, to be more consistent in what the major orientations are - for example, for organizational studies but as well for other branches in social sciences. Because, with this amount of publications, it would otherwise not be able to keep an orientation.

AK: I do not accept this thesis. Before the impact factors and rankings, we had much more variety and the scientific world managed this variety, got along with it. It was much more inspiring. This is why the top journals are getting so dumb, so boring, and so repetitive.

SB: They all have the same style or articles and there is no scope for publishing books, especially for young researchers, because you have to publish journal articles to get tenure. Yet, sometimes really good ideas cannot be put into an article. Sometimes you really need to publish a book, but you don't have the time and you don't get rewarded or tenure when you publish a book, for example.

AK: Books don't count because they don't go into the rankings.

SB: A lot of this can be traced back to the Americanization of the system. I think we, in Germany, don't have a system that supports an American style of doing research. Yet, as long as we do not have a system that supports an American style of doing research, we should not and cannot compete with the Americans.

AM: But if you are speaking about the American system, or the big US faculties that have dominated in this area for many decades, even they - with their limited variety - have limited their own potential for developing studies that go beyond fast success. More detailed studies on certain concepts, for example. I don't want to be polemic, but a concept like the balanced score card is not necessarily empirically based with the necessary or adequate methodical tools, and so what would you say about criticisms of these kinds of national research tradition? Is it something that, for example, German management sciences could repair?

AK: There is a chance. It is not so bad for Germany, because organizational theory was dead after the war really. But, as an example, Christopher Grey discusses it in an article in *Organization Studies* – you have critical management theory, which is uniquely British. They just don't adopt it at other places. There is one article in the *Academy of Management Journal*, which is about critical management theory, and the essence or conclusion is that this approach is not really good. It is biased and ideological, but not our US-ideology, which we like. So, it can't be successful because it's not rigorous enough. They have the definition power of what is rigorous, and what is not. And that's how the competition works. The bias is heavily loaded in favor of the American researchers.

AM: Speaking about the power of definition and ideology in research, let's come back to the narrative. All of the national traditions in sciences are part of the ideology of the question: Which of the stories told in the streets are true, and which ones are not? And which stories should not be told because maybe they touch a taboo? Would you judge, for example, these kinds of idea about narratives or fashion and try to identify how fashion comes into serious studies that form part of the management sciences? Do you believe that this would help to bring management sciences ahead of the very limited short-minded mainstream? Should there be a new approach – maybe a philosophical or narratological one? Talking about mythology and ideology reminds me of a theory of Roland Barthes – the everyday myth about how mythology forms part of our thinking every day. The exchange of science in communication means that there has to be an ideological level as an overall orientation without being explicitly mentioned all the time.

AK: A scientist should be capable of reflecting what he or she is doing. Of course you have ideologies, but you should be able to step back and look at your ideologies taking the perspective of other researchers and come to your own independent conclusion. But this is not what we observe in the discourse of management theory, for example. They do not judge what they do on a philosophical basis. Humboldt also had this principle: Philosophy is the basis of all sciences. And that's still true, I guess.

AM: But maybe this is the starting point for teaching entrepreneurship. Maybe it's just like the entrepreneur. He has a vision and a feeling of what his chances and possibilities are. He has the capability to look behind the facade and judge what is right or wrong, without giving too much attention to the mainstream discourse and trends. Because he looks behind the scenes and judges what is really new and what isn't. So, maybe this could be a way to conclude this interview. Thank you!

Collaborative Narrative Innovation
A Case of Public Innovation in Denmark

Anne Reff Pedersen

Introduction

Innovation in the public sector is not a new development; for many years public employees have been active innovators, building bridges, building new hospitals and changing the relationship between professionals and users in everyday life. They have done this without having a language of innovation, due to the fact that innovation has been the primary concern of private firms.

This paper has two aims: to understand public innovation as a process of collaboration and, second, to understand the concept of innovation from a narrative position. In recent years, public innovation has become the subject of a strong new discourse in many states in the western world due to the growing demands for effective problem-solving and high quality services, inspired by NPM and thereby bringing in new methods and language from the private sector, entrepreneurship as one of the new discourses.

In this chapter, I argue that there is a difference between public and private innovations. Many public innovation studies are concerned with research innovation and not with mass-production organizations such as hospitals or schools. Lundvall (Lundvall 1992) is one of the few researchers who has studied public innovation in different countries, and he argues that successful innovation is related to the degree to which the whole of the organization is driven towards innovation. This indicates that the organization level is important in understanding innovation processes.

In contrast to many private innovations, which have a natural focus on technological innovation to create new products, public innovation is concerned with developing new methods, or new ways of organizing to create more efficient organizations and focus on quality and user satisfaction. Thus organizing becomes a central concept in developing public innovation. Considine et al. (2009) raise two important questions: What kind of public organizations are innovative, and, what are the drivers in public organizations? In contrast to private organizations, public organizations are politically controlled and therefore the innovative conditions are affected by political agendas.

Public innovation can be defined as: the formation and implementation of creative ideas resulting in mutual meanings, facilitated by negotiated narrative interaction among users, professionals, public managers, politicians, consultants, interest organizations and private firms. Thus *mutual meanings* by *narrative interaction* become important elements in public innovation.

The structure of this chapter is divided into three parts: First, the paper describes the theoretical development, moving away from a technology focus in innovation to a focus on organizing by defining collaborative innovation as a narrative way of innovating. The second part focuses on a public innovation case, which illustrates how public innovation emerges with local innovators and innovative identity enabled by innovative storytelling. The case is about the idea of triage and implementing a triage model in an acute ward in a hospital. The last part discusses the possibilities for defining innovation as narrative innovation and drawing a picture of some key concepts in narrative innovation.

Collaborative innovation by organizing processes of interaction

When innovation is not understood as solely user driven or politically driven, the drivers of innovation come from the interaction of many actors. However, there is no systematic knowledge about why and when collaborative innovation leads to innovations, and the role of narrative interaction in facilitating innovative processes in organizations is hardly addressed in research literature (Pedersen and Johansen 2012). In order to gain new knowledge about the interaction processes in innovation, my focus is on interaction among users, professionals and other relevant actors in innovation cases.

The focus on interaction in innovation studies is not a new development. Since Schumpeter's (1934) idea of the entrepreneur, and the passion which drives the entrepreneur to develop new ideas, there have been many studies showing the long interactive chain of actors involved in innovations, from private firms, universities, and technical laboratories to public departments (Akrich et al. 2002). They cite Burns and Stalker's classical understanding of innovative organizations as a cluster of organizations, which favor interaction, permanent coming and going, all types of negotiation that allow for rapid adaption. Here the emphasis is not on the planned activities, but on organizing processes defined by interaction and negotiation.

The next question is: How does interaction emerge and who interacts with whom? One of the first scholars who described the innovation processes as a journey, demonstrating the chaotic processes in innovation, was Van de Ven. He described how an innovation process has different steps: first, a chaotic process and then, second, a more stable one (Cheng and Van de Ven 1996). Therefore, innovation is a very complex process involving many different stages of interaction. The two stages that are often mentioned as central to understanding in innovation are the idea process, how to obtain an innovative idea, and then the implementation process, how to implement the idea.

Akrich et al. argue against this understanding of innovation by arguing that the interaction process is in "the making", and thereby is not defined by retrospectively evaluated mistakes (Akrich et al. 2002). Instead innovation can be understood as a process of multiplicity and heterogeneous with confused decisions made by a larger number of different and often conflicting groups. In this context, decisions are made by ignorance of reason, by muddling through processes, which cannot be defined in stages or predicted, but can be explored by investigating the particular networks and stories of different interaction processes.

From a narrative perspective, interaction is not defined in stages or, in contrast, but always in "the making"; interaction can be studied in the stories that are told, which illustrate a process perspective, but at the same time allows some stories to be told and others to be quiet. Often some authors are more visible than others and these spokesmen of innovation can muddle through, but at the same time can fire others for not following instructions; thus, the innovation process can be understood as a narrative interaction and a power game.

A narrative innovation model

Micro-processes of innovation are influenced by many elements. These include leadership, social capital and forms of communication and trust (Hippel 1988; Benkler 2006). Lewis asks: Are certain patterns of connections visible in innovation processes? Or is connectivity only significant when associated with an aspect of formal structure of government (Lewis 2009)?

The answer to this question is: firstly, *the discursive drivers of innovation* in a government setting - what does innovation mean to those engaged in the public sector? By looking at these questions, it becomes possible to investigate how public actors, politicians, bureaucrats, community leaders and professionals understand innovation: maybe in a different way to how the actors in private firms understand innovation.

The second element is the informal interaction and connections that create the daily innovative processes. Innovative actions are created by local meanings and by the connections between many different actors - managers, developing consultants, street-level bureaucrats, professionals and users – by storytelling and story interaction. Thereby some *innovative stories* emerge that bring people together. A large Australian innovation study in public organizations showed that local public innovators handle information with different strategies; they often become strategic partners when other actors seek information (Considine et al. 2009). This study illustrated how some local innovators – spokespersons stories – were very important for the innovative process, working with the issue of information in informal networks. But some innovative stories can also be stories of resistance to innovation. The shared stories become storylines that define a shared understanding of innovation. Often some storytellers are central in ensuring that some of the small stories result in shared storylines.

The third element is storytelling negotiations. David Boje (1994, 1995) has been one of the advocators of a relational storytelling perspective in organization studies; by focusing on the relational part of storytelling, some tellers have certain storytelling capacities (performative capabilities, talking skills) and thereby become important story innovators. A micro interaction study of local innovation can use this perspective to gain more knowledge about the relational part of innovation, which stories become more power full than others.

In a study of patient-to-patient interaction in chat rooms, Reff Pedersen (2010) has found several important elements of narrative performance. Some actors gave themselves the *editorial right* to delete or add stories; others used *trust* and family metaphors as a way of creating common meanings and stories; others controlled the story interaction processes, while others were just involved in long interactions. It is difficult to say which kind of narrative power is the strongest, but the study illustrated how many different strategies of narrative performance manage organizational spaces and frame informal interaction.

Lastly, these innovative stories, and the way they are told, are the basis for creating *innovative identity* in a public organization. Therefore innovation emerges as a culture and as a certain way of understanding innovative practices often combined with more daily oriented practices.

My suggestion is that innovative cases in public organizations can be analyzed by a narrative interaction framework to explore the micro-processes of local innovation.

A model of narrative innovation can be made:

Narrative Innovation Model

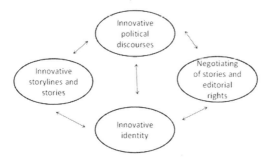

Innovative stories by spokespersons (often managers) are often the drivers that make time and spaces for other innovative stories in an organization. These managers often have some storytelling capacities (storytelling rights and telling capacities) that create the basic ground for some shared understanding of innovation (storylines). Together with the many small innovative stories, both stories of resistance to the innovation and more supporting stories, they create an innovative identity in the organization.

An innovation case: starting a triage model in an acute ward in a Danish hospital

In a Danish hospital, Hillerød Hospital, a new way of organizing staff has been developed in the acute ward. The innovation concerns the use of a triage system for the visitation of new patients in the acute ward. One of the founding fathers of this innovation was a training nurse, who had the idea of introducing this international system to Denmark, and to make local adjustments, so that the model could be used in a Danish hospital setting (characterized by a high degree of local professional autonomy and resistance to standardized work procedures). The aim of the innovation was to improve patient safety, as the doctors in the acute ward were the youngest and most inexperienced doctors at the hospital. As a result of the new triage model, patients are assessed and subsequently categorized according to standardized, predefined criteria. The patient is assigned a triage level based on vital signs as well as emergency symptoms and a signs algorithm. The most urgent ranking level of the two determines the final color-indicated triage level ranging from red (most urgent), orange, yellow and green to blue (least urgent). This categorization is visualized by placing a magnet of the appropriate color on a board, where all the patients in the ward are listed with e.g. time of arrival, name, cause of inquiry/working diagnosis and triage level indicated.

Qualitative interviews with employees in the emergency ward primarily make up the data this paper is based on. The interviews were conducted between February and April 2010, in parallel with the observation part of the study (see below). In total twenty-one semi-structured individual interviews were conducted with nurses, doctors and managers in the emergency ward at Hillerød Hospital. All interviews were conducted using a thematically arranged interview guide, where topics and issues to be covered were specified, though room was left to allow other relevant topics to surface and be explored during the interview. Each interview lasted 40-80 minutes and took place in the emergency ward. Interviews were recorded and subsequently transcribed for thematic coding and analysis.

In addition to the semi-structured interviews, observation methods were also employed during fieldwork, primarily in the form of place-based and person-based shadowing (Czarniawska 2007). The observations included a participatory element consisting mainly of questioning and reasoning together with the nurses in their triage work and of performing simple, practical tasks in relation to general nursing in the ward. Most of the observations took place during daytime hours in the emergency ward, although observations were also conducted to a lesser extent during evening and nightshifts.

In addition to these methods, data from a theater workshop has also been included in the data material. The purpose of the theater workshop was to contribute to a large research program on public innovation, CLIPS (www.clips.ruc.dk), which this hospital case study is a part of. The hospital case served as the innovation case at the workshop, allowing the collection of important data material. The theater workshop was held as an explorative approach to discussing innovation in healthcare with participants from different parts of the Danish healthcare system: politicians, professionals, representatives from interest groups, patient organizations, academics and representatives from different levels of government (municipal, regional and the National Board of Health). The theater workshop was videotaped and some of the discussions were subsequently transcribed and analyzed for use in this paper. The involved participants gave their consent for the data/material to be used for research purposes.

The reason the triage was establish as an idea at Hillerød Hospital was due to an emerging public medicine discourse about improvement of safety and quality at the hospitals and another discourse about emergency care should be a priority at the hospitals.

Several different *stories of innovation* emerged in the ward: Some stories described how the nurses in the ward collaborated differently after the triage model had been implemented; others, especially the managers, described the difficulties and struggles, the innovation processes also led to. One of the stories was about resistance and how some nurses, especially some of the older ones, had left the ward because they did not like that the work tasks were formally written down. Innovation in the public sector is not a power-free process. The managers said that innovation was more important to them than keeping all the employees. Thus, the managers expressed a dedicated and proud understanding of the innovation, "it has to be implemented" and that had employee implications. Another important innovation story is about how the nurses and the doctors working with the triage model in practice could see some benefits of the model in everyday life and therefore liked the new way of working. Especially young people felt that the triage system created security and clarity with regard to works tasks and patients' needs. The stories was negotiating when more experienced staff could see that professional judgments were still needed, because patient care and treatment can never be a standardized procedure, but always includes professional judgments. Thereby some resistance stories against the triage also appeared and the positive and negative stories interacted and made ground for polyphonic innovative stories, with both voices against and in favor for the triage idea.

The process of the implementation of the triage model created a divided *innovative identity* in the ward, expressed by one of the daily workers: "the triage model is just another change condition, and we have already had so many". The researcher who was making the observation study made a long list of changing conditions at the ward over the last two years, and it was a long list. For some of the employees this was a difficult identity to work with. Many daily workers had difficulties living in an innovative identity and culture, but the mangers liked it and were very proud of the ward and its progress. Therefore the case illustrated a stronger management innovation culture that also reflects street-level innovation identities, which is both positive and negative towards innovation.

Discussion and conclusion

Innovation is the subject of a new discourse in public organization and can be defined by narrative interaction. Narrative interaction has different steps involving public discourses, stories, storylines, storytelling capacities and innovative identities. Here identities are not defined as one shared stable organizational identity, but as bridging individual and organizational identity with many multiple innovative identities allowing innovations to emerge.

Innovation can neither be understood as a stable organizational pattern of stages or expected interactions, nor as chaotic processes. There are important sense making elements in all innovations, stories, meanings and story interaction. The spokespersons stories are not just good at persuasion, but have storytelling capacities. The innovative identities are created by multiple stories of innovation, but in an organization culture that allows many different kinds of innovative stories.

References

Akrich, Madeleine/Callon, Michel/Latour, B. (2002): The key to success in innovation. In: International Journal of Innovation Management 6, pp. 187-206.

Benkler, Yochai (2006): The wealth of networks: How social production transforms markets and freedom. New Haven: Yale University Press.

Boje, David M. (1991): The Storytelling Organization – a Study of Story Performance in an Office Supply Firm. In: Administrative Science Quarterly, vol. 36, No. 1, pp. 106-126.

Boje, David M. (1994): Organizational Storytelling – the Struggles of Premodern, Modern and Postmodern Organizational Learning Discourses. In: Management Learning, vol. 25, No. 3, pp. 433-461.

Boje, David M. (1995): Stories of the Storytelling Organization – a Postmodern Analysis of Disney as Tamara-Land. In: Academy of Management Journal, Vol. 38, No. 4, pp. 997-1035.

Cheng, Yu-Hing/Van de Ven, Andrew H. (1996): Learning the Innovation Journey: Order out of Chaos? In: Organization Science Vol. 7, No. 6, pp. 593-614.

Considine, Mark/Lewis, Jenny, M./Alexander, Damon (2009): Governance, networks and civil society: How local governments connect to local organisations and groups. In: Barraket, Jo (2009): Strategic issues for the not-for-profit sector. Sydney: NSW.

Considine, Mark/Lewis, Jenny/Damon, Alexander (2009): Networks, Innovation and Public Policy. London: Palgrave.

Czarniawska-Joerges, Barbara (2007): Shadowing and other techniques for doing fieldwork in modern societies. Copenhagen: Copenhagen Business School Press.

Hernes, Tor/Koefoed, Anne Louise (2007): Innovasjonsprocesser. Norge: Fakbokforlaget.

Lundvall, Bent-Åke. (1992): National systems of innovation: Toward a theory of innovation and interactive learning. London: Anthem Press.

Pedersen, Anne Reff (2010): Den dialogstyrede patient. In: Ledelse gennem patienten. Handelshøjskolens forlag. Edited by Peter Kjær and Anne Reff Pedersen. Copenhagen.

Pedersen, Anne Reff/Johansen, Mette Brehm (2012): Strategic and Everday Innovative Narratives: Translating Ideas into Everyday Life in Organizations. In: The Innovation Journal: The Public Sector Innovation Journal, Volume 17(1), 2012, article 2.

Schumpeter, Joseph A. (1939): Business cycles. Cambridge: Cambridge University Press.

Urban, G.L./Von Hippel, Erik (1988): Lead user analyses for the development of new industrial products. In: Management Science: 569-582.

Veenswick, Marcel (2005): Organizing innovation. Amsterdam: IOS Press.

Back Forwards

Dialogue and Innovation
World Café as a Contemporary Format for Dealing with Questions that Matter

Thomas Klug

The real voyage of discovery lies not in seeking new landscapes, but in having new eyes.

Marcel Proust

This article is a narrative about our World Café during the "Narrative and Innovation Conference" at Karlshochschule, Karlsruhe in August 2010.

It is actually two stories in one: first, the narrative about our World Café from the subjective perspective of the facilitator. This story is written in the first person and printed right-aligned in italics. Second, the article includes a description of the ingredients of a successful design of a World Café. This is written from an objective perspective, more like a scientific text, and is set left-aligned and in regular typeface for better identification.

This format has been chosen in order to reveal the fact that there are often two or more stories told when we communicate. The form of the article wants to remind us of this fact.

What is World Café?

The following characteristics will give an idea of what World Café is about:

- a "loose structure" (paradox) for hosting conversations about questions that really matter
- talking with each other, not about each other
- practicing deep narration
- holistic metaphor revealing our informal webs of connectedness
- like the Internet but in real life with real people face-to-face and heart-to-heart
- doorway to collective intelligence and wisdom

-   space of possibility
-   conversation as a co-evolutionary process creating the world anew
-   creates the magic in the middle
-   helps to connect others with each other and myself in a field of wisdom

How it started

In January 2010 I discovered Lutz Becker on the social network Xing. He was born in my hometown Solingen, Germany. That made me curious and I contacted him.
We arranged a phone call to get to know each other better. During this first call we got on quite well and he sent me a link to the conference "Narrative and Innovation" he was currently preparing with his colleague Andreas Müller. He invited me to contribute to the conference with a speech, a poster or a panel. After checking all the other contributors and their input I opted for something practical - a World Café. My reasoning was: If this conference is about narrative and innovation, it is not enough to listen to presentations and speeches. It is important to experience what narration actually is and how someone feels about it. Experiencing the power of dialogue can help to discover where to find further leverage for innovation.

Why do we need World Cafés?

In the pluralistic western world, we are currently facing dramatic changes in many relevant areas such as science, economy, education, values, politics, technology, etc. Taking these changes seriously, we are wise to elaborate modes of sustainable living. How this works is not written in textbooks: it needs to be found out by trial and error. What we can do in order to search for the most promising approaches is to talk to each other on all levels of our society in order to tap into our collective wisdom. One very successful format for these conversations is the World Café. It provides a safe place to speak from our hearts about questions that really matter to us.

Questions open the door to dialogue, conversations and discovery… and …to innovation.

Conversations and stories convey our collective knowledge. People tell stories about the "good old times"; grandmas tell fairy tales to their grandchildren (at least they used to); in church we hear about stories that are

2000 years old and older. In conversations we convey our cultural heritage and constantly reproduce culture. In dialogues we tell our stories by exchanging our ingrained culture and adding our personal view and experience. We do not only report on facts and figures. We tell the story as insiders with all our passion, our personal attitude emphasizing the aspects that matter to us. We relate these pieces of our own reality to our environment and by doing this we touch the others. They become a vital part of our story, because they are part of the relevant environment. We discover that somehow we are connected; we are part of the same community. That is the essential difference to fragmented analytical and rational talk.

The Greek word dia–logos means a free flow of meaning through a group of people. Dialogue overcomes the fragmentation that we have previously created.

The World Café allows us to be ourselves. We can talk as a whole person. We bring our entire personality to the table. This is encouraged and challenged at the same time.

How was World Café "invented"?

World Café was discovered because it was raining. In 1995 an international group of people met in Mill Valley, California, to speak about intellectual property. The meeting venue was outdoors, which is quite common in California. But weather conditions were not as planned. So the organizers Juanita Brown and David Isaacs had to re-organize. They improvised by creating a hospitable space in the host's living room. They arranged tables of four for their conversations, put white paper on the tables and some pens for doodling for new ideas and told the group to switch tables after some time talking about a subject in order to share and get fresh ideas.

They established that the success of the process had a lot to do with the attitude with which it was prepared and the safety of the space that helped people to be open to play and try new ideas with each other.

Preparation

After my discussion with the conference organizers, I assumed I would be working with an international group of about 250 people in our World Café. The advantage of World Café is that you can do it with 12 up to more than 1,000 people. So we were flexible concerning the number of participants. I checked the room conditions and the time slot that was available. For a World Café in which

the majority of participants have no or only marginal experience, you need
approximately 3 hours.
To provide the full experience of the potential of a World Café, I needed a
graphic recorder on board. I asked Lutz Becker whether they had one available
at Karlshochschule. But there was nobody available for the time of the
conference. So I had to search in my own network. Finally I found Hanno
Langfelder (Deep Dialogue), who is an active member of the European World
Café community. He was interested and had time to join me for the conference.
In order to prepare the recording properly and to benefit from somebody
else's experience, we arranged a Skype conference with Sabine Soeder, an
experienced and skillful graphic recorder and trainer. She and her husband are
also active members of the European World Café community. Together we
discussed several approaches for a suitable recording concept. Finally we
agreed on an approach that felt right for all of us. So we were ready to promote
our World Café.

The text on the conference website[1] announcing the World Café read as
follows:

A World Café on Dialogue and Innovation

In our World Café we will collectively explore our experiences with
innovation and innovation processes. In several rounds with alternating groups
we will have intense conversations about questions that matter when innovating
in our organizations, products, neighborhoods, families and lives.
This innovative communication format is based on the oldest form of
conversation – the dialogue. It will provide us with new insights into innovation
and our personal attitude. World Café offers the opportunity to talk, paint, play,
etc. Simply be creative and have fun!

---

[1]   http://narrative-and-innovation.com/panel-thomas-klug/ 18.02.2011

How is a World Café designed?

In research it was discovered that there are seven principles that if performed in interplay create the field for fruitful dialogue and a space for possibility.[2]

1. Set the context

Here are some questions to consider when preparing a World Café:
What is the topic or issue we want to address or explore?
Who needs to be invited to participate in this conversation?
Who represents both conventional and unconventional wisdom?
How long do we have for the inquiry?
What line(s) of inquiry do we want to pursue?
What themes are most likely to be meaningful and stimulate creativity?
What is the best outcome we can envision?
How might we design a path toward that outcome?

2. Create hospitable space

Most meeting places are sterile, cold, and impersonal. Consider choosing warm, inviting environments with natural light and comfortable seating. Hospitable space also means "safe" space – where everyone feels free to offer their best thinking.
Hospitable space begins with the invitation to attend a Café. Include the theme or central question you'll be exploring in your Café in the invitation. State it as an open-ended exploration, not a problem-solving intervention. Use color, hand-printing, graphics and other ways to make it stand out from the deluge of paper and e-messages we all receive.
When we ask people where they have experienced their most significant conversations, nearly everyone recalls sitting around a kitchen or dining room table. There is an easy intimacy when gathering at a small table, that most of us immediately recognize. When you walk into a room and see it filled with café tables you know that you are not there for your usual business meeting.

---

[2] The text of this paragraph is a slightly edited version of the World Café website. http://www.theworldcafe.com/principles.html, 18.02.2011. I have deliberately adopted this text as it is because it reflects the attitude and perspective of the World Café community in the most appropriate way. The current text on the website has been edited. The quoted text reflects the version referred to in this footnote.

- Creating a Café ambiance is easy and does not need to be expensive:
- Stagger the tables in a random fashion, no straight rows
- Cover these with two sheets of (flip chart) paper or a white paper tablecloth
- Put markers on the table to encourage people to write and draw on the tablecloths
- A small decoration completes the table set up
- Have some soft music playing as people arrive

3. Explore questions that matter

Knowledge emerges in response to compelling questions. Find questions that are relevant to the real-life concerns of the group. Powerful questions that "travel well" help attract collective energy, insight, and action as they move throughout a system. Depending on the timeframe available and your objectives, your Café may explore a single question or use a progressively deeper line of inquiry through several conversational rounds.

A note about the appreciative process: David Cooperrider has co-developed the "appreciative inquiry" approach. After several years of studying how people ask questions, he stated that the most important lesson from appreciative inquiry is that "people grow in the direction of the questions they ask. The questions we ask and the way we construct them will focus us in a particular manner and will greatly affect the outcome of our inquiry." We find the same position in medicine: You can focus on people's deficits and sicknesses (pathogenesis) and you can direct your attention to a patient's experience with full health (salutogenesis). "The second approach is comparable with what Cooperrider describes. If we ask: What is wrong and who is to blame? We set up a certain dynamic of problem-solving and blame assignment. While there may be instances in which such an approach is desirable, when it comes to hosting a Café, we have found it much more effective to ask people questions that invite the exploration of possibilities and connect them with why they care.

4. Encourage everyone's contribution

People engage deeply when they feel they are contributing their thinking to questions that are important to them. Encourage all participants to contribute to the conversation. As Meg Wheatley says, "Intelligence emerges as a system and connects to itself in new and diverse ways." Each participant in the Café represents an aspect of the whole system's diversity and as each person has the chance to connect in conversation more of the intelligence inherent in the group becomes accessible.

For the speakers in the conversation, the responsibility is to focus on the topic and express their thoughts about it as clearly as possible. For the listeners, the responsibility is to listen to what the speakers are saying with the implicit assumption that they have something wise and important to say. Listen with a willingness to be influenced, listen for where this person comes from and appreciate that their perspective, regardless of how divergent from your own, is equally valid and represents a part of the larger picture, which none of us can see by ourselves.

5. Cross-pollinate and connect diverse perspectives

Ask participants to offer their individual perspectives and listen for what is emerging "in the middle of the table." Use the tablecloths and markers to create a "shared visual space" through drawing and connecting the emerging ideas. Sometimes the co-created pictures can really be worth a thousand words when showing the relationships between ideas. This experience is the reason for engaging graphic recorders for the "harvesting" of the entire group.

A woman once remarked:"The most radical thing you can do is to introduce people to folks they don't know." Make sure that participants from each round all go to tables with different people as the conversational rounds progress. This cross-pollination of ideas often produces surprising results that could not have happened otherwise.

Setting up your Café in conversational rounds and asking people to change tables between rounds allows for a dense web of connections to be woven in a short period of time. Each time you travel to a new table you bring with you the threads of the last round and interweave them with those brought by other travelers. As the rounds progress, the conversation moves to deeper levels. People who arrived with fixed positions often find that they are more open to new and different ideas.

Experience shows that it is very useful to ask one person to remain at a table to act as the table host. This person will summarize the conversation of the previous round for the newcomers, ensuring that the important points are available for consideration in the upcoming round. They then invite the travelers to likewise briefly share the essence from the previous round, allowing everyone to become more deeply connected to the web of conversation.

6. Listen together for patterns, insights and deeper questions

Listening is a gift we give to one another. The quality of our listening is perhaps the most important factor determining the success of a Café. Whole books and courses have been written about how to listen. One of our favorite analogies comes from jazz: Wynton Marsalis, one of the best contemporary trumpeters, explains that when jazz musicians get together to jam, whoever is the best listener ends up contributing the most to the music, because he is able to play off of whatever is being offered by the other cats in the band. Café conversations share that jazz element of inviting each person to express themselves authentically, and those who listen skillfully are able to easily build on what is being shared.

A few tips for improving our listening:

-   Help folks to notice their tendency to plan their response to what is being said actually detracts from both the speaker and the listener
-   Listen as if each person were truly wise, and sharing some truth that you may have heard before, but do not yet fully grasp
-   Listen with an openness to be influenced by the speaker
-   Listen to support the speaker in fully expressing themselves-Listen for deeper questions, patterns, insights and emerging perspectives
-   Listen for what is not being spoken along with what is being shared

7. Harvest and share collective discoveries

Conversations held at one table reflect a pattern of wholeness that connects with the conversations at the other tables. The last phase of the Café involves making this pattern of wholeness visible to everyone. To do so, hold a conversation between the individual tables and the whole group. Ask the table groups to spend a few minutes considering what has emerged in their Café rounds and what has been most meaningful to them. Distill these insights, patterns, themes and deeper questions down to the essence and then provide a way to share them with the whole room. It can be helpful to cluster this aspect of the conversation by asking for one thing that was new or surprising and then asking people to share only those ideas that link and build on that particular aspect. When it is clear that the group has exhausted this topic, ask for another one and repeat the process until you have given each table or person the opportunity to speak about what matters to them. Make sure that you have a way to capture this. There are different ways of capturing the wealth of ideas for the group and even for others. You can use graphic recording or capture the ideas on flip charts, or by having each table record them on large post-it notes, or even on their table cloths, which can then be taped to a wall so that everyone can see them. After each table has had the opportunity to share their insights, the whole group may wish to take a few minutes of silent reflection and consider:

-   What is emerging here?
-   If there was a single voice in the room, what would it be saying?
-   What deeper questions are emerging as a result of these conversations?
-   Do we notice any patterns and what do the patterns point to, or how do they inform us?
-   What do we now see and know as a result of these   conversations?"

World Café at the conference

We started the Café after lunch. The number of participants of the conference varied around 25. So we had a much smaller group to work with than originally planned. In order to create a welcoming and hospitable space, we chose to start with an old Zulu greeting. I greeted everybody with "Sawu bona", "I see you". And the response was "Sikhona", "I am here" (Chart 2). This greeting is grounded in the Ubuntu culture and tradition of South Africa. It means that until you have seen me I do not exist. As soon as you greet me, I "exist" and can reply that I am here. This usually sets the appropriate appreciative tone for a mindful conversation. I got the message across to some of the participants, to some others I did not. It depends on how familiar a group is with these kinds of rituals and very different approaches to the implicitly known western way of behavior.

The magic of World Café is that we are allowed to be what we are: human beings. It is not only tolerated, it is mandatory to play with ideas and thoughts, experiment, improvise and have fun. With a diverse group of people it only needs a few guidelines – the Café etiquette (Chart 3) – to start and keep the process going. We introduced the etiquette to the community and it was also available on every table as a printed version.

Café Etiquette[3]

Focus on what matters
Contribute your thinking and experience
Speak your mind and heart
Listen to understand
Link and connect ideas
Listen together for insights and deeper questions
Play, doodle, draw on the tablecloth
Have fun!

Start and introduction

At the beginning of the Café, we introduced ourselves at the tables by mentioning our name, current activity/work and our most important experience with innovation (Chart 4). This helped to get to know each other better and break the ice before diving into the subject of innovation.
The overall target of our World Café was: to experience "dialogue" as a crucial resource for comprehensive and sustainable innovations. For this purpose we organized the Café into three rounds of 25 minutes focusing on questions that matter. After each round, we harvested the results of the dialogues at the different tables supported by our graphic recorder Hanno Langfelder.

Why Graphic Recording?

Graphic recording helps to visualize and memorize the main results of a meaningful conversation. It provides additional context; it is not only about what was actually said. Graphic recording can also capture the mood, the tension and emotions in the room. It can combine both levels of communication: the expressed and the silent, not expressed. By doing so, the recording taps into the collective intelligence of the group.

This integrated visualization of context and content helps to see the full picture, in particular in the western world with its fragmented language. In our languages single letters form a word; several words are put together to a sentence. Most of the time context is missing. It is different in Asian languages:

---

[3]   The World Café: Café to Go, 2008

They use images, intonation, and pronunciation to convey meaning. So we can say that the visual recording adds context to what we are saying with our words.

Questions

When preparing the World Café, my major focus was on the questions guiding the Café. Before I could create these questions, I had to ask myself some initial questions that guided and shaped the work:

Who are the people attending?
What matters to them?
How can we bring them to speak from their heart?
Do they speak English well enough in order to express what they really want to say?
Will the planned greeting open the floor for deep dialogue?
What can we do if that is not the case?
Will the participants be fresh and motivated in the afternoon to experience a good Café?

With all these questions in mind and assumptions about the answers, I had to collect questions that might be asked during the Café. I collected these questions during the period of preparing the conference while jogging, driving the car, talking to people or watching the news. The following is a collection of potential questions that needed to be checked against the criteria of powerful questions. They had to relate to each other and lead the participants more deeply into the theme of the Café with every round of questions asked. The collected questions are the following:

What is your understanding or metaphor of dialogue?
What is your experience with innovation (situations)?
Was that more a personal or a group experience?
What is important about innovation to you and why do you care?
What is our intention here?
What is the deeper purpose of working on innovation that is worth our best effort?
Why does innovation matter?
What really matters for innovation?
What do we know about innovation / what do we still need to learn?
What is the core (heart) of innovation?

How would you describe the ideal conditions for innovation?
Which assumptions and mental models do we need to test when thinking about innovation?
How do we need to think, act and sense differently?
What is needed for radical innovation?
What is the next level of thinking we need to go for?
What is missing in our picture of innovation? What is it we are not seeing?
What do we need more clarity about?
What had real meaning for you from what you have heard?
What surprised you? What challenged you?
What is being shaped here? What are you hearing underneath what has been said?
What can my personal contribution to innovation be (in work and life)?
If success was completely guaranteed, what strong steps would we take?
What challenges might we face during our journey and how might we meet them?
What seeds can each of us plant that could make the biggest difference?
From this preselected group of questions, I distilled the ones used during the Café. As a filter I asked some other test persons and myself: "What are the most powerful questions that could matter to the group?"

What are the characteristics of powerful questions?

A powerful question[4]
-    is simple and clear
-    is thought provoking
-    generates energy
-    focuses inquiry
-    surfaces unconscious assumptions
-    opens new possibilities

After each round of the World Café with a guiding question, we collected the insights gained at each table by "harvesting" the main ideas and aspects. I asked the participants what insights they had and Hanno documented the answers. In the following you can see the selected questions and the "harvest" as a graphic recording.

---

[4]   For more background see: Vogt et al. 2003

First question:
What is important to you about innovation and why do you care?

During the first round there was an intense conversation at each table. The visual record displays the diverse aspects that had been found at the individual tables and in the group as a whole.

Second question:
Which assumptions and mental models do we need to test when thinking
about innovation? How might we think, act and sense differently?

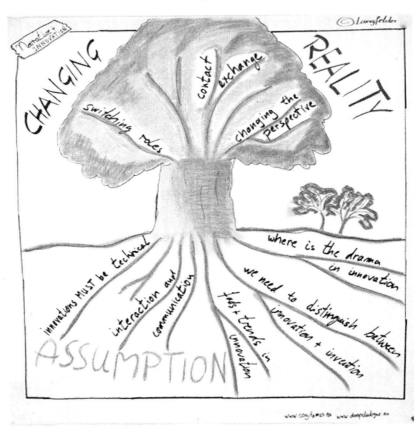

This image of a tree demonstrates to the reader how deep our assumptions
are rooted in ourselves. They influence how we see the world, how we think and
act. It reminds us also of the fact that if we want to change reality we have to
change our assumptions and deep beliefs.

Third question:
What seeds can each of us plant that could make the biggest difference in
how we innovate?

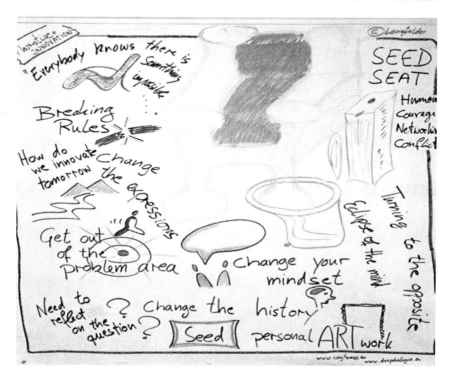

*With this question, part of the group got really energized. From a certain
point in time we did not simply talk about innovation. Some people got up and
were innovative. They broke the rule that they should only share with us what
they were coming up with and that Hanno should record what they were saying.
They started to record themselves. They played for instance with the words of the
question – seed was interpreted as seat and painted in bright colors. First,
Hanno and I as the facilitators were surprised and did not know how to deal with
the situation. But then we realized that the entire Café was about innovation.
And this consequently meant breaking rules, rules of convention. They did not
even ask whether they were allowed to paint. They just did it. In the same way
innovations are born in larger organizations. You do not ask for permission; you
just do it and excuse yourself later.*

Feedback: In one word - how did you experience the World Café?

The following picture shows one of the table cloths from the World Café. It is obvious that most of the drawing was done by one single person. Most of the little pictures face in the same direction and are drawn in a similar style. What is missing here is the connection between the images. In a conversation with a deep flow you will usually see wild scribbles that sometimes even cannot be identified by the people at that table after a while.

What if...

The future is born in webs of human conversation?
Compelling questions encourage collective learning?
Networks are the underlying pattern of living systems?
Human systems – organizations, families, communities – are living systems?
Intelligence emerges as the system connects to itself in diverse and creative
ways? We already have all the wisdom and resources we need?[5]

...just imagine!

---

[5]   Cf. Brown et al. 1998

References

Bohm, David (1987): Unfolding meaning. London.

Brown, Juanita/Margulies, Nancy/Isaacs, David (1998): Poster: Welcome to the World Café. Mill Valley, CA.

Brown, Juanita (2001): The World Café. Living knowledge through conversations that matter (Doctoral Dissertation). Mill Valley, CA.

Buber, Martin (1988): The knowledge of man. Atlantic Highlands, NJ.

Cooperrider, David/Whitney, Diana (1999): Appreciative Inquiry. Bedford Heights, OH.

De Maré, Patrick, Koinonia (1991): From hate through dialogue to culture in the large group. London.

Harbig, Andreas J./Klug, Thomas/Broecker, Monika (2007): Führung neu verorten. Perspektiven für Unternehmenslenker im 21. Jahrhundert. Wiesbaden.

Kelly, Susan (2005): The benefits of using graphic recording/graphic facilitation. http://www.theworldcafe.com/pdfs/graphicBenefits.pdf.

Schieffer, Alexander/Brown, Juanita/Isaacs, David/ Gyllenpalm, Bo (2007): World Café: Kollektive Kreativität im Kommen. In: Harbig, Andreas J./Klug, Thomas/Broecker, Monika (2007): Führung neu verorten. Perspektiven für Unternehmenslenker im 21. Jahrhundert. Wiesbaden.

The World Café (2008): Café to Go. A quick reference guide for putting conversations to work. http://www.theworldcafe.com.

Vogt, Eric E. (1994): The Art and Architecture of Powerful Questions. In: MicroMentor Corporate Learning Journal. Available through eric.vogt@interclass.com.

Vogt, Eric E./Brown, Juanita/Isaacs, David (2003): The Art of Powerful Questions. Catalyzing Insight, Innovation and Action. Waltham: MA.

For more online information on World Café visit: In German: http://de.wikipedia.org/wiki/World-Caf%C3%A9. In English: http://www.theworldcafe.com/.

For more online information on Visual Facilitation/Graphic Recording visit: http://de.wikipedia.org/wiki/Visual_Facilitation.

Practical Approach

The Tales of Institutional Entrepreneurs

Barbara Czarniawska

Abstract

In the present text, an institution is understood to be an (observable) pattern of collective action, justified by a corresponding social norm. By this definition, an institution emerges slowly, although it may be helped or hindered by various specific acts. From this perspective, an institutional entrepreneur is an oxymoron, at least in principle. In practice, however, there are and always have been people trying to create institutions. This text describes the emergence of London School of Economics and Political Science as an institution and analyzes its founders and its supporters during crises as institutional entrepreneurs. A tentative theory of the phenomenon of institutional entrepreneurship inspired by an actor-network theory is then tested on two other cases described in brief.

What, or who, is an institutional entrepreneur?

>...we do not like the complexity of real history. The authors of ideas prefer to think that they are directly responsible for realities that correspond to their speeches or writings, and the rest love simple causal explanations, not to say conspiracy theories (Dahrendorf 1995: 40).

In view of the extremely rich flora of definitions that the word institution seems to attract, it is necessary to define it at the outset. In the present text, an institution is understood to be an (observable) pattern of collective action, justified by a corresponding social norm (Czarniawska 1997). This definition is based primarily on Berger and Luckmann's reasoning: "institutions posit that actions of type X will be performed by actors of type X" (1966: 72). A constructive reciprocity is assumed; i.e. the performance of an X type of action leads to the perception that a given actor belongs to (or aspires to) type X, and vice versa. In narrative analysis, in which institution equals genre (Bruss 1976), the intelligibility of action X is achieved by referring it to a genre, where action X and actor X belong to the same type of narrative. Thus a male manager emptying waste baskets and a woman making strategic decisions in a corporation beg for explanation, as such happenings violate the institutionalized order of things.

From the perspective of an institutional order, the actors can be seen not necessary as people but rather as "legitimized social groupings": work units, profit
centers, departments, corporations, public administration organizations, associations of organizations, and all those whose interactions "constitute a recognized
area of institutional life" – an organization field (DiMaggio and Powell 1983:
148). Such actors leave or are pushed out of a field and new actors enter it (consider the powerful entry of environmentalists into political, industrial, and academic fields). Actions, in spite of the stability and repetitiveness that earn them
the name of institutions, change in both form and meaning; the narrative changes
in every narration. Finally, the process itself is recursive, as Meyer et al. (1987)
point out: whereas actors perform actions, actions create actors (or rather, their
identities) within the context of a narrative, which is created, in turn, by actions
and actors.

Thus, an institution emerges slowly, although it may be helped or hindered
by various specific acts. In narrative terms, one story does not a genre make. In
terms of actor-network theory, which is itself of narrative origins (Czarniawska
and Hernes 2005), an institution can be seen as a macro- actor of long standing
that is strengthened not only by the norm or norms, but also by artifacts (Joerges
and Czarniawska 1998). Furthermore, an institution depends for its survival on
its ability to fit into the dominant institutional order (Warren et al. 1974; Meyer
et al. 1987).

From this perspective, an institutional entrepreneur is an oxymoron, at least
in principle. A person or a group can institute, but not institutionalize: the latter
verb can only be used as past participle. In practice, however, there are, and
always have been people or groups that try to create institutions. They could be
divided into three categories:

1. those that, in their endeavors, ignore the institutional order dominant in
   their time and place: Marie Curie Sklodowska, Mikhail M. Bakhtin, and
   the founders of the Northern German University, described below;
2. those that institute a practice and count upon it being institutionalized:
   Tavistock Institute and the "company doctors" in UK; Olof Palme and the
   "you-reform" in Sweden; and the creators of the Chicago school of sociology;
3. those that construct a formal organization attempting (hoping) to turn it
   into an institution in its own right: TVA, Microsoft, LSE.

In this text I focus first on the emergence of London School of Economics and
Political Science (LSE) as an institution and treat as institutional entrepreneurs

both its founders and its supporters during crises, within a framework inspired by a combination of actor-network theory (Callon and Latour 1981; Callon, 1986; Latour, 1986; Czarniawska and Hernes, 2005) and the garbage can model (Cohen et al., 1972; March and Olsen 1976). The tentative theory that emerges from the analysis posits that a conventional theory of institutional entrepreneurship mistakes formal organization builders for institutional entrepreneurs, as the deeds of the former better fit an established narration pattern. In contrast, institutional entrepreneurs are not necessarily hero-like figures, and may contribute to the emergence of new institutions with loose connections to formal organizations. This theory is tested on two more cases described in brief: an attempt to found a private university in Germany and the formation of the Chicago school of sociology.

An idea whose time has come

The circumstances in which an idea arose in the local time/space or, even more important, how and when it decisively came to the attention of a given group of organizational actors, are often unknown (Czarniawska and Joerges 1996). It was frequently a meaningless event at the time. But when the translation of ideas into actions is well advanced, the actors involved feel a need to mythologize by dramatizing origins. Such was the case of LSE.

Breakfast at the Webbs...

Most accounts begin with the breakfast party on 4 August 1894, with four members of Fabian Society present: the wards, Beatrice and Sidney Webb, and the guests, George Wallas and George Bernard Shaw.[1] Of course, the idea was not born then and there, and Sidney Webb himself saw "the breakfast" as an invention of Wallas' imagination. The origins of the idea extend back to the Fabian Society, an intellectual movement grounded in socialist ideas (founded in 1884).

The object focus of discussion during the alleged breakfast was a bequest of £20 000[2] to the Fabian Society by Henry Hunt Hutchinson. An already existing idea of a school inspired by the Fabian spirit could materialize, but not without

---

[1] In what follows, I use Ralf Dahrendorf's history of LSE published at its 100th anniversary (Dahrendorf, 1995) and LSE's own homepage, http://www.lse.ac.uk/lsehistory, which is consistent with Dahrendorf's version.

[2] Equivalent to approximately one million two hundred thousand pounds in 2005 (acc. to http://www.nationalarchives.gov.uk/currency/results.asp#mid).

the help of others. As Sidney Webb wrote to another Fabian, Edward Pease, in 1886: "Nothing is done in England without the consent of a small intellectual yet political class in London, not 2000 in number. We alone could get at that class" (http://www. lse.ac.uk/lsehistory). Indeed, Webb's connections with the City of London and with London County Council proved invaluable.

... the Zeitgeist that set the table

How did the Webbs and their allies get 2000 people in London – or at least some of them – to listen? There is a limit to the number of issues people notice and react to, regardless of their acuity. Downs (1972) showed how public reaction to problems is subject to "issue-attention cycles", in which problems suddenly leap into prominence, remain the center of attention for a short time, and gradually fade away. A problem must be dramatic and exciting in order to maintain public interest – to survive in translocal time/space. As long as a problem is the focus of attention, all the ideas that can be related to it have a greater chance of being realized. All existing actions that can be represented as being coupled with it have a greater chance of being legitimized.

In 1890s, the public discourse in Britain was tinged with a concern that Britain's international position in business and industry was at risk because of inadequate teaching and research. In August 1894, the British Association for the Advancement of Science spoke for the need to advance the systematic study of economics. Thus the bequest met the (already formulated) need resulted in the idea of LSE: the first university organization dedicated to the social sciences. As Rorty put it, "poetic, artistic, philosophical, scientific or political progress results from the accidental coincidence of a private obsession with a public need" (1989: 37).

The original plan was to engage political science, history, and economics in the study of humanity's social relationships. Sociology, geography, statistics, and anthropology followed suit, with psychology as the latest addition. The goals and the means of LSE were to differ from those of a traditional university: it was to be a neutral and unbiased center of research, but with a pragmatic and practical bent. The advanced studies of social relationships were to be used in education for careers in administration and business.

LSE was both an invention or an imitation. The social sciences already occupied an influential position in France, and the French had their écoles educating the ruling elites. Wallas mentioned École Libre des Sciences Politiques in Paris as a model, whereas Webb was impressed by the Faculty of Political Science at Columbia University and the economics courses at MIT. The social sciences"... were not exactly invented at LSE but the School brought them together like no other university in Europe, led them to full bloom in all their variety, and then reflected the aches and pains of their maturity, in which professionalization often went hand in hand with an uncertain sense of direction" (Dahrendorf 1995: viii). The character of this invention was related to the Fabians' non-revolutionary – indeed, incrementalist – version of socialism, which was in fashion. The Webbs and GBS were undoubtedly "fashion leaders", and though individuals cannot create fashion, they can try to influence it, often successfully (Czarniawska 2005). What is more, they can use fashion for the purpose of creating new institutions. Fashion operates at institutional fringes. On the one hand, its variety is limited by the "iron cage" of existing institutions, which fashion actually reproduces; on the other hand, fashion is engaged in a constant subversion of the existing institutional order, gnawing ant-like at its bars.

Similarly, although fashion seems to sabotage and threaten established institutions, it is also an institutional playfield: new fashions can be tried and disposed of or it can become institutionalized, thus revitalizing the existing institutional order. Webb saw LSE as an experiment: "'it would make a great public sensation, and would, I am sure, 'catch on'. If not, it need not be continued'" (quoted by Dahrendorf 1995: 8).

The final say in the selection of ideas, and of fashions, is often given to the Zeitgeist who, like all holy spirits, has the double virtue of being invisible and all-encompassing, thus stopping the spiral of still further questions. This is not pure metaphysics: Forty (1986) argued that, in a sense, an idea cannot catch on unless it has already existed for some time in the minds of many people, as a part of what is called the spirit of the time. How does the spirit of the time change? Gradually and imperceptibly.

> Europe did not decide to accept the idiom of Romantic poetry, or of socialist politics, or of Galilean mechanics. That sort of shift was no more an act of will than it was a result of argument. Rather, Europe gradually lost the habit of using certain words and gradually acquired the habit of using others (Rorty 1989: 6).

Thus, although the London School of Economics and Political Science was instituted by a decision, or rather by a series of decisions, it was made possible through an initiative of institutional entrepreneurs who correctly deciphered the shift in the idiom of the day.

One more element should be added to the picture: the turn-of-the-century atmosphere. The emerging institutions become connected to existing institutions that serve as sources of ideas, stimuli for action, or both. Anniversaries, birthdays, centennials, and millennia are institutionalized celebrations that permit certain unusual actions and invite certain unusual ways of sensemaking. Turn-of-the-century is always a huge event in Europe, one that provokes enormous amounts of sense-making, which can lead to change (Joerges 1990). The time perspectives of people and organizations are turned around; courses of action are taken that break against formed expectations about what is normal, lawful, and repetitive. The unique, the unlikely, the unprecedented, even the impossible happens – or is anticipated and begins to guide action. Epochs are closed (and thereby defined), other futures are opened (and thereby tentatively defined) by breaking cleanly with the past. Such a context is favorable for turning latent ideas into projects. It entails a vast redefinition of situations, an extraordinary mobilization of resources, and the unfreezing of institutionalized resource allocations. Thus 1895 was a good year to start a new School.

An idea is enacted

The idea is objectified and attracts further allies

Sidney Webb began slowly to materialize the idea of LSE. Money first: on 8 February 1895, the Hutchinson Trustees agreed to spend most of the money on the School of Economics and Political Science, detailing its structure and the subjects of its lectures. As Webb had never intended to become a director, first Wallas, who refused, and then Hewins, who accepted, were offered the job. As Dahrendorf noted, Webb was 35 at the time, and Hewins was 29 – which may explain the pace of what happened next:

> Within six months [Hewins] found rooms for the School, designed the sylla-bus of its courses, gathered support for the new venture urbi et orbi, and at-tracted over two hundred students so that the first academic year of the Lon-don School of Economics and Political Science could start on 10 October 1895 (Dahrendorf 1995: 13).

Apart from the age of these entrepreneurs, and the fact that the 19th century was the age of founders (Gründerzeit), it was the lack of bureaucracy, Dahrendorf said, that allowed these men to put the school into operation.

Sidney Webb continued to attract sponsors: private donations and support from LCC's Technical Education Board. Webb had reorganized the board for that very purpose and had managed to have himself elected as Chairman. Hewins wrote letters to economists and social scientists in Europe and enlisted either their moral support or their direct collaboration. He coaxed the Society of Arts and the Chamber of Commerce into helping with the provision of rooms for the School. He obtained these donations by promising a neutral perspective for the School, a pledge that enraged Shaw and caused him to lose interest and withdraw from the emerging network. This was the first but by no means the last time a potentially central actor was reduced to a role of an actant (an object of the network's action).

Hewins also wrote (by hand) the academic program of the School. By July 1895, it had become a printed prospectus of 11 pages. All lectures and most of the classes were to be given between 18.00 and 21.00; men and women, British subjects and foreigners were equally welcome. There were tuition fees, but also scholarships; a publication series to secure the visibility of research results was arranged.

Hewins gave also what Dahrendorf called "a string of upbeat newspaper interviews", in which the Webbs' names were seldom mentioned. One of the newspapers called the yet non-existent LSE "one of the great English institutions of the new age" (Dahrendorf 1995: 23). Entrepreneurs, a name, rented rooms, a prospectus, money, staff, students and media testimony: everything was ready. It should be no surprise that "... words, printed and unprinted, were from the beginning the great weapons which LSE people used, weapons of attack and also weapons of self-defense, not least from the often unbearable tension of values and social science" (Dahrendorf 1995: viii).

The idea is put into practice and "a great romance" begins

And so it started. They held lectures, a departure from the tutoring tradition of Oxford and Cambridge, demonstrating from the beginning the School's in-built paradox: "Hewins in the front parlour lecturing to a dozen or so mostly men on economics; Wallas in the back parlour lecturing to twenty or thirty mostly women on Poor Law" (quoted by Dahrendorf 1995: 61). A school of commerce, and a high brow university; a school for everyone, yet educating "the captains of industry and commerce"; the Chairman to the left, the Director to the right; the Director and the Secretary aloof and disciplinarian, the Head Porter creating a domestic atmosphere; an "imperialist" staff and "social reformist" students.

What happened when it came to open conflict? In the times of the Boer War, the School divided into four factions (four being perhaps better for survival than two); and when the School was offered a Gladstone memorial endowment by the Liberal Party, its member and the main "imperialist", Hewins, said that it could be accepted only on the condition that everyone would be eligible, for "the School, like the rain, must fall equally on the just and the unjust" (quoted by Dahrendorf 1995: 68). The money went to Oxford.

Apart from formal lectures, the staff and the frequent guests conversed at the Webbs' "At Homes". Staff and students gossiped over afternoon tea arranged by the Secretary, Miss Mactaggart, and, beginning in 1897, the students debated – and danced – at the Student Union meetings. The "romance" of the title is not merely a metaphor: the School, Dahrendorf said, constituted practically a "universe of life": with many women and many foreigners, the world was present in its diversity. Unsurprisingly, there were many marriages between alumni and between staff members, and whole families frequented the School for generations. Dahrendorf noticed all this, but his explanation of the School's success gave primary credit to the entrepreneurs:

> There are several reasons why the venture of building up a new institution (...) succeeded. It benefitted, in the apt phrase used in later Calendars (...) from "the conjunction of need with an opportunity". Circumstances were favourable; a significant demand for social science education could be tapped; thanks to Henry Hunt Hutchinson and Charlotte Payne-Townshend and others the wherewithal was found; influential persons like R.B. Haldane were prepared to lend their support. But when all is said and done, no deconstruction of the history of LSE can detract from the fact that its foundation was the work of two unusual men, Sidney Webb and W.A.S. Hewins (Dahrendorf 1995: 64-65).

Why should the entrepreneurs be considered so much more important than any other actant? Elsewhere Dahrendorf said that LSE was not "merely the creature of a passing Zeitgeist" (p. 474). He was probably referring to similar attempts that had failed – a London School of Geography and a London School of Ethics and Social Philosophy – but it could just as well be that the window of opportunity had already closed (Kingston, 1984). Not to detract from Webb and Hewins, I believe that the School could have been built by two other people, and it certainly has survived both of them, or perhaps survived because it was able to rid itself of both of them. The School needed stabilization, not only in its early years, but especially then.

LSE becomes an artifact

With the exception of clandestine schools, a school is not a school without a building. Webb and Hewins understood it well, and in February 1896 a large house was rented at 10 Adelphi Terrace. Additional weight was to be added by a Library, a separate but connected building. More funds were obtained from Hutchison's Trust; from Shaw's fiancée, Charlotte Payne-Townshend, who also rented the upper, unnecessary floors of the building; and from other donors. The British Library of Political Science opened on 9 November 1896[3].

As a stabilizing artifact, a building of one's own is much better than a rented building. Webb first signed a permanent lease on 1300 m2 in Clare Market from London County Council, which, as Dahrendorf noted, he was renting as the Chairman of LSE from himself as the Chairman of the Technical Education Board at LCC. He next approached a well-known benefactor, John Passmore Edwards, for funds. Dahrendorf commented that the correspondence between them constitutes painful reading, but "quite typical of the relationship between a benefactor and an academic beggar for institutional money" (p. 54). The foundation stone for Passmore Edwards Hall was laid on 2 July 1900, and in May 1902 the School was moved to its new location. In the meantime the money proved, inevitably, to be short, and Lord Rothschild, among others, helped out. Rothschild then became President of the School.

The School also became a legal body, in a form that seems somewhat exotic to a non-British observer. LSE became a college of the new University of London and a Faculty of Economics and Political Science (including Commerce and Industry) was created, which meant that LSE lecturers became recognized university teachers. LSE was incorporated under the Companies Act as a company limited by guarantee, and registered on 13 June 1901 as the "Incorporated London School of Economics". Because the Board of Trade agreed that the School did not have to include "Limited" in its name, on 2 August 1957 "Incorporated" was dropped. Another important artifact in this context was the text defining the goal of the Corporation: "to provide for all classes and denominations without any distinction whatsoever, opportunities and encouragement for pursuing a regular and liberal course of education of the highest grade and quality in the various branches of knowledge dealt with by the institution" (quoted by Dahrendorf 1995: 58). A new institution became solidified by connections created to two other, older institutions: the university and the corporation.

Four years after its opening, the School had 1400 registered students from 16 countries, although it could not confer degrees until a year later. Most of the original teachers remained and new ones joined. The School was a fact, and an object.

Actions into routines

As Martha Feldman and Brian Pentland (2005) pointed out, routines are important but underestimated stabilizers on par with artifacts. What needed to be

---

[3] It became the British Library of Political Science and Economics in 1925.

routinized in LSE were administrative, pedagogical, and scientific activities. The person to begin this task was the next director, the geographer, Halford Mackinder (Hewins left in 1903 for his next project). A three-year undergraduate degree-day course was organized, special advisory committees were established to guarantee the continuity of research, a systematic program of visiting evening lecturers was put into operation, and the Library was turned into a research site with special emphasis on sociology and history. Postgraduate research was increasing in visibility – about 40 percent of all British postgraduates were at LSE. The Director had begun to write regular annual reports (Hewins wrote only one) – and saw to it that he had somebody to report to. Various governmental and administrative bodies were established, apart from the Court of Governors (Professorial Committee, Council of Management, Finance and General Purpose Committee). The Secretary, Miss Mactaggart, received clear responsibilities.

Beginning with Mackinder, large amounts of text were produced by the directors and many others, which seems to support the Phillips et al. (2004) thesis about the importance of texts in the process of institutionalization. At the same time, the history of LSE also exemplifies to perfection why texts are not enough, as the later case of Dahrendorf's 1974 failed project will show.

During Mackinder's time, the railways and then the army sent students in great numbers to LSE, and their fees, together with grants from public bodies and more fluctuating donations, constituted important financial input. Mackinder was quick, therefore, in responding to a cue from the Treasury Committee, which seemed to strongly appreciate the new School, and obtained a significant state grant. He was also keen on cultivating connections with the University and successful in attracting grants to support the development of the newfangled discipline of sociology.

Mackinder left his post in 1908, and the School was "better organized and academically more solid than he had found it" (p. 108). Yet Mackinder is not seen as an institutional entrepreneur. Without him, or without someone who fulfilled the stabilizing functions, the School might have failed, as others did. A question arises: Are certain persons seen as institutional entrepreneurs because they have established institutions or because they reveal traits that people associate, in the mythology of entrepreneurship, as necessary for such an endeavor – vision and enthusiasm, as opposed to mere administrative skills? Can it be that, if Sidney Webb had not existed, he would have had to be invented, and that the romance of entrepreneurship dictates the plot of its documentation? That a spokesperson is mistaken for the force behind a macro actor?

The idea is maintained and institutionalized

It is my thesis that institutional entrepreneurs, although playing a role in the emergence of institutions, do not shape them according to their will. In support of this position I briefly review the times of crisis that threatened the School and the ways in which it survived them, together with significant positive turns in the School's fate. The first crisis had, in fact, to do with its founder.

Webb resigns

On 17 September 1910, with Beatrice present, Sidney Webb gave a flamboyant talk to the railway unionists. This talk was used by the Webbs' political opponents on the issue of Poor Law to attack him as an inappropriate Chairman for LSE, which, after all, educated railway executives. Although all three Directors defended him, he used the world tour that he and Beatrice had planned as a pretext to resign. As Dahrendorf pointed out, the Webbs' actions in the matter of Poor Law were unrealistic and harmful to most of their causes; thus one can deduce that even most famous institutional entrepreneurs do not succeed with all the institutions they attempt to erect. One could claim, in fact, that the law the Webbs were trying to promote was more important than the School and that Sidney Webb cared about it more than he cared about LSE. The majority version of the law against which the Webbs rebelled was not implemented until some twenty years later.

Webb helped LSE once more, when the Director, William Pember Reeves, suffered a breakdown after the death of his son in 1917. Webb undertook the unpleasant duty of informing Reeves that his services were no longer required, assumed responsibility for the School between May and October 1919, and helped find Sir William Beveridge and convince him to become the next director.

In 1932, the Webbs traveled to the Soviet Union and described Stalin's purges in a way that Dahrendorf, in general a supporter of the Webbs, called "sickening" (1995: 268). Ernest Gellner (1995:3) thought Dahrendorf's phrasing contained "too much sorrow and too little anger", and suggested, for the good of the School, that the Founders were best forgotten.

The second foundation

Beatrice Webb coined the expression "the second foundation" describing in her diaries the Beveridge era (1919-1937), during which several things happened and several other things were produced. Beveridge introduced a commerce degree, which, he figured, had to be right, as it was criticized by both theoreticians and practitioners. A new building complex (requiring new money) has been constructed (no foundation without a foundation stone – laid in 1920 by King George V). "Staff now had rooms, there were even administrative quarters, students had classrooms as well as space for recreation, there were lecture theatres, there was a real library" (Dahrendorf 1995: 143). New faculty members were recruited and received full-time university posts, and the majority of students enrolled full time, a transformation that Beveridge called a "decasualization".

Dahrendorf shared the opinion of other biographers that all this might have happened without Beveridge, but that it would probably have proceeded more slowly and without a "Beveridge impress". The latter, Dahrendorf said, was his success with students, whom he saw as citizens of a modern state, to use his own metaphor (the faculty members, in contrast, were not fond of him).

In order to solidify, to legitimize the idea-become-action, signals had to be sent to the wider community: dramatizing, justifying, marketing, selling, and propagating. Although Webb understood all this, his choice of media was traditional: letters, articles, lectures. But an idea, locally translated into action, must be reified, for purposes of non-local communication, into a quasi-object that can travel and is recognizable as a translocal frame of reference. During Beveridge's time, the logo of a beaver and the motto, *rerum cognoscere causas* were promptly produced. The School's own journal, *Economica*, began publication in 1921.

It seems that Beveridge was a workaholic and an autocrat, two characteristics that supposedly hold the key to the governance structure he formed and survived for many decades. This structure's main trait was the delegation of governing duties from the Court of Governors (whose numbers were simply too high) to the Director, justifying it with two arguments: that the collegiate system at Oxford and Cambridge was not innovative and that academics should teach and do research and not be bothered with administration.

Beveridge was not alone: as Webb had his Hewins, so Beveridge had his Jessy Mair – first as his Secretary and later as his wife. She replaced Miss Mactaggart, who had actually run the School during the last years of Reeves' directorship, was promoted to the position of Dean, and then retired. Jessy Mair assumed both positions simultaneously.

Beveridge's perhaps greatest scoop was the grant he obtained from the Rockefeller Memorial and Foundation, which, in the years 1923-1937, constituted one-quarter of LSE's income. Interestingly enough, Rockefeller came looking for LSE and not the other way around, but once they had found each other, Beveridge took great care to preserve the connection. He established a Committee that produced serious and regular reports, sailed across the Atlantic when necessary, and, with the help of the Secretary, maintained frequent informal contacts with the foundations.

During the period 1928-1932, many of the original professors retired and were replaced by people trained at the School – a generational exchange that appears to have had a serious stabilizing effect on the School. Beveridge left in 1937.

Dahrendorf has emphasized Beveridge's single-minded pursuit of his goals, which verged on an obsession. In fact, Beveridge's undoing as Director, apart from his over-reliance on the Secretary, began with his obsession for developing "the Natural Bases of Social Science". He told the Rockefeller Foundation that that was the wish of his professors and told his professors that Rockefeller wanted it that way. Had the sociology of science and technology existed at the time, it might have fit the bill; but it did not and it had not. A zoologist by the name of Lancelot Hogben, who kept toads on the premises and disagreed with everyone, took the chair in 1930 – and left it in 1937, when it was obvious that he lacked the support of Rockefeller and his fellow professors.

I am taking Dahrendorf on his word here – the description of the events does not demonstrate why the Director's obsession for the "Natural Basis of Social Science" should have been his undoing; institutional entrepreneurs often have fixed ideas, some of them innocent. However, Dahrendorf described other undermining events, three of which occurred in 1934. There were conflicts between Beveridge and the Student Union and between Beveridge and the politologist Harold Laski, in both cases over the freedom of speech; the Director was horrified that the School might be perceived as "Red". On the other side of the political divide was a hasty promise to extract the library of the Frankfurt Institute from Germany. All these decisions were made autocratically, even if some were later accepted by his professors or his sponsors. In the same year, Beveridge was instrumental in creating the Academic Assistance Council for refugees: many refugee scientists from Germany and Austria came to LSE in the 1930s.

Beveridge wanted to resign from his post as early as 1929, and true to form, he concocted a secret plan that would gracefully retire him into a chair of economics. When the plan became known, however, the LSE professors opposed it and Rockefeller refused to finance it, withdrawing his support from the School. In the eyes of the Rockefeller Foundation's representatives, LSE was in a mess by 1935, with no rescue plan in sight. In 1937, Beveridge left for Oxford and managed to negotiate a deal permitting Ms. Mair to remain until 1938, beyond her retirement age. Professor Alexander Carr-Saunders stepped into Beveridge's post.

Should Beveridge be seen as an institutional entrepreneur in his role as the School's first successful and, in his last years, unsuccessful administrator? Or should he be seen as the Chairman of the Committee that produced the Beveridge Report in 1942, making him, at least in Dahrendorf's eyes, "the father of the modern welfare state" (1995: 154)? Observe that in his second role Beveridge did not even know that he was the founder of an institution; it took twenty years to implement the recommendations of the Report. Here again is a clash between the two meanings of the notion of "institution": that of a formal grouping of people, an organization or an association, which can truly be seen as an enterprise; and that of a collective practice that becomes justified and taken for granted.

The "door-openers"

Dahrendorf mentioned an interesting category of people who played an important role in solidifying the LSE in the first sense of the "institution", without much visibility in this role. For some reason he called them "gatekeepers", clearly unaware of the sense in which Kurt Lewin (1947) had used the term (groups or individuals who make decisions about what is allowed in or kept out). The people Dahrendorf had in mind had kept the doors open (he probably intended to say "doorstoppers") between the inside and the outside, among political factions, among academic factions, and between the mighty Director and the Secretary on the one hand and the students on the other. In the academic group, he counted Laski, in spite of his tendency to provoke scandals; Miss Mactaggart in her role as Secretary; the Registrar and, later, Secretary, Eve Evans; Dr. Vera Anstey, who took care of the student lodgings during the wartime evacuation to Cambridge; and last but not least, the porters. These people are worthy of attention because they helped a group of people who were pulled together by an institution to survive as people and as an organization, while the institutional entrepreneurs were engaged in meetings with the Zeitgeist. The metaphor of the doors – closed or open – became quite literal in 1968 when the students demolished the gates and then the doors installed at various places in the School by the then-Director, Sydney Caine.

Going on in style

"The job to be done at the School was not just one of style, much as style mattered", Dahrendorf said (1995: 337), introducing the era of Alexander Carr-Saunders that lasted for twenty years. In the recommendation sent to the Selection Committee, Carr-Saunders was described as: "admirable on Committees, practical, clear-headed and judicious, very even-tempered, and magnanimous. He doesn't inspire; but he encourages. People would like and trust him; and he would stay the course" (Dahrendorf, 1995: 334). An ideal director, it seems, but not perceived as an entrepreneur, although he led the School through difficult times for twenty years. Why not? According to Dahrendorf, because the School entered the period of "normalization", aided by the 1944 Education Act and the 1963 Report on Higher Education. LSE has become a normal university; additionally, the unrest of 1968 and the hostile political attitude toward the social sciences that began in late 1970s did not help to maintain "the style". One interpretation would be that a bigger and sturdier institution – a university – annexed the smaller one. One can see an analogy with business entrepreneurship: a small company fights for survival and then growth; its success leads to its acquisition by a large company. Is this a sign of success or the end of the entrepreneurial dream? In other words, has LSE survived as an institution?

Before I move to the next section, in which I try to answer these questions, let me point out some additional lessons that can be learned from more than one hundred years of LSE history. The presence of "stars" is not necessary for a lively and effective teaching environment, but the presence of first-rate scholars is. Clifford Geertz's memory of his years at Princeton may offer a clue as to why stars are bothersome ("such a collection of luminaries set free from real- world constraints to rub up against one another might be expected to produce [a highly personalized academic politics]", 1995: 123). Another surprising insight concerns the numbers: Gellner, in agreement with Carr-Saunders and Dahrendorf, gave the expression "critical mass" the meaning opposite to the received one: a number of people "beyond which a collection of people can no longer be an intellectual community with an ongoing and continuous debate" (Gellner, 1980: 13). In his eyes, the LSE of the post-war period became a victim of the cult of growth and turned into "a factory of degrees".

As far as the institutional entrepreneurs are concerned, many commentators have noted that their one important trait is the knowledge of when to let go, with Webb quoted as a positive example and Beveridge as a negative one.

Love, contingency and control

Why was it loved so much?

According to actor-network theory, love is a necessary requirement for an artifact in a center of a macro-actor, and therefore the macro-actor itself, to survive
(Latour, 1996). It certainly seems that LSE, as an artifact, enjoyed love in abun-
dance. In the Preface to his history, Ralf Dahrendorf claimed that one of the
alumni asked him to express "in a word the charm of the place which so many
call lovingly 'the School' as if there was no other school in the world." (1995: v).
He then proceeded, giving an explanation along the lines that Gabriel Tarde
(1890/1962) would have called "logical reasons", but soon moved to "extra-
logical" reasons:

> One word? That may be asking too much, and a word would be too little for
> an answer. One theme perhaps. There is forever an explosive relationship be-
> tween social science and public policy. Californians worry about the San An-
> dreas Fault and what its violent erruption might to do the peace of their
> homes: LSE disturbs the peace of mind of those who are directly, or more of-
> ten indirectly, affected by its doings through another fault line (...) between
> wanting to know the causes of things and wanting to change things, dispas-
> sionate study and committed action, ascetic aspirations and worldly tempta-
> tions. The very location of the School defines the fault line, at the heart of the
> polygon which includes the Law Courts and the City, Bloomsbury and Thea-
> treland, Whitehall and Westminster. (...)
> This is where the architectural as well as the geological metaphor ends, for it
> was never just the common roof which united the School. LSE may be per-
> manently threatened by quakes of one kind or another, but it is also a place
> which engenders a special kind of loyalty among its members. LSE matters
> to those who have come to it. It is not just a few lines in their curricula vitae,
> an educational experience, or even a first-rate university, but an institution
> which has laid claim to a part of the hearts and souls of many. (...)
> For the major part of its first century (...) the School was a place to work and
> to play, to spend long days in earnest seminar and corridor talk as well as on
> frivolous pursuits like lunch-hour dances, to make friends, and for not a few
> to find their partners for life. LSE creates a common sense of belonging for
> people who recognize each other wherever they meet..." (Dahrendorf, 1995:
> v-vi).

The first part of Dahrendorf's utterance is a description of specificity of the School as an idea; it is hardly an explanation of its success, however. A great many academic organizations that were trying to combine "dispassionate study and committed action" have either vanished or have given weight to the one side. The location of the School in the center of the city is already a clue, and far more than a metaphor. What is in the center of the city is in the center of public attention. To move out of the city, unless to a city of its own, as Microsoft did, is equal to moving out of that attention, as both the directors and the porters fully understood.

Even more explanatory power can be attributed to the "extra-logical" reasons explored by Dahrendorf: the love and loyalty of the School's alumni. But why did they love it so much?

I think that Dahrendorf provided an answer, both in the quote and in the book, but did not label it. I would say that the School, unlike many other academic organizations, constituted a complete world. He mentioned "work and play", but only in another place did he mention an aspect central to my view: from the inception, women constituted a natural and integral part of the School, not only as students, but also as people in high positions, formally or informally. Additionally, because of the evening students, the age of the student population varied, unlike the situation in other universities. This complete world was also due to the high percentage of foreign faculty and students; again, they were not there as tokens of some alien group (Austrian émigrés, Indian exchange students), but as full-fledged members of the School who brought their alterity – their defining difference – with them and mixed it into LSE. Granted, the code of conduct was very "British", but it was, and is, a theatrical Britishness, at which the foreigners can actually beat the locals. LSE was thus a micro-world, and a world easy to love: full of variety, based on irresolvable tensions (between theory and practice, between political left and right), and turning this tension into a source of energy rather than disruption (a "tamed paradox", as it were).

Additionally, as Dahrendorf pointed out, it was never "an ivory tower": "on the contrary, truly academic pursuits always involved a battle to keep the noise of the outside world out" (1995: 301). No wonder that it felt like taking part in history just to be there. What role had the institutional entrepreneurs in all of this?

Contingency or control? An anthill

Does the emergence of LSE conform to the model of institutionalization as a contingent process, or to the idea of instituting – the result of effective control exerted by the entrepreneurs? Both.

Let me first review Dahrendorf's reasoning: I was, after all, piggy-backing on his work, and he was a great sociologist who had his own explanation. He started with the lucky complementarity of Webb's visions and Hewins's hard work: necessary but not sufficient. He also noted alliances, but these are also a work of entrepreneurs, and I would give them greater weight. He even brought fashion into the equation: "The 'five Es' which made up the field of intellectual forces in which LSE came into being – Education, Economics, Efficiency, Equality, Empire – were associated with the great or at least fashionable names of the time" (1995: 25).

So what did the institutional entrepreneurs actually do? They recruited, enrolled, translated the interests, and stabilized the connections, just as actants and actors building a macro actor do. The interesting aspect of this case, however, is that the allies practically begged to be enrolled. Dahrendorf himself comments on the Treasury Committee's cue to LSE: "Those were the times!" (1995: 93). Indeed, the times when he was the Director were very different.

In this light, the relevance of the garbage can model becomes evident. In a given time and place, a Zeitgeist met the institutional entrepreneurs who picked up/translated/invented an idea that fit both it and the sponsors who were willing to respond to the call. The rest is history, one is prompted to say, but that would be too glib. The garbage can theory does not exploit its own metaphor on one point: what reaction is occurring to produce an effect (a decision or, better yet, an institution – after all, a decision seems to be momentary whereas an institution "ferments" for a long time). One could ask: What is the role of the institutional entrepreneurs in this metaphorical picture? Are they enzymes? I would like to suggest a metaphor that might combine both models: an institution as an anthill[4]. It is not a building erected according to a plan; it is a practice of long standing, taken for granted by the ants; and if the ants might not know what justifies its existence, the biologists certainly do. The anthill is a part of an ecosystem, and can be built only in specific places where specific materials are available, and at specific times. It takes many ants to build it, and as individuals they are indispensable but not irreplaceable. Who are the institutional entrepreneurs? The ants who start the building – the idea being the queen? It is tempting to say that they

---

[4]   The metaphor was previously used to describe open-source communities (Lefkowitz 2002).

are warriors – male ants with wings. This would be unfair, however, as warriors do not work and institutional entrepreneurs do.

Each metaphor reaches the end of its usefulness at some point. As for now, however, the metaphor of an institution as an anthill and the observation that institutional entrepreneurs are not necessarily those individuals who become heroes of popular narratives rest on the history of LSE only. In what follows, I briefly present two other cases to support my analysis. In the spirit of grounded theory, I first report an effort similar to that of establishing LSE, which failed. Second, I briefly recall the history of building a school without building a School – the Chicago school of sociology.

How anthills emerge

Young universities in old Europe

This section is based on a study of an attempt to establish a new university in Northern Germany, as reported by Czarniawska and Wolff (1998), which we called the NGU. It originated in the wave of the EU initiatives to stimulate growth in what was considered underdeveloped regions of Europe. Thus in 1983, the Christian-Democratic Regional Government of the Northern Province approached (or was approached by) what was then the only private university in Germany. Compared with other parts of Germany, the North had an inadequate educational system, and the rate of innovation lower than in the rest of the country. The investment rate was also low during the 1980s. It was believed that a new university could rejuvenate and stimulate the region. The provincial government and the representatives of the university agreed on a plan of cooperation for the province.

By engaging in the launching of a private university, the government was solving some of its own problems as well as those of the province. During the 1970s, the previous government had promised one of the cities in the region that they would found a polytechnic there. The land had been acquired and developed, it was formally dedicated in a symbolic opening ceremony, and the necessary legislation was enacted. As a consequence of a budget squeeze, however, the government had been forced to postpone the establishment of the university, although the legal arrangements were still valid.

The years 1983-84 were dedicated to generating support for the idea and creating networks of people and institutions to make its implementation possible. No professional academics were involved during this phase, which was dominated by politicians and administrators. On 26 September 1984, the university was officially founded. The act of incorporation declared that one of the fundamental functions of the university was to create a bridge between Scandinavia and the continent. Further, all faculty members and all students were to engage in a philosophical discourse as an obligatory part of the courses and research program. Theory and practice were to be combined at the various levels inside and outside the university.

The founding act was followed by intensive negotiations with the government. On 7 June 1985, the provincial government announced its endorsement of a second private institution of higher education in the Federal Republic. The act contained specific rules for such things as the organization of the university; the design of the curriculum; the structure of the faculties; and, in particular, overall control exercised by the government. There was a stipulation that no faculty should start teaching without confirming to the ministry that its financial basis was secure. It should be mentioned that the act itself required a change in the law concerning higher education.

The emerging university was dependent on a fund controlled by a board including representatives from well-known German multinational companies. These people were supposed to act as ambassadors for the university, while guaranteeing (or at least contributing to) its financial basis. A formal opening ceremony attended by government representatives marked the formal start of the university's life. In August 1985, the first professor was engaged for the Faculty of Economics to speed the process of designing the curriculum and organizing the Faculty.

In the autumn of 1985, the board decided that the head of administration was allowing his private business commitments to mingle to too great an extent with those of the university. His unfortunate combination of personal and institutional interests had been criticized by some of the sponsors and led to the termination of his employment. The vulnerable process of building a new organization had been disrupted. Reactions varied. The still small group of academics sought to launch the image of a private university governed by professional academic norms. Networks of supporting colleagues were activated in order to demonstrate the honesty and seriousness of the emerging organization. This external support was needed, particularly to combat the gathering criticism from the other university in the province, which was a state organization. All this turbulence, however, served to speed up events.

On 1 October 1986, the NGU welcomed its first students in a ceremony held in a church. On 3 October, 400 selected guests from Germany, Austria, and Scandinavia gathered on the Faculty's premises to celebrate its formal opening. Symbolically, the university had now come into being. This meant, however, that the NGU started operating before a steady resource basis had been secured. At the same time, the original idea of the "university as a profit-making machine" had disappeared with the entrepreneurial head of administration. The leadership now counted upon the support promised by the provincial government, which in turn was expected to elicit supplementary support from the private sector. The university ended its first year of operations (1986-87) with a deficit of 1.2 million DM. Although the difference was covered by the provincial government, the newspapers had dramatic headlines: "Is the private university founded in 1984 nearing its end? A gap of millions: NGU facing bankruptcy." The reaction from the university was to close ranks, at least in public: "The University is strengthened by the crisis," claimed the leaders. The attacks continued, however. The University Presidents' Conference in the province was unanimous: "Don't pay for the NGU!"

In March 1988, the headlines cried: "NGU needs more money than ever!" The articles referred to the NGU's estimate that a further 5 million DM were needed to survive for another academic year – something, it was suggested, that had been previously concealed. In fact, the figures matched the estimates published by the same newspapers two years earlier, when 10 million DM was the amount given as the annual budget. The difference lay more in the long-range budget, which showed a tendency to increase – a characteristic of all big projects, which always turn out more expensive than predicted. A broader political consensus was sought on the question of financing the university. It was noted in some quarters that stricter financial control should be exercised over its operations. On the whole, however, the attitudes were positive and, in May 1988, a third faculty was opened. The crisis seemed to be over and the stabilization on course.

The same year, however, one of the most spectacular postwar scandals, involving a leading figure in the government, shook the Northern Province and its stable political order. The new government had a different ideology regarding both privatization and anthroposophy. Private universities in particular were regarded as contradicting the Social Democratic Party's idea of higher education as a public concern. After approximately six months of negotiations, the NGU was closed down by a special Regional Government Act. Some of the consulting activities were transferred to a research institute situated in one of the cities. Some of the students were admitted to the neighboring university and some to other schools in the country.

Rolf Wolff and I offered a detailed analysis of the NGU story, of which only one aspect is relevant here. The institutional entrepreneurs (and there is no doubt that the founders of NGU deserve such a label) underestimated an institutionalized union of states and schools in Europe (Ramirez and Boli, 1987). Also, one can claim with the hindsight, they enrolled weak allies: the Scandinavians instead of US schools, as their followers did. And the translation of interests – the companies that were to become sponsors – did not hold. Does it mean that they failed as institutional entrepreneurs? Not from the anthill perspective.

In January 1999, Gary Wolfram, analyzing the situation of private colleges in USA, pointed out that Germany still had only one private university – the one mentioned above. He was probably not well informed, or else the new anthill was build practically overnight. By 2002, there were 46 private universities in Germany (Steghaus-Kovac 2002; Wallace 2002). All the commentators come with a similar explanation: the declining reputation of public universities in Germany. From the model to the world in the 19th century, only Heidelberg made it to the 2004 *Times Higher Educational Supplement*'s top fifty best universities – in 47th place (Bhatti 2005). So, although the NGU failed as an organization, it contributed to a rise of a new institution.

Need a school to be a School?

In this section, I briefly recapitulate the history of the Chicago school of sociology, as an illustration of an institutional entrepreneurship that did not involve or concentrate upon the building of formal organizations. The institution in question is, as most people agree, "the first successful American program of collective sociological research", which, rather than launching a specific approach, propagated commitment to a firm connection between theory and field research (Blumer 1984: xv, 224) and to a thesis that social life must be always located in a time and place (Abbott 1999). It is necessary, however, to confront a likely critique first: wasn't Chicago school of sociology (a school of thought) dependent on the existence of University of Chicago (a formal organization)? Yes it was; John D. Rockefeller, Sr. (the main sponsor) and William Rainey Harper (the first president) are legendary entrepreneurs – one in finance, the other in academia (Feffer 1993). Yet they have not established either the institution of a university, which goes back to Middle Ages in Europe; the institution of modern higher education, which is usually attributed to Wilhelm von Humboldt (1767-1835); or even the US university focusing on research, following in the footsteps of Johns Hopkins and then Clark (Bulmer 1984). University of Chicago has been highly successful, however, in that it first saw the birth of the pragmatist school of philosophy; then the Chicago school of sociology; and, finally, the Chicago school of economics (McCloskey 1994). As William James put it facetiously but acutely, speaking of philosophy: "Here [at Harvard] we have thought, but no school. At Yale a school but no thought. Chicago has both." (1903, as quoted by Bulmer 1984: 28).

Andrew Abbott (1999) located the beginnings of his story of the Chicago school at 1892, when Albion W. Small founded the first-ever Department of Sociology; Bulmer (1984) focused on the years 1915-1935, when William I. Thomas and then Robert E. Park and Ernest W. Burgess set the grounds for what became a legend.

The legend of a school of thought has its standard narrative, too. It is usually a story of a giant mind, followed by mediocre-minded crowds of disciples. As an aphorism, it takes the form of what Merton (1965/1993) called OTSOG, or "on the shoulders of giants", tracing it back to the 12th century. And yet the strong suspicion is that this is yet another stylized story of science, as opposed to the actual one – that the science stands on a pyramid of midgets – an anthill image, after all. Chicago school is a perfect example of "the power of associations", as Latour would have called it. How did Thomas convince Znaniecki, a philosopher, to read thousands of letters of Polish peasants? Most likely, because he had an unusual argument: perhaps the first-ever research grant[5]. They were clearly good at enrolling but they also had a boundary object (Star and Griesemer 1989): the City of Chicago. Bulmer put it succinctly: "The dense, highly integrated, local network of teachers and graduate students carrying out a program of research in one city centered around common problems" (1984: 1). Was that their invention? No; as Jazbinsek et al. (2001) convincingly demonstrated, Chicago's scholars were inspired by Charles Booth's seventeen volumes on *Life and Labour of the People of London* from 1892 and followed the blueprint of *Großstadt-Dokumente* edited in the years 1904-1908 by Hans Ostwald in Berlin. Although this latter research made no impact on German sociology (judged by German sociologists as too journalistic) and did not produce a school in the sense used in science studies, scholars like Louis Wirth translated it, in many senses of the word, to fit US circumstances.

One important aspect of the Chicago school was its mouthpiece, the *American Journal of Sociology*, with its first editor, Albion W. Small; and its connection to an emerging macro actor, the American Sociological Society (16 presidents of the Society in the years 1924-1950 were either Chicago graduates or Chicago faculty). In 1915, a year after the Chicago library acquired all 51 volumes of the Berlin series, Robert E. Park explicated, for the first time, the ideas

---

[5]   Znaniecki was the Director of the Polish Emigrants' Protective Association in Warsaw; they met in 1913. Until then, Znaniecki kept his scientific work (on Henri Bergson) separate from his administrative duties (with the help of Russian authorities who did not allow Poles to become university professors). When visiting USA in 1914, Znaniecki became stranded because of the war, Thomas arranged an appointment for him at Chicago. Znaniecki returned to Poland in 1920 and became the first Polish professor of sociology at Poznan University (Kaczynski 1997).

of urban research to be conducted in Chicago. It was an innovative way of doing research, but its attractiveness may have been based on other reasons as well.

The Chicago school might have become popular for what it missed, at least in the eyes of Abbott: "Chicago writing lacks the Latinate literacy and high tone of the Europeans" (1999). Chicago writers wrote plain, realistic prose, but they were closer to the novelists than to the natural scientists:

> Chicago urban sociologists and novelists intellectually rubbed elbows, and conceptually and methodologically, aesthetically and thematically stood as primary reference points for one another. They felt no qualms about acknowledging this kinship (Cappetti 1993: 32).

The Chicago school of sociology is often compared to LSE, particularly by its historian, Martin Bulmer, who studied at LSE. There were similarities: a vision of a close connection between theory and practice, translated to fit local realities, a community of scholars of different ages, sexes, and nationalities (both elements also present in the NGU), persuasive self-presentations, and a superb ability to associate. The difference was that Thomas, Park, and Burgess left most administrative and financial arrangements to others (mainly to Small, who was decisive in creating both the Department and the Local Community Research Committee); did not have a political mission on a national level (but did have a social mission towards the local community); and, in spite of internal tolerance and openness to external influences, were confined to one discipline. The later schism between the proponents of quantitative and qualitative scholars cut deep, therefore, and shook the fundaments of the school (although Bulmer sees causes of decline even in Parks's unwillingness to deal with administrative matters, and the increasing irritation with Chicago's dominance in the rest of USA).

However, the networking skills of the Chicagoans were unparalleled. Not only did they start a national association and a national journal, but they also had dining clubs for graduate students, the Sociology Club, and the Society for Social Research with its three main activities: evening meetings, the Summer Institute (which reassembled Chicago alumni), and the Bulletin.

Bulmer thus summarizes his history of Chicago school of sociology:

> At the heart of any academic school are one or two individuals with a body of ideas or a compelling vision that attracts others, binds the group together, and gives it a greater degree of intellectual cohesion than is usual among col-leagues in academic social science departments. A „school" is ultimately the product of that personal quality of intellectual passion or self-confidence that emanates from one or two individuals who stand out at some distance from their colleagues. In sociology, (...) leadership was shared, initially between Thomas and Park, then between Park and Burgess. (...) Thomas alone would not have created the Chicago school, and Burgess alone could not have sus-tained it (1984: 214).

Note that the first sentence is a perfect description of a formation of an actor-network (omitting only the artifacts, especially *American Journal of Sociology*, but its role has been emphasized before): a heart composed of one or two actants, a body of ideas, and the forces of attraction and binding that result in stabiliza-tion. But the second sentence lapses into the traditional narrative of entrepre-neurship: there must be a hero figure; and if here are several, it is only because together they possess this outstanding quality that distinguishes entrepreneurs from other people. This oxymoron is present already in the definition of a "school" that Bulmer adopted at the outset: "The paradigm's core formulations are those of the founder-leader, but the full blown paradigm is typically a collec-tive enterprise" (quote on p. 2). An actor-network needs a figurehead.

Do institutions require entrepreneurs?

The final conclusion to be drawn from the three cases might be, therefore, that the quality that distinguishes institutional entrepreneurs from other people is that they are entrepreneurial. This is hardly surprising, but what does it mean? It seems that such people are equipped with a great deal of energy, that they are very good at forging alliances, and that they have a special sense that allows them to feel "what is in the air": the smell of the Zeitgeist.

Are these skills or traits learnable or teachable? Hardly so. As with artists, one can improve the technique, but not learn a talent. But do institutions require entrepreneurs? This is not certain, as most of the reasoning about their role is post hoc, ergo propter hoc: when an institution has been established, people who were involved in establishing it are seen as decisive for its establishment (cher-chez le entrepreneur!). As suggested before, most practices that have not been institutionalized probably also had their ardent proponents, but they have been forgotten. Also, as seen in the case of NGU, the practices can become institutionalized, even when entrepreneurs fail. In a sense, as the subsequent decline of Chicago school of sociology well illustrates, they all fail sooner or later. A school of thought cannot be dominant forever, but its impact – in this case, a transformation of the discipline that survived the subsequent schools – might last, and this is the emergence of an institution.

There can be no doubt that "institutional entrepreneurs" are characters in a narrative of the emergence of institutions. They are attributes of such genre, and are required to achieve the narrative coherence. The question might then be asked: who is interested in this genre and why? The answer seems obvious to me: people who, like the founders of LSE, of NGU, and the Chicago school of sociology believe that society needs a change and that it is possible to change it through research and education. Allowing the narrative of institutional entrepreneurship to be enriched with the image of an anthill might make it more realistic – not diminishing the heroism of ants, only multiplying their number and character and stressing the connections.

References

Abbott, Andrew (1999): Department and discipline: Chicago sociology at one hundred. Chicago: University of Chicago Press.

Berger, Peter L./Luckmann, Thomas (1966): The social construction of reality. A treatise in the sociology of knowledge. Harmondsworth, Middlesex: Penguin.

Bhatti, Jabeen (2005): Private universities take hold in Germany. Deutsche Welle, 13 June.

Bruss, Elizabeth W. (1976): Autobiographical acts: The changing situation of a literary genre. Baltimore, MR: John Hopkins University Press.

Bulmer, Martin (1984): The Chicago school of sociology. Institutionalization, diversity, and the rise of sociological research. Chicago: University of Chicago Press.

Callon, Michel (1986): Some elements of a sociology of translation: Domestication of the scallops and the fishermen of St Brieuc's Bay. In: Law, John (ed.) (1986): Power, action and belief. London: Routledge and Kegan Paul, pp. 196-229.

Callon, Michel/Latour, Bruno (1981): Unscrewing the big Leviathan: How actors macro-structure reality and how sociologists help them to do so. In: Knorr-Cetina, Karin/Cicourel, Aaron V. (eds.) (1981): Advances in social theory and methodology. London: Routledge and Kegan Paul, pp. 277-303.

Cappetti, Carla (1993): Writing Chicago. Modernism, ethnography and the novel. NY: Columbia University Press.

Cohen, Michael D./March, James G./Olsen, Johan P. (1972): A garbage can model of organizational choice. In: Administrative Science Quarterly 17(1), pp. 1-25.

Czarniawska, Barbara (1997): Narrating the organization. Chicago, IL: University of Chicago Press.

Czarniawska, Barbara (2005): Fashion in organizing. In: Czarniawska, Barbara/Sevón, Guje (eds.) (2005): Global ideas. Malmö/Copenhagen: Liber/CBS, pp. 129-146.

Czarniawska, Barbara (2008): How to misuse institutions and get away with it: Some reflections on institutional theory(ies). In: Greenwood, Royston/Oliver, Christine/Sahlin, Kerstin/Suddaby, Roy (eds.) (2008): The SAGE handbook of organizational institutionalism. London: Sage, pp. 769-782.

Czarniawska, Barbara/Hernes, Tor (2005): Constructing macro actors according to ANT. In: Czarniawska, Barbara/Hernes, Tor (eds.) (2005): Actor-network theory and organizing. Malmö/Copenhagen: Liber/CBS, pp. 1-8.

Czarniawska, Barbara/Joerges, Bernward (1996): Travels of ideas. In: Czarniawska, Barbara/Sevón, Guje (eds.) (1996): Translating organizational change. Berlin: de Gruyter, pp. 13-48.

Czarniawska, Barbara/Wolff, Rolf (1998): Constructing new identity in established organization fields: Young universities in the old Europe. In: International Studies of Management & Organization 28(3), pp. 32-56.

Dahrendorf, Ralf (1995): LSE. A history of the London School of Economics and Political Science, 1895-1995. Oxford: Oxford University Press.

DiMaggio, Paul J./Powell, Walter W. (1983): The iron cage revisited: Institutional isomorphism and collective rationality in organizational fields. In: American Sociological Review 48, pp. 147-160.

Downs, Anthony (1972): Up and down with ecology: The issue-attention cycle. In: The Public Interest 28, pp. 38-50.

Feldman, Martha/Pentland, Brian (2005): Organizational routines and the macro - actor. In: Czarniawska, Barbara/Hernes, Tor (eds.) (2005): Actor-network theory and organizing. Malmö/Copenhagen: Liber/CBS, pp. 105-131.

Feffer, Andrew (1993): The Chicago pragmatists and American progressivism. Ithaca, NY: Cornell University Press.

Forty, Adrian (1986): Objects of desire. Design and society 1750-1980. London: Cameron.

Geertz, Clifford (1995): After the fact. Two countries, four decades, one anthropologist. Cambridge MA: Harvard University Press.

Gellner, Ernest (1980): The LSE – a contested academy. In: The Times Higher Education Supplement, November 7, pp. 12-13.

Gellner, Ernest (1995): No school for scandal. Dahrendorf's LSE and the quest for a science of society. In: The Times Literary Supplement, May 26, pp. 3-4.

Jazbinsek, Dietmar/Joerges, Bernward/Thies, Ralf (2001): The lin "Großstadt-Dokumente" A forgotten precursor of the Chicago school of sociology. In: WZB Working Papers, FS II 01-502.

Joerges, Bernward (1990): Global 2000: Social Science, Ecology and the Bimillennium. In: Futures 1, pp. 3-20.

Joerges, Bernward/Czarniawska, Barbara (1998): The question of technology, or how organizations inscribe the world. In: Organization Studies 19(3), pp. 363-386.

Kaczynski, Grzegorz J. (1997): Znaniecki come immigrato. Una retrospettiva biografica. In: Sociologia 3, pp. 5-22.

Kingdon, John W. (1984): Agendas, alternatives and public policies. Boston: Little, Brown and Company.

Latour, Bruno (1986): The powers of association. In Law, John (ed.) (1986): Power, action and belief. London: Routledge and Kegan Paul, pp. 261-277.

Latour, Bruno (1996): Aramis, or the love for technology. Cambridge MA: Harvard University Press.

Lefkowitz, Jason (2002): Lessons from the anthill. Online Community Report, June 15.

Lewin, Kurt (1947): Frontiers in group dynamics II: Channels of group life: Social planning and action research. In: Human Relations 1(2), pp. 143-146.

MacIntyre, Alasdair (1981/1990): After virtue. London: Duckworth Press.

March, James G. and Olsen, Johan P. (eds.) (1976): Ambiguity and choice in organizations. Bergen, Norway: Universitetsforlag.

March, James G./Olsen, Johan (1989): Rediscovering institutions. The organizational basis of politics. New York: The Free Press.

McCloskey, D.N. (1994): Knowledge and persuasion in economics. Cambridge, UK: Cambridge University Press.

Merton, Robert K. (1965/1993): On the shoulders of giants. A Shandean postscript. Chicago: University of Chicago Press.

Phillips, Nelson/Lawrence, Thomas B./Hardy, Cynthia (2004): Discourse and institutions. In: Academy of Management Review 29(4), pp. 635-652.

Ramirez, Francisco O./Boli, John (1987): On the union of states and schools. In: Thomas, George M./Meyer, John W./Ramirez, Francisco O./Boli, John (eds.) (1987): Institutional structure: Constituting state, society and the individual. Beverly Hills CA: Sage, pp. 12-37.

Rorty, Richard (1989): Contingency, irony and solidarity. Cambridge, UK: Cambridge University Press.

Star, Susan Leigh/Griesemer, James R. (1989): Institutional ecology, "translations" and boundary objects: Amateurs and professionals in Berkley's Museum of Vertebrate Zoology, 1907–39. In: Social Studies of Science 19, pp. 387-420.

Steghaus-Kovac, Sabine (2002): Private universities: Better than the rest? In: Science, October 25.

Tarde, Gabriel (1890/1962): The laws of imitation. Gloucester MA: Peter Smith.

Wallace, Charles P. (2002): Germany's Ivy League. In: Time Europe, March 31.

Warren, Roland L./Rose, Stephen M./Bergunder, Ann F. (1974): The structure of urban reform. Community Decision Organizations in stability and change. Lexington MA, Lexington Books.

Wolfram, Gary (1999): Private college under siege – need to end direct subsidies to public universities. In: USA Today, January.

Resolving Collective Disputes in Poland: A Narrative Perspective

Leszek Cichobłaziński

Introduction

Conflicts are an integral part of collective relations in company management and their resolution is one of the most important elements of the managerial function. In Poland, since 1991, conflicts between trade unions and employers have been regulated by law in the Statute on Collective Dispute Resolution. Before this period, under communism, officially there was no such thing as conflict in the workplace because in the framework of Marxist ideology conflicts could not take place. All citizens were the owners of the means of production (employers and employees as well) and therefore, theoretically, there was no structural cause for creating conflicts in industrial relations. In reality, it was not true and hidden conflicts blew up from time to time with a very high intensity and sometimes these conflicts were suppressed by communists in a bloody way. It is a very well known and described phenomenon in sociological literature (Dahrendorf 1959: 3-35; Staniszkis 1992) and it is interesting in itself; however, this problem is not the subject of this analysis. It was mentioned only to describe the historical background of the legal and social institutions for resolving industrial conflicts, which is the mediation process for collective bargaining in Poland.

Scientific reflection concerning mediation as a useful tool for resolving conflicts is relatively new in Poland in general and in industrial relations in particular, unlike in western countries where much research has been conducted and many different theories have been tested. In this paper, one of many theoretical concepts of mediation will be presented, namely a narrative approach to mediation, whose most representative adherents are John Winslade and Gerald Monk (2000).

The author of this paper is a mediator in collective dispute resolution in Poland and the paper is partly based on his experiences in this role.

Institutional and Theoretical Background: The Institution of Mediation in Collective Relations in Poland

The role of mediation in the whole process of collective dispute resolution is very important for this research. The Act on Solving Labor Disputes defining the procedure of resolving collective disputes is as follows:

- Negotiations – at this stage of collective disputes, both parties must try to find a solution by themselves. Negotiations end upon the signing of an agreement or with records of divergences indicating the position of each party.
- Mediation - in the latter case, "the parties shall conduct the dispute with the assistance of a person who ensures to be impartial, further referred to as the mediator". Mediation and negotiations end with an agreement or a record of divergences.
- Arbitration and strike – if mediation has ended in failure both parties may submit the dispute to the Social Arbitration Committee or the trade unions may go on strike. The procedure for preparing a strike has its conditions. The crucial condition is a referendum. "A strike in the establishment shall be declared by the trade union organization after an approval by the majority of voting employees, providing that at least 50 percent of employees employed in the establishment participated in the voting" (Cichobłaziński 2004).

As described above, mediation in resolving collective disputes in Poland – which is important – is a part of a bigger process and this factor is very significant for the explanation of the mediator's effectiveness. Mediation in resolving collective disputes is an obligatory procedure in Poland, which distinguishes this kind of mediation from others because, according to the majority of definitions, this process should be voluntary (Moore 1996).

Definition and Main Approaches to Mediation

Mediation is a very complicated process of reaching agreement with a third-party intervention. This paper is based on the Bush and Folger definition of mediation. They understand mediation "as an informal process in which a neutral third party with no power to impose a resolution helps the disputing parties try to reach a mutually acceptable settlement" (Bush and Folger 2005: 8). One can observe one important difference between this definition of mediation and the procedure of mediation in resolving collective disputes. The authors of "The Promise of Mediation" state that mediation is an informal process, but mediators who deal with trade unions and employers in conflict must act within the framework of a procedure precisely determined by law. Despite that difference, other elements precisely mentioned above also describe mediation in collective bargaining.

Mediation is a complicated process, consisting of many stages, which should be described for further analysis. Wall and Lynn created a model of mediation consisting of eleven elements (Wall and Lynn 1993: 163).

The Elements of the Mediation Framework:
1. Mediation Determinants
2. Parties' Interaction
3. Decision to Mediate
4. Techniques and Strategies
5. Technique Determinants
6. Outcome Determinants
7. Mediators' Outcomes
8. Parties' Outcomes

In the framework of this model, mediation techniques and strategies are a central element of the whole process of third-party intervention, which is determined by other elements and which directly influences the outcome of the mediation. The basic question which is posed in this research concerns the conditions of choosing mediation tactics, i.e., which factor should be taken into consideration by mediators in order to accomplish their missions.

Some approaches to mediation can be indicated (Picard and Bishop 2004):
- Interest-Based Approach
- Transformative Approach
- Facilitative versus Evaluative Approach
- Social Norm Approach
- Restorative Justice Approach and Victim – Offender Mediation
- Narrative Approach

A brief description of these approaches follows:
The interest-based approach is focused on the individual concept of social interaction and mostly takes into consideration the material interests of the parties in conflict. The solution of the conflict has mainly a compromise shape.
The transformative approach is based on the collective concept of social interaction and takes into consideration the relational context of group existence.

Conflict resolution in this case not only leads to a compromise but, first of all, is an opportunity to improve relations between the parties. Two dimensions of interaction in the transformative approach are crucial: empowerment and recognition.

The facilitative and evaluative approach to mediation concerns two basic mediator attitudes to conflict resolution and to the parties. The facilitative mediator focuses mostly on the process of communication between the parties and tries to manage this process so that the parties may reach an agreement by themselves. The evaluative mediator acts partly like a judge. He influences not only the process, but also the understanding of the interests by the parties, often using evaluations of their proposals of resolutions. Sometimes the mediator even creates proposals of solutions himself.

The social norm approach refers to social norms existing in society, for example social justice or customs, tradition and religion. This kind of mediation is similar to the evaluative approach.

The restorative approach is used in court and its goal is to restore the harm committed by the offender. It is important in the rehabilitation process in the case of young people.

The narrative approach to mediation focuses on stories about the causes of conflict that are told by the parties to the mediator, but not as an account of the real situation. It does not matter whether the story is true or not. It is important how the story creates the party's perceived understanding of reality and how this story can be changed. In this approach, it is the story that creates conflict interaction rather than the conflict creating the story.

Narrative theory and practice

The authors of the best known book on narrative mediation describe this approach in the following way: "Mediators who use a narrative orientation are interested in the constitutive properties of conflict stories. In other words, whether a story is factual or not matters little to the potential impact it has in someone's life. Our emphasis is on how the story operates to create reality rather than on whether it reports accurately on that reality. Stories therefore are not viewed as either true or false accounts of accounts of an objective <out there> reality. Such a view is not possible, because events cannot be known independently of the dominant narratives held by the knower. It is therefore more useful to concentrate on viewing stories as constructing the world rather than viewing the world as independently known and then described through stories" (Winslade and Monk 2000: 3).

The main problem in this approach to conflict resolution is that parties in conflict have their own narrations of the situation. The mediator deals with two different stories, which usually have few common points or little common ground. The first stage of the mediation process is to "bring the disputants to a place where they could at least hear and understand the other person's story" (Johston 2005: 278). Then the so-called "deconstructive phase" follows, during which the mediator asks the parties questions that should allow them to open up to each other's stories and to reconstruct their own stories into less conflict-causing ones.

This process is presented in Figure 1.

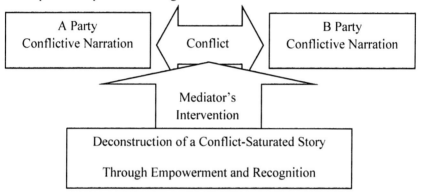

Figure 1: Mediator's Intervention in the Narrative Approach
(Adapted from Winslade and Monk, 2000: 73; Bush and Folger, 2005: 55)

It should be stressed that, in general, the narrative approach to mediation, which is also called "storytelling" (Cobb 1994: 49-63), has its roots in symbolic interaction theory, which emphasizes the process of social creation of reality and is based on the following tenets that are particularly important for mediators (McCorckle and Reese 2005: 109; see Manis and Meltzer 1978; Lanigan 1988):

1. Individuals act according to how they understand the world based on their own subjective interpretation of their circumstances.
2. People understand and interpret their world through language (symbols).
3. Through social interaction we construct (and re-construct) meaning.

The crucial task for the mediator in this approach to conflict resolution is how to break the grip of the dominant story and create the alternative story? These are tools which might be used by the mediator in narrative mediation (Winslade and Monk 2006: 224):

1. Mapping the effects of the conflict story on the participants and on the relationship between them.
2. Asking questions that attempt to deconstruct the dominant story by bringing into the foreground the taken-for-granted assumptions on which the conflict story relies.
3. Mapping the discursive positions that have been crafted within the discourse of the conflict story.
4. Asking the participants to evaluate the conflict story and its probable future trajectory.
5. Inviting the participants to articulate their preferences for a future that is not limited by the conflict story.
6. Asking about the existence of unique outcomes that would not be predicted by the conflict story.
7. Listening for the implicit story of cooperation, or understanding, which is always present in the midst of a conflict story, and inquiring into its possibilities.
8. Building the significance of these unique outcomes into a narrative that stands a chance of competing with the conflict story.
9. Fashioning, in collaboration with the participants, an agreement that expresses the spirit of their preferred relationship story.

The Case of Using the Narrative Approach in Collective Dispute Mediation

Mediation in the Coal Mining Industry
1. The legal status of the company X Industries is a "one-person company of the State Treasury", which means that the company belongs to the Government, but its operations are based on the Commercial Code, a special statute for private companies. State-owned companies do business based on the state-owned company code.

The differences are in the organization of power in the company. In a state-owned company, power is jointly held by the director and a board of workers. In a "one-person company of the State Treasury", power is midway between a state-owned and a joint stock company. The state owns it, but power lies with the stockholders. This has been one of the solutions to the privatization of formerly fully state-owned industries. It is similar to the privatization that took place in the United Kingdom under Margaret Thatcher's government.

2. The problem causing the conflict was the distribution of the social fund. The social fund is part of a company's budget that is designated for workers, but not payable directly to them. Derived from workers' incomes, the social fund may be distributed as loans for restoring houses or flats, money for summer holidays, or subsidies (given to workers without obligation to repay). The president of the company and representatives of all the labor unions in the company make decisions about how to divide up the fund. In this case, they had already made an agreement, but one of the labor unions rejected it and decided to renegotiate. The issue concerned whether to withdraw money designated for loans and share it each year among the workers. If the money was not given as a loan but as a distribution, it would not need to be returned. The objecting labor union held a referendum among workers concerning this problem and members voted that the proposal prepared by the labor union was acceptable.

3. The first meeting was with the president of company, who after one hour invited the vice president for finance and legal counsel to participate. They described the conflict as having been begun by the smallest, least influential of the six labor unions in the company, and the only union to voice any objections to this distribution of the social fund. The company president also characterized the referendum as illegal and as having been worded in such a way as to lead voters to choose particular answers. He and his team described the methods used by the labor union as tactical actions in order to obtain popularity and influence among workers. This seemed to be a typical employer's strategy: attempting to destroy the credibility of the other party. The mediator asked the management, "Why don't you want to make this agreement with the labor unions?" The president's answer was, "Because I do not violate the law. This was reached with the participation of all unions." The mediator then asked, "Why did you announce this as a collective conflict?" His reply: "Because there was no other way to resolve this conflict." After this two-hour meeting, another meeting was held with representatives of the labor union.

4. The first meeting with representatives of the labor unions took place in a large conference room that could seat around 100 people and also served as a center for managing rescue actions. The central square of the coal mining plant was visible from the window. The president made a telephone call to representatives of the labor unions asking them to meet the mediator. At the beginning of mediation, the representatives of the labor union argued that the social fund should be renegotiated for two reasons. First, the referendum showed that this is what workers wanted. Second, they argued, the old agreement was dishonest and not in the workers' best interests. Money from the loan fund had to

be returned, and the company profited from interest charged on the loans. Furthermore, this fund helped only people with a flat or house to renovate. They felt it should be divided equally among workers in the company without having to be returned.

The conversation with labor union representatives took slightly less time than the conversation with management. The mediator asked the following questions:

a) The agreement was made by all of the labor unions in your company. Why has only your union raised this objection?
   Answer – We do not know and this question does not interest us. We do not pay attention to what is being done by other labor unions. The outcome of the referendum is the most important thing for us.

b) What about the objection of management that your referendum was not conducted according to the law?
   Answer – If you want to find a reason to criticize, you can always do so.

5. Next, there was a meeting between the management and the representatives. This took place in the same conference room. The tables were set up in a "U" shape. The representatives of one party sat along one long "wing" of the table across from the representatives of the other party. The parties asked the mediator to sit at the head of the table—the place usually occupied by the management. This placement was a visible symbol that the parties in the collective conflict agreed on the role of the mediator.

The mediator began by explaining his role in this situation and outlining some principles of negotiation. Both parties explained their positions. After lengthy discussions and exchanges of opinions, it seemed to the mediator that the arguments presented by the management were more reasonable. Despite this, the labor union representatives stayed with their position.

The mediator asked the parties to take a break. People went willingly, not only because he asked them to, but also for a smoking break. During this break, the labor union representatives stayed in the conference room while the management representatives went to the president's office. The mediator went from one room to another, talking with both parties. During this break some people from the labor union had a conversation with the company's lawyer in the hall, based on the common bond that they were all smokers. In this informal conversation, the lawyer was able to find some common language with the workers and could convince them of an important point. The money they sought was not actual money, but was only circulated among people who had taken out loans for renovating houses.

After the break, the atmosphere for bargaining was quite good and the parties soon reached an agreement. The labor representatives made two points. First, the money they had argued about should be available to share; it was not real money (this is what had been explained to them during the break). Second, the agreement could not be changed without involving the other labor unions, and changing it would necessitate waiting to meet with them. This last point was placed in the final report written after the mediation session. It was a classic example of finding a reason that allowed one of the collective bargaining parties – the representatives of the labor unions – to save face. The entire amount of time that this mediation had taken was around six hours, a little less than a standard workday of eight hours.

In summary, key questions include:
1. What was the role of the mediator in this case?
2. Why could this conflict not have been resolved earlier between parties?
3. Why was a mediator necessary?
4. How did the conflict grow to such a magnitude to be called a "collective conflict"?

The answers include the following:
1. Insufficient understanding of the economic issues by the labor union representatives.
2. Weak communication between management and labor unions.
3. Even the actual presence of the mediator had an important function. The parties tried to be polite to each other.
4. Other remarks - whenever the members of the labor union did not understand what was being said by the management, the answer was "no".

Discussion

1. Mediation in the coal mining industry is an example of mediation that was necessary due to poor communication and not enough prior knowledge concerning economic issues on the part of labor union representatives.

2. Both parties had their own stories. The management was convinced that the main goal of the trade union was to create a good image among employees and to weaken the authority of the management. On the other hand, the trade union stated that the management administrated the social fund in a way that was harmful to the employees. These stories were contradictory.

3. What the mediator did in order to resolve this conflict was:

a) Brought the parties to one room and enabled them to tell their stories.
b) Asked the parties questions that allowed them to deconstruct their stories.
c) Created an atmosphere of mutual trust, which was necessary for constructing the alternative story.

4. Questions that were posed to the unions by the mediator enabled them to understand their own narrations and understand each other's narrations.

5. Under these conditions, the parties constructed the alternative story by themselves, without the mediator's participation, during the "smoking break" initiated by the mediator. Stories are always modified during informal discourse. The main communication tactic for a mediator is to create various occasions for informal discourse of this kind.

References

Bush, Robert B./Folger Joseph P. (2005): The Promise of Mediation. The Transformative Approach to Conflict. San Francisco CA: Jossey-Bass.

Cichobłaziński, Leszek (2004): Collective Bargaining in the Industrial Relations in Poland. In: Industrial Relations in Europe Conference <IREC> 2004", 9. Utrecht: Utrecht University, pp. 9 -10.

Cichobłaziński, Leszek/Glenn, Phillip (2004): Labor-Management Mediation in Poland: Two Case Studies. In: Częstochowa University of Management Journal, No. 5, pp. 15-24.

Cichobłazinski, Leszek (2009): Effectiveness of Mediation in Resolving Collective Disputes. In: Bylok, Felicjan/Cichobłaziński, Leszek (eds.) (2009): Chosen Aspects of Managing Human Resources in Modern Organizations. Częstochowa: Częstochowa University of Technology, pp. 57-64.

Cobb, Sara (1994): A Narrative Perspective on Mediation. Toward the Materialization of the "Storytelling" Metaphor. In: Folger, Joseph P./Jones, Tricia S. (ed.) (1994): New Direction in Mediation. Communication Research and Perspectives. Thousand Oaks CA: Sage, pp. 48-63.

Dahrendorf Ralph (1959): Class and Class Conflict in Industrial Society. Stanford CA: Stanford University Press.

Johston Linda M. (2005): Narrative Analysis. In: Druckman, Daniel (ed.) (2005): Doing Research. Methods of Inquiry for Conflict Analysis. Thousand Oaks CA: Sage, pp. 277-292.

Lanigan Richard (1988): Life – History Interviews: A Teaching and Research Model for Semiotic Phenomenology in Phenomenology of Communication. Pittsburgh: Duquesne University Press, pp. 144-153.

Mains Jerome G./Meltser, Bernard N. (1978): Symbolic Interactionism: A Reader in Social Psychology. 3rd ed. Boston, Mass.: Allyn and Bacon, Inc., pp. 1-9.

McCorckle, Suzanne/Reese, Melanie J. (2005): Mediation Theory and Practice. Boston: Allyn and Bacon.

Moore, Christopher (1996): The Mediation Process: Practical Strategies for Resolving Conflict. San Francisco CA: Jossey-Bass.

Picard, Cheryl/Bishop, Peter (2004): The Art and Science of Mediation, Toronto: Emond Montgomery Publications.

Staniszkis, Jadwiga (1992): The Ontology of Socialism. Oxford: Clarendon Press.

Wall, Jr., James A./Lynn, Anna (1993): Mediation. A Current Review. In: Journal of Conflict Resolution. Vol.37, No. 1, pp. 160-194.

Winslade, John/Monk, Gerald (2000): Narrative Mediation. A new Approach to Conflict Resolution. San Francisco CA: Jossey-Bass.

Winslade, John/Monk, Gerald (2006): Does the Model Overarch the Narrative Stream? In: Herman, Margaret S. (ed.) (2006): The Blackwell Handbook of Mediation. Bridging Theory, Research, and Practice. Malden MA: Blackwell Publishing, pp. 217-227.

Tangible Business Model Sketches to Facilitate Intersubjectivity and Creativity in Innovation Encounters

Robb Mitchell

The coming together of diverse viewpoints has been heralded as fruitful for innovative ideas. But for innovation to actually happen, collaboration and effective communication are required.

Sharing narratives can be helpful for innovation in two, often overlapping ways. Firstly, narratives provide a means for different perspectives to be understood. Narratives can be deployed or called upon to explain current situations from one or more viewpoints. Secondly, narratives can be a fruitful route to new ideas. Narratives can provide the spark and/or the fuel with which to create or propose a new state of affairs.

Although accounts of innovation often involve descriptions of how organisations and processes are structured, it can also be revealing to take a more micro approach and look at what maybe happening at the level of an individual person or small group interactions (Buur and Larsen 2010; Heinemann et al. 2011).

Innovation requires going beyond an existing situation. But how can and do people think beyond their own immediate experiences? Particularly relevant to innovation is how can people go beyond their own perspective and take into account or attempt to predict the thoughts and feelings of other people?

The social psychologist Alex Gillespie in his account of how human agency develops outlines two routes for transcending the immediate here-and-now: *distanciation* and *identification*. Distanciation refers to an actor "stepping out of ongoing action by reflecting upon one's self and mediating ongoing activity" (Gillespie 2010: 2) whilst identification is "identifying with, empathizing with, or participating in the feelings and experience of someone else" (ibid).

In recounting a narrative about one's own experiences, one must be at least implicitly involved in distanciation. One cannot avoid engaging in self reflection as one chooses what and how to describe the experience. Narratives recounted by others, when at least moderately engaging, normally result in a degree of identifying with the experience of the teller of the narrative and/or subjects of the narrative. Gillespie argues that perspective taking is central to these processes of stepping outside of (what he calls *extrication* from) one's immediate and present experiences.

Maps and frameworks for intersubjective snapshots

Understanding the perspectives of others is key to harness the social dynamics for the purposes of business. Operating within the emerging field of Participatory Innovation (Buur and Matthews 2008) the author has been engaged in ongoing research that can be seen as attempting to aid distanciation and identification when discussing business dilemmas. These activities have centered upon using tangible materials that attempt to enable industrialists and others to step outside and individually and collaboratively reflect upon their own situations whilst also provoking better understandings of the perspectives of other people such as colleagues, customers, suppliers, competitors (Buur and Mitchell 2011). This includes making three dimensional maps of a company's value network (Heinneman et al. 2009) and rearranging bricolage objects on work surfaces (Heinneman et al. 2011) which depict well known two- dimensional frameworks for describing companies such as the business model canvas (Osterwalder 2009).

Such depictions are largely static, so we started exploring if it would be possible to build interactive artefacts that could provide an impression of the dynamics of business.

Tangible business model sketches to evoke innovation dynamics

Here we present two examples of what we call "tangible business model sketches" (further described in Mitchell and Buur 2010).

Hearing Aid Pinball Machine

From a distance, this model might resemble a homemade version of a pinball machine. Two receptacles at the base of an inclined surface are labeled with the name of a hearing aid supplier and its competitors:

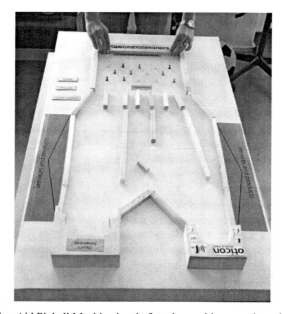

Figure 1: Hearing Aid Pinball Machine just before the marbles are released

Figure 2: Marbles representing hearing aid users roll towards one of the receptacles representing an audiological manufacturer.

From the opposite end several dozen marbles – representing the hearing impaired customers – will roll and bounce off various obstacles towards either receptacle when a release gate is lifted. The obstacles represent the various entities and opportunities such as clinics, product features and services, which mediate the indirect relationships between the hearing aid companies and potential individual users of audiological devices. The "flippers", for instance represent audiology clinics which depending on their history or ownership may have a preference for leading customers to specific manufacturers. Manipulation of these obstacles could cause different numbers of marbles to end up in the receptacle of one company or the other.

Sales Effort Balance

The second model was developed to illustrate some of the business dilemmas experienced by a lighting technology company. It took the form of a suspended mobile comprising a 2m long dowling pole, and two shorter poles suspended at either length of the main pole (see Figure 3-4).

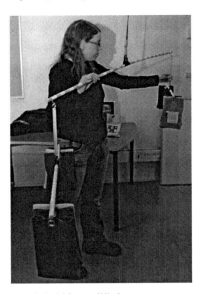

Figure 3: Sales Effort Balance is held in equilibrium

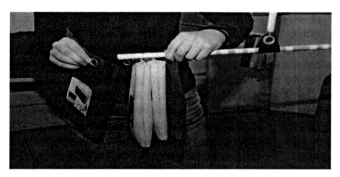

Figure 4: Making adjustments to the position of the differently weighted bags

The Sales Effort Balance has the appearance of a set of balancing scales with another set of smaller balancing scales at each end of the pivot. All three poles feature a measurement scale along their length and the point at which they hang is adjustable. The large uppermost pole is labelled to indicate *sales effort* at one end and *development effort* at the other. The two lower poles are labelled with respective subdivisions of these two kinds of effort. Screwed into the ends of the two secondary poles are four small hooks. A number of filled cloth bags of different weights and colours are labelled to indicate in further detail the kinds of effort (i.e. resources) that may be expended within the categories and subcategories delineated by the poles. The sketch thus proposes to show how the company putting different emphasis (or weight) upon different areas of development may need to be balanced by amounts of effort in sales and marketing.

Both these tangible business model sketches can seen as enabling extrication from the here-and-now through both reflecting upon self and promoting identification with the feelings of others.

Distanciation

Both *Sales Effort Balance* and *Hearing Aid Pinball Machine* appeared to provoke distanciation at several levels, both social and strategic. Each of these tangible business model sketches provided an engaging physical "what will happen?" experience. Such a physically unpredictable situation is distinct from the normal activities of a business meeting or seminar. Many of the industrialists who encountered the model commented along the lines of how different this was to their typical meetings and described (in brief) how such encounters were normally structured. These comparisons with normal practice which this provokes, elicits the sharing of narratives of what is normal and enables reflection on such typical practices. Those encountering *Sales Effort Balance* can be seen as experiencing extreme distanciation – they forget temporarily about the business dilemma and focus instead on trying not to break, get tangled up with, or be hit by the artefact. However, once more comfortable with and comprehending of how the artefact moved, the CEO and directors of the lighting technology company experienced distanciation in that they came to realize that they were unbalancing the business through not devoting enough resources to the sales department. The sales manager had previously attempted to argue this point through more conventional means but it appears that the interactive and physical presence of *Sales Effort Balance* made this narrative more compelling.

The designers of both models can also be seen as having experienced distanciation through its repeated use. One of the developers of *Sales Effort Balance* commented: "releasing the marbles is a bit like what happens when we let people use the model – we didn't really know what people's reactions would be". This observation was reported by the designers as bringing them greater awareness of their own disciplinary challenges and positioning.

Identification

As mentioned, above the CEO of the company could see that the sales department when under resourced can "float off" uncontrollably. The different weights of sales effort balance provoked expressions of sympathy as to how managers could predict the weight of many decisions about resources in advance.

Hearing aid pinball machine, although giving a somewhat detached "helicopter view", could be seen as facilitating identification with a greatly range of stakeholders, albeit less richly so. Because it is not possible to unilaterally adjust the activities of other entities in an organization's supply chain.

As an innovation researcher who encountered this model in a workshop commented when adjusting some flippers halfway down the marble run "it would be helpful if the audiological dispensers made this change, but the competitors would find out and respond to this".

Collaborators from other companies and university researchers reported that *Hearing aid pinball machine* increased their empathy with the design and development personnel of the audiological device firm in terms of how their product development effort could only be understood within a larger systemic view. In particular the "challenge" of influencing the destination of the marbles provoked empathy with the position of hearing aid marketers and overall business strategy developers. Likewise, the dilemmas faced by management of the lighting technology company were brought to life and easily understood by less senior employees and graduate students undertaking a collaboration with this firm.

Open ended nature enabled lively enactments of various "what if"-situations e.g. adjusting the gradient of the *Hearing Aid Pinball Machine* to provoke exploration of "faster or slower markets". Participants could thus reflect upon and discuss how they themselves may behave under different economic conditions and also hear how others might respond

The artefact provoked brief narratives, but narratives also provoked further (novel) interactions with the model and the co-creation of new narratives with other people

Hearing Aid Pinball Machine also provoked reflection as to how users and potential users of a hearing aid experience the process of acquiring audiological devices. For instance participants in one workshop with industrialists concurred with the question "How would hearing aid users react to us talking about them as downward rolling balls that have no agency in themselves?"

Conclusion

This paper outlines some promising ways to engage and provoke stimulate the comparison and co-creation of narratives in innovation. They provide an aid to narrative recounting and thus provide greater shared understandings of complex situations. The fresh perspectives that emerge by extricating participants from the here-and-now can also inspire new narratives and thus may help innovative thinking regarding developing and implementing innovation.

Gillespie suggests infants playing with dolls (Gillespie 2010) offers a route to explaining how intersubjectivity develops. Through such play, a child experiences a reversal of social position from recipient of care (being looked after by adults) to that of care giver ("looking after" the toy). It is interesting to speculate that the physical nature of encountering tangible business model sketches may tap into related properties of objects in terms of enabling reflection upon self and others.

Children are natural, creative and uninhibited story tellers, and dolls and other toys play an important role in scaffolding and inspiring their narratives. Likewise it is hoped that innovation narratives maybe inspired by adults through their engaging in the playful encounters afforded by tangible business model sketches.

Acknowledgments

Thanks to industrial partners for volunteering the business cases, and the graduate students of the IT Product Design and Innovation & Business programmes at the University of Southern Denmark for developing the tangible business models - particularly Torben Jessen and Daniela Santos for the *Hearing Aid Pinball Machine*, and Magdolna Puskás and Soila Oinonen for the *Sales Effort Balance*.

References

Buur, Jacob/Matthews, Ben (2008): Participatory Innovation. In: International Journal of Innovation Management 12(3), pp. 255-273.

Buur, Jacob/Mitchell, Robb (2011): The Business Modeling Lab. Proceedings of PINC 2011 Participatory Innovation Conference. Sonderborg, Denmark.

Gillespie, Alex (2010): Position exchange: The social development of agency. New ideas in psychology, pp. 32-46.

Heinemann, Trine/Mitchell, Robb/Buur, Jacob (2009): Co-constructing meaning in innovation workshops. In: Objets et Communication, MEI 30-31, pp. 289-304.

Heinemann, Trine/Landgrebe, Jeanette/Mitchell, Robb/Buur, Jacob (2011): Narrating value networks through tangible materials. In: TAMARA, Journal of Critical Organization Inquiry (forthcoming).

Mitchell, Robb/Buur, Jacob. (2010): Tangible business model sketches to support participatory innovation. Proceedings of the 1st DESIRE Network Conference on Creativity and Innovation in Design (pp. 29–33).

Osterwalder, Alexander/Pigneur, Yves (2009): Business Model Generation: A Handbook for Visionaries. Game Changers, and Challengers. Amsterdam: Modderman Drukwerk.

How Innovations Become Successful through Stories

Michael Müller

Introduction

Social systems are systems that consist of communications (Luhmann 1988: 192). The types and contents of the respective communications define the different systems. Every social system possesses various types of communication: everyday communications, descriptive communications (through which the system's knowledge is defined), performative communications through which realities within the system are created ("I declare you husband and wife"), and others. For the identity of every social system, narrative communications play a central role: the stories that circulate in the system about itself, about other systems and about its environment. In addition, stories that are told about the system outside of it, in its environment, and that are, so to speak, processed, modified, adapted or rejected in the system as an intervention, are meaningful for the identity of a social system. A family that continually hears stories about its own anti-sociability from outside has to deal with these stories one way or another - perhaps the family incorporates them as its own stories and wins important values, using its state of being ostracized as a means of shaping its identity, or the family dismisses the stories as the "lies" of others.

Stories of the past and the future

By far the largest part of stories that are told within social systems are stories of the past: stories that describe "what happened a short or a long time ago" or stories about "how we have become what we are today". The identity of individuals, but also of social systems, is defined by stories of this type saved in autobiographical memory. The predominance of stories of the past is confirmed by the fact alone that the past tense is the prevailing tense of narration, for example in literature. In companies, too, a lot of stories of the past are told: stories of founders and foundation, stories about key events, individual or collective experiences. Apart from that, however, it is characteristic of companies that they also produce an above-average number of stories about the future compared to other systems.

One only has to take a look at the statements of managers during company events or on brochures or on the Internet presence of companies in order to get the impression that one of the central tasks of corporations is to develop visions of the future and to take steps to make these visions become reality: We are going to be this or that; we are going to achieve this or that; we are going to do this or that. Therefore, it is possible to claim that companies are social systems that – apart from other narrative communications – tell stories of the future. "We are going to be like that" is a common type of story of the future and usually refers to processes of change. "In the future we will be positioned even more creatively, even more globally". "We are going to be this and that". "We are going to have flat hierarchies". Or stories of the following type: "In 20 years time we are going to offer the 1.5-liter car", because innovations are also stories told about the future.

Innovations as stories

At the beginning of every innovation there is a story based on an idea that is told about the future. This is often a story with a variety of narrative strands that affect the innovation process itself ("how we set up the innovation process"), the final state ("how it will be when this new product/this service is on the market") and also the use of the new product by the customer ("how the innovation is going to change the everyday life of our customers"). To some extent, the story is the backbone of the innovation process: It is a map and a vision at the same time. In subsequent analyses of successful innovation processes it is very easy to recognize the stories behind them.

The question that companies now ask themselves is how it is possible to write new, successful stories of innovation: How can we become more innovative? The most frequent aberration occurring within companies is the borrowing of stories of innovation from others. Under the keyword *Best Practice* one looks up how other companies or individuals have achieved their innovations and tries to copy it. Management guidebooks with titles such as *What would Google do?*, *The Edison principle* or *What we can learn from Steve Jobs* (Jarvis 2009; Meyer 2008; Gallo 2011) are proof of this. Subsequently, one tries to apply the promised recipes for success to one's own company – obviously with moderate success, otherwise new innovation guidebooks would not have to be written time and time again. Google's innovation story has worked for Google and that of Steve Jobs has worked for Apple, because Google and Jobs wrote these stories in their own, individual way on the basis of their own backgrounds. Looking at *Best Practice Examples* for innovations and *borrowing* stories of innovation and the future both misjudge an essential characteristic of stories of the future. If they are supposed to be more than mere science fiction, they have to be deeply rooted in the present of the company that writes them. In order to understand what this means, a short digression into narrative theory is called for.

What is a story?

A lot of research has been conducted regarding narrative theory in recent decades, and semiotics and literary studies have very sophisticated tools today, which can be used to describe and analyze characteristics of narrative utterances (Krah and Titzmann 2011; Sottong and Müller 1998). Since Aristotle, however, there has been unanimity as far as the basic elements of every story are concerned: Every story has a chronological sequence of events and thus a beginning and an end and between these two poles something happens that causes a change. Stories are always about transformations: The final state of the story is different from the initial state regarding at least one feature, and this altered final stage is caused by the transformative event in the *middle* (Aristoteles 1982). In the beginning the protagonist is lonely, then he meets the woman of his life, and in the end he is a happy family man. Or, the protagonist learns of a treasure, embarks on a search, finds it and is rich at the end. Or, somebody sets up a company, fights against numerous obstacles and finally establishes his product on the market. Stories are about changes. If nothing changes, it is not a story but a description of the status quo. Therefore, the three basic elements that every story needs are the following:

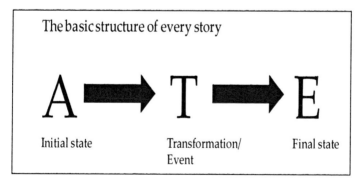

Figure 1 (own source)

Stories dangling in midair

The problem of many stories of the future, which are told by companies, is that they do not consider one of these elements or at least do not do so sufficiently: the initial state. Most of the stories of the future or stories of innovation in companies paint a vague or a detailed picture of the final state, but often they do not take into account the way from the current state to this innovation. Their stories lack a central element, namely the initial state. However, the initial state of a process of change and innovation can only be the present of the system, of the company. Very many processes of innovation fail exactly because of this, because the story "is dangling in midair", because it has no real beginning, is not rooted in the present of the company, in the conditions which form the basis for innovations. As mentioned before, stories of innovation without a starting point are mere science fiction and, if at all, merely successful by chance. So innovative companies, companies with a culture of innovation are those that know their present state very well and are able to develop stories of the future starting at this point.

Knowing the present

At first glance, the postulation that a system, a company has to know its present in order to write successful stories of innovation might seem banal. Of course, one is of the opinion that one knows the present of one's own company. The capacities are known as well as the amount of money and resources that are available, how the company is positioned in the market, and whatever there might additionally be when it comes to key figures. Certainly it is important to know about these matters, too. Nevertheless, for innovations the mental state of the company is much more significant, the "company in the mind" ('Unternehmen im Kopf') (Frenzel, Müller and Sottong 2005) of the employees when it comes to being creative, to developing ideas of innovations and to getting these innovation processes going right. And in the end this means that one has to grapple with the identity of one's own system, one's own company. The answers to questions such as "Who are we? What do we stand for? What are we doing? What are our strengths?" are of central importance for successful stories of innovation. It is now possible to answer these questions more or less arbitrarily by forming a *concept workgroup*, which then, in a theoretical approach, finds nice wordings, which are subsequently labeled as the new *CI* or *culture* of the company. However, this usually has very little to do with the actual identity of the company: artificial identities remain, which are hardly connected with the actual (mental) realities in the company. Precisely because they are for the most part nothing more than pipe dreams, the *CIs* and *mission statements* of most companies are very similar to each other: They all place the human being, the customer, in the centre of attention, contribute actively to the improvement of society, play a leading role within their market segment, etc. The true identity of a system, of an organization, of a company is not written on paper, but is hidden in the minds of the employees, in the communications between them. And all these communications and ideas are conveyed by the history and the stories of the company.

Identity: How we have become what we are

Psychology and brain research have agreed by now that the identity of an individual largely consists of the stories told by the individual about himself and those told about the individual in his environment (cf. Markowitsch and Welzer 2006: 259f; Bruner 1997: 121f; White 2010: 79-80; Kotre 1996: 133; Kast 2010: 13; McAdams 1993: 5). If the concept of identity – which originally, as we know, was only meant for individuals – is transferred to social systems, to organizations and companies, the following applies here as well. The identity of the system is fundamentally determined by the stories that are told within it and about it. Primarily the stories about "how we have become what we are" are the ones that make up the identity of a company. The stories transport the unofficial mental system rules of the company. They cannot, however, be investigated simply by questioning employees and managers, because they are usually not aware of them. The identity that is experienced is not a set of opinions, but based upon stories that have been experienced and deal with how the system has become what it is now. So in order to get to know the present of a company (which then again serves as the starting point for a story of the future, an innovation process), one has to step into the past: into the stories that the employees tell. In doing so it is necessary to let these stories, first of all, come into being within the process of telling, and to analyze them afterwards with regard to the collective mental system rules (i.e., those that appear in all the stories of a system) lying under the surface of the story/the stories that have been told.

Storytelling analysis

In storytelling analysis (Frenzel, Müller and Sottong 2005, 2006a, 2006b) a sample of employees, put together based on qualitative criteria, is asked to tell their stories in the company, their professional biography. Experiences that are told within their respective contexts (What happened? How did this happen?) and their derivations (Why did this happen? Why was it done like this and not any other way?) give hints as to how the system – in our case the company – has become what it is. The stories are collected in individual narrative interviews, which, in an ideal case, do not need any questions but merely a stimulus that triggers the telling: "Go ahead and tell us what has happened since the first day when you started here until today". People then tell their personal biography in the company. The interviewer accompanies the narrative by giving support, for example by digging deeper if the narrator tells a certain phase very quickly, but he does not dictate topics (such as: "How do you handle the matter of customer orientation?"), because what is not told, is also significant. Therefore, it does happen quite often, for example, that in a company, which sees itself as customer oriented, neither the word nor the mental concept *customer* appears in 40 one-hour narrative interviews, neither in the narrations of the employees nor in those of the managers. The interlocutors are guaranteed total anonymity; the client is not presented with the individual narrations, but only with the results of the analysis. As the presentation of the results targets comprehensive, supra individual statements, the individual narration steps back with regard to the narration of the whole system. The system is examined from a large number and variety of individual perspectives, and in this way one gets a broad and extensive range of system rules and mentalities.

Making system rules visible

The transcribed interviews are then analyzed using methods of semiotics, narrative and structural text analysis (Titzmann and Krah 2011; Titzmann 1977; Sottong and Müller 1998; Lotman 1972; Frenzel, Müller and Sottong 2005). In doing so, the interest is primarily focused on the experiences and descriptions that are similar in all the narrations. The system rules are to be described and not the (certainly existing) individual facets of these general rules. In storytelling analysis, these stories are in a way put on top of each other like overhead transparencies, and one concentrates on the structures that all of them share, which become visible when looking through the transparencies. Subsequently, on the basis of this analysis, the system rules are reconstructed, the so-called *company in the mind*.

Results of an analysis: an example

One of the most important tools in storytelling analysis is the search for the *central event*, the event highest in hierarchy. The central event marks the transition and the turning point from the initial state ("earlier") to the final state of the system – which means the current state in the narrations of the employees ("today"). What is surprising at first sight is that this central event is always positioned in the same spot by various narrators from the same system. Although every employee naturally tells his individual sections of stories and weighs them individually, all the narrations from a system coincide regarding the central event (in terms of the story of the company, not the individual professional biography). Thus, the *central event* seems to be an important narrative system that is invariable regarding the construction of reality within the system. An indicator as to where this central event is located is the occurrence of the terms/concepts "earlier" and "today/now", for example in statements such as: "In earlier days it was so and so, but today it is so and so". The central event that has transformed the system can be found where the narrators switch from "earlier" to "today". Apparently, the *great narrative* of the system is depicted in the individual professional biographies within a social system after a relatively short time of membership. Indeed, the narrations of interviewees who have been in the company for no more than a year show the same rules and regularities as the stories of people who have belonged to the company for years or decades.

The central event in the narrations of a system is always a function of the present; it can change over time. In a company we collected and analyzed stories twice during the course of some years. The first time the central event could be described with the following sentence: "In earlier days we were a creative and funky company, and then the stiff suits came, now we are a bureaucratic company". In this case the stiff suits stood for the introduction of controlling. In the second interview, a couple of years later a stock market flotation, which had taken place in the meantime, was the central event. Therefore, the central event in the stories of a system is always a function of the present and that way ultimately of the present identity. This means, the stories of an individual or of a system, which are told with a certain time lag, are not simply an addition or a prolongation of the stories told before in the sense of a supplement or an appendix. Indeed, it is more frequently the case that everything experienced to date can appear in memory in a whole new light, because it is evaluated differently in light of new experiences: Every present has its own past.

From the present back to the future

To say it explicitly, in order to be able to write successful stories about the future and innovation, the initial state of these stories has to be known – the present. And in order to know the present mental state of a system, a company, one has to know the stories that are told about its past. This is why stories are collected in storytelling. Many managers misconceive this intention and repeat the mantra: "We know that a lot has not worked out ideally in the past. But let's rather focus on the future now. There is no need here to dish up an old story". Only if one is able to face one's own past, is it possible to understand the present and based on this to march efficiently into the future. Often the analysis of the stories alone makes the potential for innovations visible. Alternatively, one realizes which obstacles have prevented successful innovation processes until now. For example, it does not happen all that rarely that employees are deeply convinced in their minds, due to a variety of respective experiences and incidents, that innovation processes do not stand a chance "in our company". They have experienced too often how concepts have vanished without a trace, how processes have been stopped halfway down the road or how innovations, that were almost finished, were not put into practice after all. The employees "know" now that it is not worthwhile to invest energy into innovation processes in this company. If the storytelling analysis produces a result that indicates that the current state of the "company in the mind" is shaped by such convictions, then the story of the future towards innovation will certainly have another starting point than in a company where this is not the case. You have to know the present to be able to determine the steps that lead from this initial state to the final state of the story, the fulfilment of the vision.

Innovative companies: open story culture

Every successful innovation process is thus a story, a narrative structure, which is rooted in the present and is told about the future. The question now is how the likelihood can be increased that successful stories of innovation are written in a system, an organization, in a nutshell: how a company can become an innovative company.

The answer: A company significantly increases the chances for innovations by tackling stories that circulate in the company openly and actively. Of course, the basic prerequisites, which usually exist within a certain culture, have to be created; these are the basis for creativity and innovative ideas, for example an anxiety-free, motivating and failure-friendly corporate culture, as well as enough time for the employees to take the wrong paths and detours, which every story of innovation entails. But the company and, even more, its stories have to face their narrative roots in order to avoid that inside a creative culture only science fiction develops or ideas that are not feasible, leading ultimately to a failure of the innovative processes. Innovative companies are companies with an open story culture. The way there:

1. To get to know one's own present:

To get to know one's own present means, as described above, to collect and to analyze the stories told by employees about the past (storytelling analysis). I think it has become clear that this step cannot be skipped. To believe one knows the present state of one's own company can have disastrous consequences, as it is the "hidden rules", the regularities and characteristics of the system that are not visible at the surface, in particular, that determine the ability for innovation of a company. Anybody who thinks he knows the present, without having it analyzed with the help of the stories of the past, is running the risk of falling victim to his own blind spot.

2. To create a "stream of stories":

A company can only be innovative if experiences are shared within it. The old saying: "If Siemens knew what Siemens knows" proves that this is obviously not possible in every company. And experiences are handed down best through stories. Therefore, an innovative company sustains a continuing "stream of stories" by opening spaces where employees can share stories. There are companies that hold, for example, two-hour storytelling workshops in each department twice a year, which serve as a possibility for the employees to exchange various kinds of experiences that occupy their thoughts. It is often the case that already at this point ideas for innovations arise.

3. Picking up approaches to stories of innovation and differentiating them:

Should approaches to an innovation become evident in the stories or at some other place in the company, these approaches should be verified according to the story model, and then the following should be planned: What is the initial state, what is the final state and which transformations are necessary in order to get there?

In this way companies connect the future with their own past and strategically benefit from potentials that can be found in their own company.

References

Aristoteles (1982): Poetik. Griechisch/Deutsch. Stuttgart: Reclam.

Bruner, Jerome (1997): Sinn, Kultur und Ich-Identität. Zur Kulturpsychologie des Sinns. Heidelberg: Carl-Auer.

Frenzel, Karolina/Müller, Michael/Sottong, Hermann (2005): Das Unternehmen im Kopf. Storytelling und die Kraft zur Veränderung. 2nd ed. Wolnzach: Kastner.

Frenzel, Karolina/Müller, Michael/Sottong, Hermann (2006a): Storytelling. Die Kraft des Erzählens fürs Unternehmen nutzen. München: dtv.

Frenzel, Karolina/Müller, Michael/Sottong, Hermann (2006b): Storytelling. Das Praxisbuch. München: Hanser.

Gallo, Carmine (2011): Was wir von Steve Jobs lernen können. Verrückt querdenken – Strategien für den eigenen Erfolg. München: Redline.

Jarvis, Jeff (2009): Was würde Google tun? Wie man von den Erfolgsgeschichten des Internetgiganten profitiert. München: Heyne.

Kast, Verena (2010): Was wirklich zählt, ist das gelebte Leben. Die Kraft des Lebensrückblicks. Freiburg im Breisgau: Kreuz.

Kotre, John (1996): Weiße Handschuhe. Wie das Gedächtnis Lebensgeschichten schreibt. München: Hanser.

Krah, Hans/Titzmann, Michael (Hrsg.) (2011): Medien und Kommunikation. Eine interdisziplinäre Einführung. Passau: Stutz.

Luhmann, Niklas (1988): Soziale Systeme. Grundriss einer allgemeinen Theorie. Frankfurt/Main: Suhrkamp.

Markowitsch, Hans J./Welzer, Harald (^{2}2006): Das autobiographische Gedächtnis. Hirnorganische Grundlagen und biosoziale Entwicklung. Stuttgart: Klett-Cotta.

McAdams, Dan P. (1993): The Stories we live by. Personal Myths and the Making of the Self. New York, London: The Guilford Press.

Meyer, Jens-Uwe (2008): Das Edison-Prinzip. Der genial einfache Weg zu erfolgreichen Ideen. Frankfurt/Main: Campus.

Müller, Michael (2004): Das „erzählte Unternehmen". Die Rekonstruktion von System-Regularitäten aus Erzählungen von Mitarbeitern. In: Frank, Gustav/Lukas, Wolfgang (Hrsg.) (2004): Norm – Grenze – Abweichung. Kultursemiotische Studien zu Literatur, Medien und Wirtschaft. Passau: Karl Stutz, pp. 431-445.

Müller, Michael (2010): Auf der Suche nach der Core Story: Im Kern steht immer eine Geschichte. In: Wirtschaftspsychologie aktuell 3/2010, pp. 58-60.

Sottong, Hermann/Müller, Michael (1998): Zwischen Sender und Empfänger. Eine Einführung in die Semiotik der Kommunikationsgesellschaft. Berlin: Erich Schmidt.

White, Michael (2010): Landkarten der narrativen Therapie. Heidelberg: Carl-Auer.

Interview: Narratives of Unity and Identity in Ambiguous Environments – A Case of Internal Business Communication

Florian Menz

Andreas Müller: I am sitting here with Mr. Florian Menz. Mr. Menz is a researcher and Professor of Linguistics at the University of Vienna. He has published a series of papers on the recent developments of organizations, the role of discourse and language in organizations.

Florian, how did you perceive the conference and the topic "Narrative and Innovation"? What were, for you, the most productive questions and results of the conference?

Florian Menz: I very much appreciated the interdisciplinary approach to the topic of the conference. What I found most inspiring was the combination of (academic) theoreticians from many different disciplines and practitioners. On the one hand, it was interesting to hear how theoretical models are transferred to the practice of management by CEOs of innovative enterprises; on the other hand, there were quite a few extremely stimulating demonstrations of training concepts. This mixture appears very productive to me and is indeed innovative.

AM: What did you think when you were invited?

FM: Interdisciplinarity always entails the risk of talking at cross-purposes. Therefore, my main concern was how to make clear that qualitative research on microstructural aspects (as interaction usually is) may add new insights to the working of large-scale approaches that dominate the study of organization. The concentration on narratives in organizations, however, necessarily entails a different perspective on organizational problems. Within narrative approaches, discourse analysis focuses especially on a level that can easily be identified as microstructural. My primary interest lies in the question as to how larger changes can be identified and/or observed in everyday interaction at a personal face –to – face level. By combining different data such as natural conversations, on the one hand, with interviews, and long-term observations of the success of the enterprise I analyzed, on the other hand, I hope to have reached this goal, at least partially.

AM: Have there been aspects that you could easily recognize and identify as being relevant for your own work?

FM: Discourse analysts are obliged to conduct interdisciplinary research as they work at the interface of different scientific approaches. It was astonishing, however, how easily many of the macrostructural approaches presented could be combined with my own, more interpretive model of "balanced discourse".

AM: Narratives of unity and narratives of identity in ambiguous environments— what are the results of your most recent research?

FM: Karl E. Weick was one of the first to point out, in a brilliant manner, that organizations must not only absorb uncertainty, but must also produce new insecurities in order to be able to survive. From a discourse-analytical point of view, this means that interaction must contain elements that reduce ambiguity as well as features that maintain equivocality (Menz 2000).

Many enterprises nowadays are characterized by uncertainty that arises from turbulent, ever-changing environments. Routines and planned processes have become brittle; exceptions as well as disturbances from outside and inside thwart standard processing. In fact, we could speak of a routine disturbance of the routine. The employees constantly have to deal with increased flexibility.

But there is some danger in this increased flexibility and uncertainty. It lies in the loss of identity as an organization. What would the recognizable image, the "sameness" of an organization, be if every standard process, every routine was doubted or turned out to be inadequate? Along with its identity, therefore, the organisation would also lose its unity, its status as an organization.

The employees in an enterprise I examined found a very creative solution to the paradoxical dilemma of increasing flexibility, on the one hand, and the danger of losing their identity as members of a specific organization, on the other hand.

The default way to attempt a solution would be the reinforcement of structures, routines, hierarchies: in a nutshell, the bureaucratization of the organization. However, doing so would bring to threatening proximity precisely that condition which was no longer adequate to handle growing problems.

The unity of the organization, when threatened by chaos, flexibility and contingency, must therefore be achieved in some other way. The solution that the employees "found" is astonishing, as they turned the thing that threatened identity into the central identity-endowing factor. "Chaos" and competence are regarded as unique characteristics by the members of the organization. They are consequently construed as an essential, central component of the identity of the business.

Thus, the answer to the question as to how identity can be achieved in turbulent, chaotic environments that demand ever- increasing flexibility, is -with special types of narratives that "glue" the members together with the help of membership categorization device.

AM: In your work, you very often speak about post-bureaucratic organizations. Can you explain what you mean?

FM: The early organization theoreticians, especially Max Weber and Frederick Taylor, conceived of organizations as bureaucracies, hierarchically structured entities that performed their tasks with the help of routines. At the same time they were seen as relatively independent of the persons acting within them. The personality of their members was only interesting for the organization as far as their work and their abilities relative to their work were concerned. Only the contribution of this partial identity (cf. Allport 1962; Weick 1995: 131) was demanded and expected by the organization. Bureaucracies were characterized by centralization, standardization, division of labor and specialization. Communication was primarily conceived of as compliance with rules and instructions.

Modern forms of organization need other, sometimes converse, qualities of their members. Along with communicative skills, qualities like spontaneity, initiative, commitment, enthusiasm and pragmatic decision-making are expected of the members; indeed, the member is expected to contribute his entire (or at least a considerably larger part of his) personality as a resource to the organization. Donnelon/Heckscher and Iedema call this type of organization post-bureaucratic.

AM: Would you say that the loss of structures is related to our society or is it to do with changes in the demands that organizations have to meet?

FM: Definitely the latter. To talk about changes in society on a global level and their influence on single people is far too long an explanation chain. And, actually, I don't see a loss of structures, but rather a change of their nature – a change which might be conceived of as a loss at the moment, but I'm pretty sure that in the not so long run we will discover a new nature of these structures.

AM: Communication (including new narratives) and, along with it, qualities such as spontaneity, initiative, commitment, enthusiasm are becoming more and more important. What implications does this have? How should organizations react?

FM: Since the introduction of Management Science by Max Weber and Frederick Taylor, management's first and almost instinctive reaction to chaos, uncertainty and structure – deficiency in organizations has been the implementation of new rules and regulations – i.e., more structure and instruction, an increase of bureaucracy and emphasis on routine formulas according to their classic if-then scheme. Recourse to what was successful in the past has also promised success for the future. In this conception, an organization works like a trivial machine (cf. Foerster 1990), whose output can be predicted by the input if it is correctly programmed, i.e., provided with the right rules and instructions. In classic structuralism (Taylorism, Fordism), this view of the business reached an early climax.

For economic reasons, reinforced bureaucratization and the development of new routines is not a lasting solution. In the not so long run, it would end with the organization's departure from the market.

On the other hand, conflicts that occur due to increasing involvement, communication, and commitment also endanger the existence of the organization: In the end, the loss of structures and routine procedures means the loss of its identity as an organization, because it offers no recognizable appearance to both external and internal observers.

So how, other than by means of bureaucratization, can identity management be practised, stability be gained, continuity and unity be maintained or produced, without jeopardizing adaptability?

The "solution" to the problem is to find a balance between retentional, bureaucratic, past-driven routines, and spontaneous, flexible solutions "against the rules". Successful enterprises practice this by adopting and using specific communicative styles: They (subconsciously split their interactions up into parts that contain elements of uncertainty (expressed, e.g., by elements of vagueness and doubt), and parts that communicate security and safe knowledge. This splitting can be observed at any level of organization: in face-to-face interaction in a meeting, in the "cultures" of different departments, in the different management approaches of different board members, etc.

AM: What are the advantages or values of the approach that you use? How can discourse analysis bring you insights for organization theory or its methodology?

FM: Using naturally occurring data (e.g., actual conversations) provides the researcher with what Geertz has called thick descriptions. These data are very rich and open to thorough interpretation; they therefore provide more information than, e.g., simple counts. If data from different sources are triangulated, i.e., statements from interviews are compared to actual communicative behaviour in everyday or organizational interaction, not only the descriptions but also the data become "thick".

Conclusions drawn from these data are very plausible and comprehensible for the practitioner. And talking about communication: Communication is a form of practice, like playing the piano, which has to be exercised and cultivated. Examples of good and bad interaction practices combined with the theoretical approaches that enable their evaluation may be a good basis for changing the management (as opposed to change management).

AM: Organization studies very often rely on positivistic empirical research. Can your study be understood as a criticism or are combinations possible?

FM: In principle, critical discourse analysis is to be seen as a corrective to positivistic research, as its roots lie in the critique of precisely these affirmative approaches. But, of course, in order to be credible, critical discourse analysis (CDA) must not repeat the mistake of presuming to know the truth, or at least the right and only way to it. In this sense, CDA is self-reflective – a characteristic that unfortunately is frequently missing in other scientific models.

AM: Would you say that your kind of research opens a new path for critical research in management and organization sciences? What can strategic management learn from it?

FM: As communicative skills gain more and more importance in modern organizations, it seems obvious to me that discourse analysis may contribute interesting facets to the analysis of organizational communication. What seems most important to me is the conviction that the balance between innovating aspects and retentional aspects, which are both indispensable for the survival of any organization, can only be reached via a special type of interaction practices – a practice that allows for both communication of certainty and communication of uncertainty and doubt. How this can be enacted, as it were, through communication, is one of the most interesting fields of research within organization theory and, therefore, most relevant for the practice of strategic management.

References

Allport, F.H. (1962): A structuronomic conception of behavior: Individual and collective. In: Journal of Abnormal and Social Psychology 64: pp. 3-30.

Donnelon, A./Heckscher, C. (1994): The Post-Bureaucratic Organization. New perspectives on Organizational Change. Thousand Oaks: Sage.

Foerster, H. von (1990): Kausalität, Unordnung, Selbstorganisation. In: Kratky, K./Wallner, F. (eds.) (1990): Grundprinzipien der Selbstorganisation. Darmstadt: Wissenschaftliche Buchgesellschaft, pp. 77-95.

Iedema, R. (2003): Discourses of Post-Bureaucratic Organization. Amsterdam: Benjamins

Menz, F. (2000): Selbst- und Fremdorganisation im Diskurs. Interne Kommunikation in Wirtschaftsunternehmen. Wiesbaden: Deutscher Universitätsverlag.

Weick, K. E. (1995): Der Prozess des Organisierens. Frankfurt/Main: stw (Engl. 1979: The Social Psychology of Organizing. Reading, Mass. Addison-Wesley).

Life and Innovation – A Practitioner's Narrative

Philippe Rixhon

Combination – how the new combination of existing narratives leads to the declaration of groundbreaking purposes

> To produce means to combine things and forces which exist in my domain. To produce different products or to produce differently means to combine these things and these forces differently. As long as the new combination can be achieved through time, through little steps, through continuous adaptation, there is a certain change, perhaps a certain growth, but, according to me, there is no new phenomenon, no innovation. To the contrary, when the combination can or does only occur disruptively, then there is an innovation as I mean it – a breakthrough of new combinations.

This was Joseph Schumpeter, one hundred years ago, still the best definition of innovation.

Combinations of things, combinations of forces, combinations of narratives

Twenty five years ago, Artificial Intelligence is all over the place – the science and engineering of making intelligent machines. What a narrative! Let's call it *Narrative One*. The story tells that a central property of humans, intelligence, the sapience of Homo sapiens, can be so precisely described that it can be simulated by a machine. We start to study and design intelligent agents, systems that perceive their environment and take actions to maximize their success.

By fortuity, *Fortuity One*, I advise a manufacturer of high precision equipment in Germany. By fortuity, *Fortuity Two*, I attend the first conference about Artificial Intelligence ever organised in Switzerland. By *nature*, I'll come back to *nature* later, I combine the needs of my client with the speeches of the conference, something from one country with something from another country, something from one domain with something from another domain. I invest a lot of time, a lot of money, and come up to speed. I develop a configurator for hydraulic systems. It fails, it fails, it works. I communicate. By fortuity, *Fortuity*

Three, engineers from Areva, the French builder of nuclear power plants, listen to what I'm saying. They call me.

We meet. We work together, weeks, months, years. We develop a relationship. A strong development relationship focused on *the* task of the nuclear industry: maintenance. *Narrative Two*. This story tells that corrective maintenance is not good enough for nuclear power. Correcting is, most of the times, simply too late. The story tells further that these systems are so complex that humans can only find root causes with the help of computers. The story tells finally that the faults are so rare, that human experience cannot be built, well, should not be built. This narrative has a sequel. Preventive maintenance. Making sure that the maximum credible accident, the *GAU*, does not happen. Shut the power plant for weeks, replace many systems, most of them in perfect functioning order, and hope for the best. Correcting is good, preventing is better.

So far, two narratives, Artificial Intelligence and Maintenance. The first one rather ambitious, the second one, obviously weak. So far, two narratives and three fortuities.

I continue to fail, to fail, to succeed and to communicate. Another conference. *Fortuity Four*. For some reasons, I speak about technical diagnostics and sensors; for some other reasons, Boris, professor at a Belgian University and CEO of a spin-off, speaks about simulation and sensors. *Narrative Three*. The story of simulation, modelling, forecast, prophecy, prediction. My domain – at the time – complex electro-mechanical engineering, Boris' domain: complex chemical plants. Coffee break. Within ten minutes we connect diagnostic and simulation through sensors.

Can't sleep that night. Call Areva in the morning.

- We need to talk.
- Come to Paris.

Aside.

You know that we built a strong relationship. They trust me as I trust them. I know them. They know me. They know that – in the morning – I don't drink anything else than coffee. They know that I don't smoke any grass, don't take any pill, and stay away from magic mushrooms.

I begin.

- Theoretically, we could build the unbreakable machine.
- Tell us more...

I continue – that's *Narrative Four*, a four-time fortuitous combination of three existing narratives from three different domains, information technology, nuclear power plants, chemical plants. Here is the story:

- If we can assess exactly the status of a machine, through sensors, X-rays, oil analyses and what have you; I mean if we have a perfect picture of the current status; and if we can know everything about the planned use of the machine, rotations, forces, wear and tear, well everything; I mean if we have a perfect prediction of every situation, let's say within the next six months; and if we can mine the combination of these two tremendous sets of data through technical diagnostic systems; then, we can go beyond preventive maintenance. Instead of acting preventively on a machine on the base of past experiences collected from other machines, we can act preventively on a machine on the base of the current, *known* status of this very machine and on the base of the future, *known* situations of this very machine.
- You mean we can act predicatively on the machine...
- Yes, that's exactly what I mean. And if we can act predicatively on the machine, theoretically, the machine is unbreakable.
- Wonderful!
- But only a theory.
- Why?
- Because it's much too expensive.
- Philippe, we will worry about the money, you will worry about the team.
- It's a deal!

The four-time-fortuitous, new combination of the three existing narratives of Artificial Intelligence, maintenance and modelling lead to the declaration of the unbreakable machine, truly a groundbreaking purpose. The rest is history – I assembled the team who realised the idea. The idea has been implemented first on nuclear submarines, then in nuclear power plants, recently, it has been tried on airplanes.

Life – how innovation is disruptively inherent in life, be it individual or corporative life

Where there is life, there is change. As soon as you breathe, there is a change, a molecular transformation in your lungs. As soon as you digest, there is a change, a chemical transformation in your stomach and intestine. The same for all humans, all animals, all plants.

And, as you know, climate changes too. It always did. And the Earth and the universe are in permanent change too. I think we can say they are well alive, they struggle for life.

> – I use the term *Struggle for Existence* in a large and metaphorical sense, including dependence of one being on another, and including – which is more important – success in leaving progeny. Owing to this struggle for life, any variation, however slight and from whatever cause proceeding, if it be in any degree profitable to an individual of any species, in its infinitely complex relationship to other organic beings and to external nature, will tend to the preservation of that individual, and will generally be inherited by its offspring. The offspring, also, will thus have a better chance of surviving, for, of the many individuals of any species which are periodically born, but a small number can survive. I have called this principle, by which each slight variation, if useful, is preserved, by the term *Natural Selection*, in order to mark its relation to *Man's Power of Selection*.

That was Charles Darwin, one hundred and fifty years ago and still the best definition of evolution.

Let's hit the pause-button – a first time.

There is the dead. And there is the living. And Darwin says the one best adapting to change – not the strongest, not the fittest, the one best adapting to change – that one will survive and its progeny will inherit the necessary characteristics to survive for a while. And that is *Natural Selection*, in another word, evolution. And Darwin opposes *Natural Selection* to *Man's Power of Selection*. Fifty years later, Schumpeter opposes continuous adaptation to innovation.

Let's hit the pause-button – a second time.

I have met the parasites – amateurs, charlatans and thieves – and the useful creatures – producers and innovators. Life would be easier without the parasites. Life would be impossible without the producers. You cannot run a railway network without them. You cannot bake bread or manufacture cars without them. And, life would be impossible without the innovators. You cannot solve problems without them. You cannot break ground without them. Both, production and innovation people, are equally necessary. And I have observed that life is not black and white. Most producers are also more or less innovators. Most innovators are also more or less producers.

Let's hit the pause-button – a third time.

A company which does not change is a dead company. So, change – Darwin would say *evolution* – is necessary. So, change management is a condition for survival – a necessary condition of corporative life. It is also – necessarily – a struggle, because the producers – the drivers of the bread-and-butter machine – are allergic to change. They manage the existing production process and optimize it slowly and surely. That is their necessary role. They must be conservative, here and there with a zest of evolution.

I had the privilege to serve one client – Swisscom – ten years long from 1988 until 1997. It was the deregulation of telecommunications, when Swisscom changed identity, ownership, business model, territory, service portfolio and technology. Without evolutive producers and disruptive innovators, that company would have gone bust.

I served Swisscom wearing four different hats. The first was mine; the second was the hat of senior vice president at Zühlke Engineering, the Swiss Denkfabrik; the third, the hat of CEO of AT&T Solutions Switzerland and the fourth, the hat of partner with Andersen Consulting. My role was always the same: agent of innovation, at least agent of change. My platforms were very different: a company which generates ideas, a company which empowers ideas, a company which delivers new systems, and a company which improves management. Not only, I could observe the necessity of evolutive production for the survival of Swisscom and the necessity of disruptive innovation for their success; but, I could also observe the unstable balance between production and innovation forces within the companies I was operating from.

My company and Zühlke Engineering are still led by innovators, dedicated to innovation, and well alive. AT&T Solutions has been sacrificed 15 years ago on the altar of Wall Street and, 10 years ago, the producers took over the power at Andersen Consulting, transforming the disruptive consulting company into Accenture, another stock exchange story. Innovators live longer.

Allow me to mix my limited practitioner's experience with the vast researches of illustrious scientists such as Darwin and Schumpeter. There is a difference between, on one side, *Natural Selection* and continuous adaptation, and, on the other side, *Man's Power of Selection* and innovation. Both production and innovation are inherent in life. Producers manage and tune. Innovators disrupt. Evolutive producers assure survival, disruptive innovators assure success, exciting survival.

Transcendence – how innovators transcend their condition, in particular the ego, the unknown and the complexity

Why do we innovate? Who is an innovator?

A narrative.

Spring 1987. The textile machine industry prepares its main exhibition which takes place every four years. Rieter – at that time one of the duopolists in spinning machines – understands that Schlafhorst, the other one, will present something new... and Rieter has nothing to show. Crisis. Urs leads the R&D department. He convenes 20 people at a briefing. Some people are from Rieter, some not; some from established suppliers, some without commercial relationship; some are freelancers, some delegates of large companies. Urs explains

- An important labour cost at a spinning mill is generated by the handling of doffers; let's build a robot and automate the manual operation.

Urs speaks with each attendee, one by one, mechanics with the mechanicians, electronics with the electronicians. My turn comes.

- Philippe – can you build an embedded diagnostic system?
  I do not know, but say – yes.
- Philippe – there is no keyboard on that robot, can your system work without a keyboard?
  I do not know, but say – yes.

- Philippe – the users of the robot are all over the world, Germany, Turkey, Malaysia, most of them are illiterate, can illiterate people use your system?
  I do not know, but say – yes.
- Excellent Philippe. You get the contract.

And Urs continues with the next attendee. I'm driving back to my office, feeling *high*. Why?
Is it because I'm again member of a big thing? Fun? Is it because I belong to the great community of engineers? Pride? Is it because I got a contract? I do not know. Driving, I go from high to low. I realise the technical challenge. And I see a picture. You could say *I have a vision*. I clearly see a washing machine. That is my blueprint. I have a few weeks to realise it. But I'm missing a key element. I call Urs.

- Urs, many thanks for the contract. We will deliver on time, but we did not agree on the price.
- Philippe, the price will be the amount stated on your invoice.
  I do not quite understand, but nevertheless say – yes.

The rest is again history. I find that Philips is developing interfaces with an institute in Nancy. One engineer of that team accepts to work with us. The robotics engineers fit a touchscreen and a CPU board according to our specs. We work day and night. We go to Paris. The night before the opening. Our system does not work; <u>we</u> continue to work. Opening. The first visitors walk along the alleys. Suddenly, the system works! One or two days later, Urs is interviewed. The journalist is impressed by our system. Urs says:

- I wanted to test them, I was sure they would fail, but they succeeded.

He was sure he would not have to pay, but he did. He gave me the chance, intuitively, irrationally; and I took it, intuitively, irrationally.
Let's come back to some rationale.
The psychologist Abraham Maslow is famous for positing a hierarchy of human needs, ranging from *deficiency needs* (needs for food, safety, love, and self-esteem) up to a *being-need* (the need of self-actualisation, to engage in meaningful, helpful work and service, to promote justice, to creatively express oneself, to find spiritual fulfilment in realising what is true, beautiful and good).

At the end of his life, Maslow exceeded the *being-need* of self-actualisation with his ideal of self-transcendence based on his observation of people he called *transcenders*. Here are seven of his observations:

1. *Transcenders* are much more consciously and deliberately meta-motivated. That is, the values of being, truth, beauty, goodness... are their main or most important motivations...

2. They seem somehow to recognize each other, and to come to almost instant intimacy and mutual understanding even upon first meeting...
   (Comment: so far I came to almost instant intimacy with all innovators I met, but also with few others who were not innovators).

3. There is more and easier transcendence of the ego, the self, the identity...
   (Comment: for an innovator, the *thing* is important, not the self. Two years ago an already famous person joined me on an innovative project. Sadly, it was all about him, how he would be interviewed, how he would be on stage and – I do not make this up – how we would get a Nobel Prize. Utter non-sense. When he discovered that it was not about him, but about the *thing*, he resigned).

4. *Transcenders* are far more apt to be innovators, discoverers of the new, than are the healthy self-actualisers... Transcendent experiences and illuminations bring clearer vision of the *being-values*, of the ideal... of what ought to be, what actually could be...
   (Comment: two of the most important words for innovation are German, and they do not translate easily in other languages. The first one is *Auseinandersetzung*, the skill of putting something together out of the pieces from something you de-constructed, a wink to Schumpeter's combination theory; and the word Maslow is here referring to, *Vorstellungskraft*, the force to project in front of you something which is not yet there, then the ability to see it, and finally the opportunity to realise it).

5. *Transcenders* show more strongly a positive correlation between increasing knowledge and increasing mystery and awe... For *transcenders*, mystery is attractive and challenging rather than frightening...
   (Comment: for an innovator there are few things he knows, many things he knows he doesn't know and infinity of things he doesn't even know that he doesn't know. An innovator is not frightened by the unknown; he does not fill gaps with stories but with substance).

6. *Transcenders* are interested in a *cause beyond their own skin*, and are better able to *fuse work and play*. *They love their work*, and are more interested in *kinds of pay other than money pay…*
(Comment: There is no glory about being a *transcender* or an innovator, it is in their *nature*, a simple fact of life, and there is a price…)

7. Maslow wrote – I have a vague impression that *transcenders* are less *happy* than the healthy self-actualisers. They are more prone to a kind of cosmic sadness over the stupidity of people, their self-defeat, their blindness, their cruelty to each other, their shortsightedness… No wonder they are sad or angry or impatient at the same time that they are also *optimistic* in the long run.

(No comment. I quote Curt Goetz:

According to the rule that the antidote of a sickness will always be found when that sickness has reached its peak and become unbearable, the germ of human stupidity must be found today or tomorrow.

Unquote).

We reach the interval. We had Act I – three observations, the innovative power of combining narratives, life and innovation, transcendence and innovators. Let's move to Act II – three suggestions.

Human touch – how mechanical organisations and processes should be replaced by bio-logical structures and codes of conduct

Have you ever considered the number of books we have about innovation management? Many of them are written by intelligent people according to accepted scientific or academic methods. Nevertheless, another book will be published next week, few more next month and many more next year. Why? Why can't they encapsulate once and for all the essence of creation, the nurturing of innovators and the process of innovation?

I do not know. But I might have two *Denkanstöße*, some food for thought. Thought number one – for the moment, mankind cannot codify innovation and even less creation; for the moment, this scientific quest is doomed to be as productive as the quests for the Golden Fleece, the Holy Grail or the Philosopher's Stone. Thought number two – the managerial methods currently used to apprehend innovation are inappropriate. Here and tonight we leave the first thought to artists and philosophers and focus on the second one.

Management – the art of getting things done through people – has three main sources: Sun Tzu's *The Art of War*, Niccoló Machiavelli's *The Prince* and Adam Smith's *The Wealth of Nations*. Military, political and productive backgrounds – no innovative or creative backgrounds.

War, politics and production deal with power. No matter if it is legitimate, traditional or charismatic power, not even if it is the power of expertise, it is power. Innovation deals with the thing, not with the self, not with power. Power needs organisation. Power needs process, power transmission, transmission process.

Innovation is life. Life appears and develops in complex, dynamic eco-systems. Evolution occurs through slight changes reacting to slight modifications. Innovation occurs through disruptive changes reacting to dramatic modifications. Management hates drama, innovation lives from drama.

Innovators are attracted by the unknown and by the mystery. Managers mitigate risk and model the future. They hate the unknown and replace the mystery by powerful, fictional narratives. They have to.

I think that you cannot manage innovation. I think that you can nurture an eco-system which is prone to innovation. Innovation needs liberty. The liberty of self-determination. The liberty of altruistic objectives. The liberty of communication. The liberty of failure. The liberty of intuition. The liberty of irrationality.

The liberty of self-determination.

Early 80's. I'm a financial analyst at Procter & Gamble. The boss of my boss reads somewhere that PCs are good for business. Instead of asking his boss for permission or a consultant for feasibility study, he buys an Apple II and brings it to the office. Because I am an engineer – at least here there is some logic – I receive the box and a simple brief.

– Philippe, try to figure out how this thing could be good for our business.

VisiCalc is in the package. I try. My productivity goes through the roof. Soon all analysts get an Apple II on their desk. And I get more and more frustrated. We are entering vast amounts of data which we are reading from listings, outputs from mainframe computers. This is stupid. As the data are on a computer, we must be able to link the mainframes and the PCs and have the data flowing from the ones to the others. I explain that to the boss of my boss and tell him that the missing cable would transfigure the life of analysts at Procter & Gamble and all over the world.

He says:

- Philippe your future is in finance, you can become a comptroller, forget about these computers.

I say

- Alan, it's not about me; it's about the cable, it has to be developed.

Few weeks later, I resign, for the cable. Twelve months later, I have it. Tedious implementation of unproven hardware and software. Tremendous help from Hewlett-Packard – both divisions, the instruments and the computers. The liberty of self-determination. The boss of my boss bought an Apple II, simply because he – independently – decided to buy an Apple II. I got my cable, simply because I – independently – decided to resign and focus on the cable.

You remember the liberty of communication and failure from the maintenance story. You remember the liberty of intuition and irrationality from the robot story.

You may already observe the emergence of a recurring pattern. I have some ideas and few of them have been realised. But I never realised any of them alone. Not only there have always been others to help me or even to realise my ideas without me, but these others have always been groups of others. These groups were most of the times composed of people from different disciplines and from different types of institution, freelancers, SMEs, universities, large corporations.

If there is one word to bridge idea and innovation, for me, it is collaboration. I think that you can have a mental set and a physical environment which foster the type of collaboration required by innovation. I do not think that you can manage this particular type of collaboration. I even think, based on my limited experience, that if you attempt to manage this collaboration, it will not produce any innovation.

Chance and necessity – how breakthroughs should not be obstructed by management and monthly reports

Let's continue to review our innovation vocabulary. We already have *Auseinandersetzung* and *Vorstellungskraft*. Let's go now to few English words.

Serendipity.

Serendipity is the propensity for making fortunate discoveries while looking for
something unrelated. Everyone knows that the discovery of X-rays came as the
result of several incidences of serendipity. You cannot manage serendipity in the
sense that you cannot plan and control serendipity, and surely not a sequence of
serendipities.

January 2008. I have prepared an art festival with some colleagues. We need
only to sell it. Hum, hum. We target one venue in London. One man can decide.
He is not approachable. I need to catch him somewhere. I know that he will
attend an important conference about performing arts. I go to New York. After
two days, I meet him, briefly, one or two minutes – it will never come to fruition.
I browse the exhibition. On a table, I see two brochures. One in German, one in
English. The strange thing is that the title of the German brochure is in English.
This is what catches my attention. This title is *Broadening the Scope of Choral
Music*. I start to read. Hans-Hermann comes to me:

- Can I help you?

January 2008. Hans-Hermann and I start to communicate. September 2010. We
are still in communication. It keeps me awake at night. A Londoner goes to New
York to meet another Londoner, and he meets a Berliner. As William
Shakespeare said:

- All things are ready if our minds be so.

Readiness. That's what it is. Readiness vs. planning. Innovation is more linked to
readiness than to planning.

Little aside.

Scenario techniques are not planning the future but raising the readiness to face
probable events. That's the mastery of chess.

Serendipity does not work without sagacity. Sagacity is the ability to link
together apparently innocuous facts to come to a valuable conclusion.
Serendipity and sagacity are now recognized as significant in the advance of
science, in particular in pharmacology. Cancer was known by the Greeks and the
Romans. Cancer was already treated by the Arabs in the 11th century and
scientifically researched by the English in the 18th century. A lot is at stake, but
nobody in his right mind would ask a team of researchers to manage the

innovation necessary to develop the remedy against cancer, to produce a feasibility study, to make a business plan, to present a budget and to tell by when the remedy will have been found. To find the remedy against cancer is in the realm of disruptive innovation, serendipity and sagacity. It is not in the realm of management.

Necessity.

2,500 years ago, Democritus says:

– Everything existing in the universe is the fruit of chance and necessity.

40 years ago, Jacques Monod recycles the sentence for the title of his book *Chance and Necessity*, and 2 weeks ago, Stephen Hawking declares that:

– Because there is a law such as gravity, the Universe can and will create itself from nothing.

In other words *it is necessarily so* – George Gershwin would have contradicted that.

27 May 2010. I discuss a new TV format with Gary. He knows the industry like the back of his hand. Gary tells me:

– Philippe, if you don't do it, and if you keep it absolutely secret, someone else will do it, because all possible TV formats will be produced. It is necessarily so.

17 July 2010. I discuss innovation with Solomon, a Chinese philosopher. We talk about creation and discovery. We touch parallel developments and parallel discoveries. People who have absolutely no contact whatsoever work on the same things and find the same things, at the same time. Solomon tells me:

– The thought doesn't need the thinker.

The innovation doesn't need the innovator. If that is not keeping you humble, what will?

Serendipity, sagacity, necessity. Three words, three swords, but the three musketeers were four, weren't they? Serendipity, sagacity, necessity and fortuity.

A monthly report on serendipity? A monthly report on sagacity? A monthly report on necessity? And of course, the speciality of the management house, a monthly report on fortuity!

What are then the levers that open new paths to opportunity recognition, entrepreneurial innovation and business development in uncertain and contingent markets? What are the bio-logical structures and codes of conduct?

Theoretically, that's easy to answer – eco-systems where liberty can flourish; eco-systems where collaboration can emerge spontaneously; eco-systems where serendipity and sagacity can blossom; eco-systems where readiness supplants planning; eco-systems where necessity and fortuity are respected.

Practically, that's difficult to realise – because innovation is cultural, socially located – some principles transfer from one culture to the next, some principles are culture-specific. I would suggest, at the beginning, focusing on the effectiveness of the eco-system, not on the efficiency. I would also suggest, at the beginning, that it is probably easier to kill an innovation parasite than to give a planned birth to an innovation gardener.

Dialogue – how the exchange of narratives between creators and users should prop up the success of innovations

You remember the robot to handle doffers in spinning mills. Next instalment of that story. The robot did not sell, for the simple reason that the mills did not want it, did not ask for it. It was a supplier's reaction to the competitive threat from another supplier. It was not a supplier's reaction to a customer's need.

Seven years later, Percy has merged ASEA and Brown Boveri and launched an ambitious change programme called *Customer Focus*. Now, they want to go the extra mile and add innovation to that programme. They need help. They send a request for proposal to their three most innovative suppliers. Zülke Engineeering empowers ABB's ideas. I'm with Zühlke Engineering at the time. Work reasonably late. Just before closing the office, I pass by the fax machine and find ABB's request. Too lazy to put it at the right place. It can wait for tomorrow. Take the request home. Read it. Start to write. All night. The next morning go to Gerry, the boss. He says:

– Philippe this is not our line of business, we will not get the contract, but we are not in a position not to answer ABB, you are right to make an offer, send it and forget it.

So he says, so it is done. Two weeks later, Zühlke Engineering is invited to defend the offer. Gerry calls me:

- You wrote the offer, now you go and defend it.

So he says, so it is done. Two days later, Zühlke Engineering gets the contract. Gerry calls me:

- You defended the offer, now you go and deliver it.

Easier said than done. I need help. The Swiss Federal Institute of Technology, the ETHZ, they must know. I have three buddy professors there. Visit them one by one:

- Philippe, we do search and find, but we do neither search nor teach about searching and finding.

One of them is Urs, Rieter's Urs, all his live spent in searching and finding:

- Philippe, I cannot help you, go and do it, but when you are done come back.

So he says, so it is done. I deliver. Once to the top bosses of ABB, a second time to the in-house trainers, then I go back to Urs. He offers me to continue with his department. Gerry accepts as long as I do not work less for him. And here I am, digging into past and present to try to find out why and how an innovative process can be successful. I take ABB's point-of-view: *Customer Focus*. Urs says:

- Start with the past.

I become an expert in the Swiss textile machine industry – focus: 19th century. Amazing! I go further and I'm very intrigued by the parallel development of technologies in France and Great Britain during the 18th and 19th century. They find many similar things at the same time, but the industrial revolution happens in Great Britain, not in France. The British are empiricist and mercantilist. The French are rationalist and idealist. Well – in general. The English and Scottish innovators innovate to make money; they need to sell the innovation to a user, a user who has a mission-critical need to be satisfied. The French innovators innovate for innovation, *l'art pour l'art*. Well – in general. I sketch the first version of my thesis – *the success of an innovation depends on the quality of the relationship between innovator and users*. Urs – the one who decided to build a robot to handle doffers without asking spinning mills – likes it. I embark on a 10-year observation of the textile machine industry – from 1995 until 2004. And I can confirm – *the effectiveness and efficiency of the innovation process is directly linked to the quality of the relationship between innovator and users*. What is this relationship? It is exchange – machine against money. It is not only an exchange of machine against money. It is communication, an exchange of one story against another story. A narrative against another narrative. A vision and a mission against another vision and another mission. A purpose against another purpose. A dream against another dream. A *raison-d'être* against another *raison-d'être*. A life against another life. A man-made-up story against a man-made-up story.

Narrative and innovation. Yes, they are linked. More than you think. Story telling is a children's thing. Being curious, risking and discovering are other children's things. Wake up your sleeping inner child. Wake up the sleeping children in your team. You will be surprised.

References

Darwin, Ch. (1859): On the Origin of Species. London: John Murray.

Frayn, M. (2006): The Human Touch. London: Faber and Faber.

Maslow, A. (1969): Theory Z. Palo Alto. In: The Journal of Transpersonal Psychology. 1 (2), pp. 31-47.

Monod, J. (1970): Le hasard et la nécessité. Paris: Éditions du Seuil.

Rixhon, P. (2008): Innovation leadership: Best practices from theatre creators. In: Becker, L./Ehrhardt, J./Gora, W. (eds.) (2008): Führung, Innovation und Wandel. Düsseldorf: Symposion, pp. 197-216.

Schumpeter, J. (1911): Theorie der wirtschaftlichen Entwicklung. Berlin: Duncker & Humblot.

Intercultural Awareness in Business and Literary Works

Kinuyo Shimizu

Introduction

The purpose of this paper is to introduce an activity and materials concerned with raising learners' intercultural awareness of marketing through literary works in graduate-level classes. People constantly create different realities in their own ways. These realities depend on their sensory and selective perception. They perceive what they value in their lives. Each culture has its own unique values with regard to survival or well-being. For people in business, who must interact with others from different cultures on an everyday basis in this globalized world, it is often difficult to understand and work properly within the value systems of other cultures.

In the international business world, many companies try to sell their products as they are, without considering any modifications for foreign markets. They make a few changes to the product name, color, size, advertising and so on. There are different reasons for this: the cost of the changes, their strong belief in the quality of their own products, and a lack of awareness of the different ways others may perceive their products. The result of this failure to make necessary modifications could be a withdrawal of the products from the foreign market.

Literary Works and the Business World

Business books or articles are full of successful, positive stories or negative starts with happy endings. However, literary works often also describe the dark side of human life or its nature with unhappy, ambiguous endings. They portray life-styles of people in a certain place or time. We can find the particular values of a culture through its literary works. Negative stories and the lifestyles of different cultures may provide a new perspective for those involved in international business.

Einbeck (2002: 62) designed a literature course for study-abroad students to help them develop cultural awareness and coping skills while discovering the literature of the host country. According to Einbeck, literature is a magnificent cultural lens: It focuses our gaze, filters out the extraneous details, and concentrates the emotional impact of what it portrays (Einbeck 2002: 59). There are many culture-related cases with "fact". However, they are a sum of the pieces of the facts, not a holistic entity.

Bloch (1995: 4) discusses the use of literature to teach cross-cultural management, providing examples of topics found in literature that seem to be well-suited for teaching culture, such as: attitudes towards strangers, the cultural meaning of a situation, how cultural perceptions influence communication, ambiguity in cross-cultural interactions, and attitudes towards material possessions. These topics are deeply connected to not only cross-cultural management, but also to marketing. In order to successfully sell products internationally, one should know the culture of the market.

Specifying the target and analyzing the market bring about efficient and effective marketing plans. However, at the same time, there is a chance that this creates an overly narrow view of the market and of the people who are purchasing the products or the services. Moreover, literary works can introduce other views of human behavior and culture, which have no direct connection with business. Harold Bloom claims that, "by reading, people can become more aware and acquire a broader range of sensibility" (Coutu 2001: 65). Lack of sensitivity towards foreign markets may result in unproductive marketing plans. A balanced view is necessary in this globalized market.

There are business school instructors who emphasize the importance of literary works in the business world. David White points out, "Good poetry can open up areas of everyday business life that remain impervious to the jargon we have created to describe it. Executives are hungry for this larger language" (Burrell 2007). The jargon that business people use limits their thoughts and tends to narrow their view of life. The meaning of a word in poetry may be deeper and wider than a word in business. According to James March, topics in his leadership and literature course can draw illumination from the social sciences, but they are more profoundly considered in great literature. Additionally, he said, "One issue, which I used to talk about by looking at George Bernard Shaw's Saint Joan, is how madness, heresy, and genius are related" (Coutu 2006). Topics in business schools are full of measurable or objective "facts". There is not enough time for discussion of the human mind and emotions. The drama of life is missing in business school topics.

Joseph L. Badaracco mentions the subjectivity of literature; however, he insists, "It actually provides us with some of the most powerful and engaging case studies ever written. Serious fiction that has survived the test of time raises more questions than it answers" (Badaracco 2006: 48). Many case studies at business school become outdated quickly and are used temporarily. They may explain the recent business matter clearly, but their relevance may not be long lasting. Thus, business students may be learning how to analyze the business world with a short-term view. The balance of a short- and a long-term view is necessary for learners.

According to Sandra J. Sucher, in her Harvard Business School's literature class "The Moral Leader": "Because the books we read are not about business, executives can distance themselves from their biases and only later, upon reflection, see how their own choices might mirror those in the narratives" (Peebles 2008: 21). The learners need time to connect the messages found in literary works to their business reality. It may be demanding in some cases to try to connect literature and reality during the available class time. There are not many opportunities for learners to distance themselves from the business world while in business school. The main focus of their lives and the subjects they study in school are usually strongly connected. They spend most of their time concerned with business-related pursuits during their years in business school. Therefore, introducing literature into their classes provides a valuable opportunity for business students to gain insight into other perspectives that can be applied to the business world.

Activities

This activity consists of two parts, and uses Franz Kafka's *The Metamorphosis (Die Verwandlung)* and Arthur Miller's *Death of a Salesman* as reading material. The first part of the activity is to read the stories, find business realities of today in the stories, and record the results on a spreadsheet. This activity enables learners to make a connection between themselves and the stories, which then gives them new perspectives regarding their ordinary business practices. The second part of the activity is to discuss the results of the first part, and uncover the differences of culture that people should not ignore in globalized markets.

In the story *The Metamorphosis*, the main character Gregor Samsa found himself transformed into a monstrous insect one morning. The transformation separates him from society and his family. The story demonstrates over and over again the highly elusive nature of the cultural and aesthetic encoding of the key signifier, the vile body around which the constellation of this family drama endlessly gyrates (Ryan 2007: 1). The elusive expressions in the story enable one to find the meanings of the signifier in different ways. It is possible for readers to create another story from *The Metamorphosis.*

Arthur Miller's *Death of a Salesman* is a play that describes the life, work, and family of the main character (Willy Loman). Carson and Carson (Carson, K. and Carson, P. 1997: 62) point out that Loman's grim and futile situation is all too familiar to some contemporary workers. People can identify with the character in the play. According to Garaventa (1998: 535), plays more sharply address the interactions of characters, and the reader becomes more involved in their situations. In order to balance the expressions in literary works, both a novel and a play were chosen for this activity.

Activity 1: Connecting with the Story and Creating One's Own Story

First, the learners are required to read Franz Kafka's *The Metamorphosis (Die Verwandlung)* and Arthur Miller's *Death of a Salesman* and to analyze the plots using the spreadsheets. One spreadsheet is used for both stories. Next, the learners create their own stories which describe today's business problems by using the plots of both stories.

Title	Title
Characters	Characters
When?	When?
Where?	Where?
Incident(s)	Incident(s)
Insight(s)	Insight(s)

Activity 1

Activity 2: Uncovering the Differences of Culture

The second part consists of discussing the following three questions.

- What are the situations or incidents that you couldn't understand or identify with in the story? Explain the reason by referring to your cultural backgrounds.
- What are the situations or incidents that you could understand or identify with in the story? Explain the reason by referring to your cultural backgrounds.
- What are the cultural values in the story which you may not have noticed before now?

For outsiders there is always something very difficult to understand about each culture. Realizing one cannot understand everything about different cultures is significant.

Conclusion

Business cases, papers and books are full of measurable facts. This makes it difficult for people to obtain a holistic image of another culture. Cultural matters need both the facts and one's imagination to understand the meaning of the situations. There are many things in culture that cannot be explained and expressed with measurable facts. In order to do business globally, people should realize the alternative ways of understanding foreign markets.

References

Badaracco, Joseph (2006): Leadership in Literature. In: Harvard Business Review 84, pp. 47-55.

Bloch, Brian (1995): Using Literature to Teach Cross-Cultural Management: A German Perspective, In: Unterrichtspraxis/Teaching German, 28, pp. 146-152.

Burrell, Lisa (2007): A Larger Language for Business, Interview with David Whyte, Lecturer, an Associate Fellow at Templeton College and Said Business School at the University of Oxford. In: Harvard Busi-ness Review 85, pp. 28.

Coutu, Diane (2006): Ideas as Art, Interview with James March, Professor Emeritus at Stanford University. In: Harvard Business Review 84, 82-89.

Carson, Kerry D./Carson Paula P. (1997): Career entrenchment: A quietmarch toward occupational death? In: Academy of Management Executive 11, pp. 62-75.

Einbeck, Kandace (2002): Using Literature to Promote Cultural Fluency in Study Abroad Programs. In: Unterrichtspraxis/Teaching German 35, 59-67.

Garaventa, Eugene (1998): Drama: A Tool for Teaching Business Ethics. In: Business Ethics Quarterly 8, pp. 535-545.

Peebles, Ellen M. (2008): Conversation, Interview with Sandra J. Sucher Senior. Business - Administration Lecturer at Harvard Business School. In: Harvard Business Review 86, pp. 21.

Ryan, Simon (2007): Fanz Kafka's Die Verwandlung: Transformation, Metaphor, and the Perils of Assimilation. In: Seminar 43:1, pp. 1-18.

Beatles & Co: Creativity as an Emergent Phenomenon

Stephan Sonnenburg

Introduction

Although creativity had been a significant driver of human development for centuries, it crystallized as a practical and theoretical topic in the 1950s. Since that time, creativity has gone up and down until Murakami and Nishiwaki (1991) proclaimed the fourth revolution after agriculturalization, industrialization and computerization: the age of creativity. However, personalities such as Florida (2002) or Leadbeater (2008) are needed so that creativity, as the fourth economic revolution, can become reality and no longer a vogue word or a mere attribution to (ingenious) individuals. Creativity is a co-created phenomenon. However until now, it is not clear theoretically and operationally what creativity is. The challenge of this paper is to show a new way to study and manage creativity. Therefore, the article has three interrelated objectives: to develop a different theoretical approach; to document how famous people engage in joint efforts; and to identify main dynamics that contribute to success in the "real world", especially in business settings.

A Snap Shot: From Individual Creativity to Group Creativity

The main research field is psychology (Mayer 1999), which mainly prefers a psychometric and experimental access to creativity. Until now, individual creativity has been the main research topic, but in the last few years it has been studied in a broader context. You may think of important researchers such as Amabile (1996) with her componential model, Csikszentmihalyi's (1996) systems approach, Harrington (1990) with his ecology of human creativity or Sternberg's and Lubart's (1991) investment theory. As a result of the complexity of society and business, new research areas are becoming more important, above all collaborations.

Owing to their synergetic potential of knowledge and diversity, human beings can often find better solutions for innovations in collaboration than when working on their own (Kelley 2001; Sawyer 2003; Schrage 1995). Especially in business settings, where the development of products expects too much of an individual, group creativity characterizes success. Bennis and Biederman (1997: 199) put this fact in a nutshell:

The Lone Ranger, the incarnation of the individual problem solver, is dead.
And Sawyer comments:

> The lone genius is a myth; instead, it's group genius that generates break-through innovation. When we collaborate, creativity unfolds across people; the sparks fly faster, and the whole is greater than the sum of its parts (Sawyer 2007: 7).

Early academic research makes group creativity a subject of discussion. However, researchers did not develop models or even a theory, but only focused on single aspects, in particular creativity techniques such as brainstorming (Osborn 1963), group dynamic factors in educational settings (Torrance 1972), or group training procedures (Stein 1975). Since the 1990s, group creativity approaches have been developed with a more complex design. According to Sonnenburg (2004), researchers analyze creativity in teams (Kelley 2001; Kurtzberg and Amabile 2000/01; Puccio 1999; Rickards and Moger 1999), in groups (Leonard and Swap 1999; Nijstad and Paulus 2003; Rubenson and Runco 1995; Sawyer 2007; Woodman et al. 1993), in partnerships (Clydesdale 2006; John-Steiner 2000), in couples (Chadwick and de Courtivron 1996), in improvisational genres of performance (Sawyer 2003), in virtual teams (Nemiro 2004) or in laboratory collaborations (Paulus et al. 2001).

There is no doubt that the various social entities have an effect on the quantity and quality of creativity (Moran and John-Steiner 2003) and that there is no logical evolution from individual to group creativity, as the research understanding of creativity in an individual context is different to creativity in a collaborative context. To approach a theory of creativity (Magyari-Beck 1990) based on multidisciplinary research (Montuori and Purser 1999: 20-23), it is helpful to find something in common in all of its forms.

The Rise of a Paradigm: Project Creativity

To create this common point, creativity is freed from individuals or social entities. Creativity is an emergent phenomenon which is not reducible to an individual, a dyad, or a group. However, this does not mean that it occurs in a sociocultural vacuum. Creativity emerges in specific intentional and time-limited situations. Therefore, I would like to speak about *project creativity*. And in this context, creativity is defined as the human potential for meaningful innovation that unfolds in action (Sonnenburg 2007: 150). For this reason, project creativity does not focus on the creativity of groups such as The Beatles, it focuses on the creativity in a specific situation such as the making of Sgt. Pepper by The Beatles. What is the research benefit of this understanding of creativity? More attention is paid to the creative act itself than to the social entities such as teams or partnerships.

The potential for meaningful innovation can be paraphrased in a wider sense as power, quality, capability, or energy. It is not rigid, isolated, and self-contained. It depends on a specific situation or context; thus the project can be regarded as the overarching parameter (Buijs et al. 2009; Sonnenburg 2004). Creativity can emerge only by action or performance in a project. Therefore, creativity is a dynamic phenomenon that changes during the project. Although each creativity project is unique and individual, general tendencies in typical cases can be observed, as a project starts with a problem and in best case ends with a product called an innovation. The project can last for a few hours like a workshop session, or some years, which is generally the case for business inno-vations.

Figure 1 illustrates the relevance of the Ps with regard to the development of creativity in a project. The arrow and dotted shape of the illustration indicate the interdependency and continual change of creativity during the project. For each P, I have intentionally used the plural in brackets to point towards the complexity and diversity of creativity projects and what is involved. For example, is there a single problem or are there multiple problems? Is there one company or are there joint ventures, different levels or departments of the organization, other involved institutions such as universities? And are individual or group projects undergoing the process to produce one or several products?

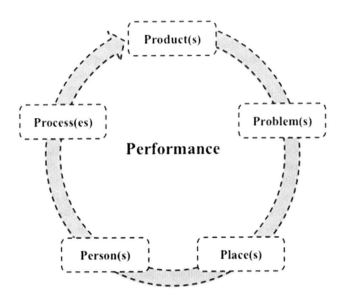

Figure 1: The Emergence of Creativity in a Project

In most organizations, a creativity project starts with a problem and, respective-ly, with problem-finding. Either the problem is given by the place, e.g. an organ-ization, or it is self-initiated at the beginning of the creativity project. According to van Gundy (1984), a problem can be extracted and classified by eight dimen-sions: (1) magnitude, (2) history, (3) location, (4) multiple causes, (5) threat, (6) time horizon, (7) people affected, and (8) complexity. This helps to forecast tendentiously the outcome.

In our times, the most innovative places are organizations and their creative power is characterized by co-creation (Henry 2004; West 1997). Due to global dynamics, innovations and creativity are becoming more important as the poten-tial to develop innovations is essential for business success. According to Csikszentmihalyi (1990), an organization can be regarded as the domain for which the participants of the creativity project develop a product. In a wider sense, the market in which the company operates is the enlarged domain. Csikszentmihalyi also uses the term "field" of experts, who are a kind of gate-keepers for the success of a new product in their domain. In business, the first field of experts is inside the company such as the department head or the board. Overall, the project and its performance have to fit in the organization.

As each project is unique, its process is unique as well. Just as the structure of the problem has an important influence on the process, so do the people (persons) as well as their engagement during the process. Their performance is a parameter that is decisive for the creative outcome and has to be handled adequately so that creativity can flourish. As said before, most creative acts occur in a collaborative context. Therefore, a creativity project is a co-creation project.

Co-creativity comes from synergetic knowledge potential and diversity. Human beings can find better solutions in collaboration than by working on their own. As said before, the lone ranger is no longer a formula for success. However, co-creation gives rise to new challenges, often including conflict and discouragement, which arise from the disparity of group members and must be handled. To put it to a nutshell at this moment, interaction becomes an eminent quality in creativity projects.

The overall aim of a creativity project is the development of a product called an innovation. I use product in a wide sense that spans from ideas and prototypes to marketable products. It depends on the overarching task for the creativity project and in general, although not predictable, the market relevance of the product. According to the "propulsion model of kinds of creative contributions" (Sternberg et al. 2002), eight ideal types can be differentiated: (1) replication, (2) redefinition, (3) forward incrementation, (4) advance forward incrementation, (5) redirection, (6) reconstruction/redirection, (7) re-initiation, and (8) integration. Without being too detailed, this model can be regarded as a typology showing different qualities of innovation. They have to be considered when managing a creativity project and with regard to the acceptance of the product in the market.

Exploring Project Creativity: A Case Study Approach

Due to the uniqueness of each creative project, a case study approach is the best alternative of investigation. In lab studies, items are created in isolation and the research design is not structured sufficiently complexly to achieve the richness of creativity. Thus, real life remains the best lab to study creativity (Schrage 1995). I follow Howard Gruber (1988; 1999) and his evolving systems approach. This approach draws attention to the way a creative person is organized as a system. Uniqueness and development are the central goals of investigation. The only difference is that he focuses on the individual, and the focus of this paper is on collaboration.

What are the main criteria for a case decision? First, the solution has to be accepted as a creative product in the relevant domain; second, the project has to be of great value for all participants; third and very importantly, there must be sufficient case material. The last point is the Achilles' heel of studying creativity (Clydesdale 2006). Only in a few public cases, the projects are well documented as far as creativity is concerned, and this is the reason why insights are best gained by analyzing famous collaborations.

The choice of cases is motivated by differently structured collaborative situations, various domains and cultural backgrounds. Before starting, it has to be said that generalizing copy-cat predictions do not approach the complexity and uniqueness of project creativity, but tendencies, learnings, and inspirations can be obtained. The creative projects are The Beatles and their revolutionary album project Sgt. Pepper's Lonely Hearts Club Band, Picasso and Braque with their pioneering of Cubism, and the Prada flagship store in Tokyo designed by world-famous architects Herzog & de Meuron.

Sgt. Pepper: The Sound of a Generation

On June 2nd 1967, The Beatles released Sergeant Pepper's Lonely Hearts Club Band, one of the most famous albums in music history and a time capsule of what the world was like during the Summer of Love (Belmo, 1996: 4). Its outstanding status crystallizes not only in the music, but also in the making of a gesamtkunstwerk of concept, songs and record sleeve design. Sgt. Pepper characterizes The Beatles at their best. None of the Fab Four subsequently surpassed the musical and artistic standard of that time.

Figure 2: CD Cover of Sgt. Pepper
(Grasskamp 2004: 98)

> Like its creators, *Pepper* was greater as a whole than as the sum of its parts. Individually, the tracks could be grappled with. In some cases they were quite straightforward. Together, though, they added up to something rich and strange (Martin 1994: 4).

The Beatles started recording at the Abbey Road Studios in London on November 24th 1966. The project took over four months to complete and ended on April 2nd 1967. At that time, this was considered an amazingly long recording period and expensive for the studio. By way of comparison, the album "Please Please Me" was recorded in one day and even "Revolver" took less than three months (Lewisohn 1990). For Sgt. Pepper, however, The Beatles spent more time because they wanted to create an album never seen and heard before:

> Why should we ever want to go back? That would be soft. It would be like sticking to gray suits all your life. I suppose everybody would like to do this, to try something different every time they do any work. We do, because it's just a hobby, that's all. We put our feet up and enjoy it all the time (McCartney cited in Davies 1968: 283).

The Abbey Road Studios were a perfect place for project creativity. As far as possible, The Beatles' requests were fulfilled; for example, they loved working at night. The studio became a playground for their production:

> One of the great things about Abbey Road was that it almost became our own house, especially by the time Sgt. Pepper was going on (McCartney cited in Lewisohn 1990: 8).

The making of Sgt. Pepper was characterized first of all by open communication. Although Lennon and McCartney were the leaders, especially in composition, Harrison and Starr played unrestricted parts during the project. The Fab Four were able to work with criticism and conflict in a creativity-enhancing way because they focused on the creative process. This was not possible in later projects, as interpersonal conflicts grew (Moore 1997: 71).

In most cases, Lennon and McCartney composed the raw material for the songs on their own, before The Beatles refined them in face-to-face collaboration. It is noteworthy for Sgt. Pepper that composition and recording were in interdependency, and together The Beatles brought the songs to perfection. Associative accident acted an important part during the project, which Martin illustrates in his description of the making of "Getting Better":

Paul had been running through the song on the old upright piano in No. 2 studio so we could all learn it. He had got to the part where it starts again, and was singing, 'I've got to admit it's getting better, A little better all the time', when John strode through the doors at the far end of the studio. Instantly, and having never heard a note of the song before in his life, he started singing the perfect musical and lyrical counter: 'It can't get much worse.' And his line gave the song just that little edge it needed (Martin 1994: 112).

It was during the making of Sgt. Pepper that the different personalities fitted in an ideal way: Lennon acted as bandleader and intellectual, McCartney as perfectionist and instigator, Harrison as sound expert and Starr as a balancing participant with regard to music, but also between the Fab Four. Lennon and McCartney, however, had a special relationship, as they were the composers for the most part, either on their own or in collaboration. They became each other's main rivals, and a creative power emerged, unleashed by the desire to top each other's innovations. The outcome was a productive constellation, which was a counterbalance neutralizing each other's weaknesses and a kind of a friendly competition:

John Lennon and Paul McCartney in particular were extremely good friends; they loved one another, really. They shared a spirit of adventure, and a modest little childhood ambition: they were going to go out and conquer the world. You could, though, almost touch the rivalry between them, it was so intense and so real, despite this overriding warmth. No sooner would John come up with an outstanding song […], than Paul answered him straight back with a winner in the same vein (Martin 1994: 70).

Cubism: A Paradigmatic Approach to Painting

Figure 3: Picasso: Accordionist
(Rubin 1989: 190)

Figure 4: Braque: Man with a guitar
(Rubin 1989: 191)

Pablo Picasso und Georges Braque first met in 1907. In the following years, their contact led to an intensive and creative friendship culminating in an epochal art movement in the 20th Century called Cubism. This was a new approach to painting that focused on the correlation of objects. The word "Cubism" was created by the art critic Louis Vauxcelles who described Braque's paintings, which were exhibited in November 1908, pejoratively as cubes (Richardson 1996: 101). Thereupon, the term was established in the public sphere. The creative collaboration between Picasso and Braque started in winter 1908. It ended with the French mobilization at the start of World War I because Braque went to war. This artistic project of two great artists at the beginning of the 20th Century was remarkable, as style and creativity were attributed to the individual genius:

> The fact that Cubism unfolded essentially through a dialogue between two artists extending over six years makes it a phenomenon unprecedented, to my knowledge, in the history of art (Rubin 1989: 15).

They were not only a working team in that period, but they also formed a competing friendship, which Françoise Gilot describes in this way:

> With Braque, it was always like two brothers, [...] each striving to demonstrate his independence and autonomy and – in Pablo's case, at least – superiority. The rivalry was all the stronger because underneath it they were linked by a real bond of affection and their consciousness of having worked almost as one during the Cubist period before going their separate ways (Gilot and Lake 1965: 138).

Their friendship was based on a creative balance between homogeneity and heterogeneity regarding painting. Both artists were influenced by Cézanne, which led to a common attitude and the artistic expression necessary for the development of Cubism. Besides that, Picasso and Braque had different talents and working methods. Picasso's painting was characterized by spontaneousness and a figurative preference, whereas Braque concentrated intensively on abstraction and composing aspects. In the long run, they managed to harmonize painting through their artistic dialogue. But how could project creativity unfold in this case? During their collaboration, Picasso and Braque were able to become attuned to one another in such a way that they reached a symbiotic level. This was the main precondition for the unfolding of their project creativity. In this context Picasso commented:

> At that time our work was a kind of laboratory research from which every pretension or individual vanity was excluded (Picasso cited in Gilot and Lake 1965: 69-70).

And Braque expressed himself in the following way:

> Pablo Picasso and I were engaged in what we felt was a search for the anonymous personality. We were inclined to efface our own personalities in order to find originality (Braque cited in McCully 1981: 64).

Their symbiosis was sometimes so distinctive that the creative process was more important than the paintings themselves, and it was impossible to distinguish their works. They did not sign their outcomes to prioritize the idea of Cubism in comparison with the artist's identity:

> You know, when Picasso and I were close, there was a moment when we had trouble recognizing our own canvases. [...] I reckoned the personality of the painter ought not to intervene and therefore the pictures ought to be anonymous. It was I who decided we should not sign our canvases and Picasso followed suit for a while (Braque cited in Cox 2000: 251).

And Picasso commented:

> Almost every evening, either I went to Braque's studio or Braque came to mine. Each of us had to see what the other had done during the day. We criticized each other's work. A canvas wasn't finished unless both of us felt it was (Picasso cited in Gilot and Lake 1965: 69).

Both artists spent the summer of 1911 in Céret, a small village in the Pyrenees. Their collaboration reached its peak when they harmonized their different artistic abilities to a complementary equilibrium. This can be seen in paintings that have an extraordinary similarity. According to Rubin (1989), the paintings "Accordionist" and "Man with a Guitar" show uniqueness in their similarity. Picasso and Braque swapped roles: Picasso painted a "Braque" – the strongly abstracted "Accordionist"– and Braque answered with a "Picasso" – the gloomy and untypically sculptural "Man with a Guitar".

Prada Aoyama Epicenter: A Visionary Shopping Experience

 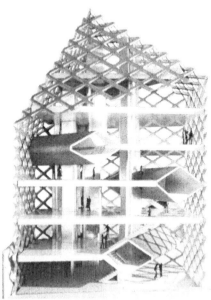

Figure 5: Prada Flagship Store in Aoya-   Figure 6: Working Model in April 2000
ma (Herzog and de Meuron 2003: 345)   (Herzog and de Meuron 2003: 183)

Aoyama is one of the most expensive shopping areas in the world with
"Omotesando-dori", the main street with luxurious brands such as Issey Miyake,
Martin Margiela, or Comme des Garçons. Surrounded by inconspicuous buildings of stones and ceramics, a complex polyhedral form towers over Aoyama:
the Prada flagship store. Opened in spring 2003, it is the first building by Herzog
& de Meuron in which structure, space, and façade form a single unit. Three
vertical cores, three horizontal tubes, floor slabs, and grilles define not only the
space, but also the structure and the façade (Herzog and de Meuron 2003: 125).
Above all, the clear glass elements glitter and draw attention to the passersby:

> The façade becomes almost a sort of interactive screen. Really low-tech.
> When the glass bends towards you, you are being observed. You are being
> pushed back. But when it curves away from you, it invites you in. It actually
> draws you in physically. The glass is really between the world of Prada, Pra-
> da goods, and the observer. And it's between the visitor and the city. And the
> world. It involves every player (Herzog and de Meuron 2003: 105).

The specific feature in the partnership of Jacques Herzog and Pierre de Meuron is its duration, as they have known each other since their childhood. They went to the same school and university and started their professional career collaboratively. Their lives have proceeded in a kind of deliberate twinship, which has a direct effect on their creative work:

> Because we know each other since we are children, it's like having another brain, like a computer where you have more power because the communication goes faster, so that's the ideal thing. Sometimes you do not even know where an idea comes from, and very interesting things come from a discussion and you don't know exactly who brought that in (Herzog cited in Sabbagh 2000: 39).

Although their friendly collaboration is close and intensive, Herzog and de Meuron are open-minded to (junior) partners and artists such as Adrian Schiess or Thomas Ruff realizing projects. They believe in the power of collaboration and Herzog and de Meuron's success mainly stems from the renunciation of individuality (Moneo 2004: 364). Both architects are like "hubs" with regard to communication and the unfolding of creativity (Sonnenburg 2007: 160). Herzog describes their role in this way:

> Each of the partners has responsibility for certain projects whose progress they follow on a daily basis and for which they organise the work to be done by the teams. Our role, Pierre and myself, is to inspire and assist all the projects. The pace is not dissimilar to that of a university or a school: we see each team one a week or every fortnight. [...] It is important to work with partners whose options and cultures are different. That is a way of working that guarantees there will be differences within the office itself, more than if we worked in a more hierarchical way, with invisible teams who put up no resistance (Herzog in an interview with Chevrier 2006: 26).

Herzog and de Meuron were contacted by Prada in the late summer of 1998. A few months later, they met for initial talks about their plans and projects. In comparison with the making of Sgt. Pepper and the pioneering of Cubism, the Prada project was largely different and more complex as more parties were involved, which is a typical situation for architects. Each project has a certain potential, "which depends on the client, the budget, the landscape, the program, and the possibilities of changing it" (Herzog in an interview with Chevrier 2006: 27).

Although a construction project is not manageable without algorithms, Herzog and de Meuron's working style is characterized by a heuristic approach and sensitivity for the contextual conditions of the site. There are only a few rules, but each project determines its own creative rhythm (for the conceptual Prada process, see Herzog and de Meuron 2003: 57-119). Indeed, in the case of Prada, the process did not take a linear course and did not culminate in one big idea. The innovative development was based on a combination of many small sparks and even "wrong paths" were fruitful during the creative process; for example, the brilliant idea of the augmented reality window became the virtual window (for this development, see Herzog and de Meuron 2003: 300-313).

Insights: Dynamics for Real Life

The main objective of this part is to describe important patterns to enhance and manage project creativity in real settings. It is beyond argument that results from only three cases are empirically limited and they have an illustrative more than a conclusive character. However, tendencies and analogies can be observed and are helpful for the future. Four essential dimensions for project creativity, which are mutually dependent for practical settings, are under consideration: *open communication, democratic leadership, productive conflict* and *friendly competition.*

First of all, project success is characterized by a creative working style that is distinguished by open communication (Bennis and Biederman 1997; Kylén and Shani 2002; Sawyer 2007; Sonnenburg 2004). This means that contributions can not be excluded beforehand by bureaucratic rules or supervision. In open communication, each collaborator has the same chance to contribute to the project and the same right that his contributions are taken seriously. This is very important because to solve complex problems a project needs the free flow of a variety of knowledge and perspectives (for the importance of diversity, see Gassmann 2001; Milliken, Bartel and Kurtzberg 2003).

Picasso and Braque created such a communication situation during their stay in Céret, and The Beatles reached their peak performance during the recording of Sgt. Pepper in the Abbey Road Studios. This working style prevents typical creativity inhibitors such as passivity (Davies 1996) or evaluation apprehension (Paulus et al. 2001). In contrast, open communication supports mutual trust (Chadwick and de Courtivron 1996; Moran and John-Steiner 2003) or risk-taking and experimentation (Kylén and Shani 2002), which increase the quantity and quality of contributions.

In all three cases, open communication was possible because strong personalities such as Lennon, McCartney, Picasso, Braque, Herzog, or de Meuron kept in the background to bring the project collaboratively to success. The formula for success is a creativity-enhancing kind of leadership. It can be observed that there is not a leader who dominates the creative process. The project is the work of equals and has a self-organizing and improvisational momentum, although one or two persons are, I would say, "focal figures" in each case. Lennon and McCartney, for example, were the collaborative songwriters, but input by Starr and Harrison was always welcome. In this case and regarding Picasso and Braque, one can talk of distributed leadership (Sawyer 2007: 13).

Generally speaking, a democratic leadership is desirable, and two leadership styles might be relevant for project creativity: first, the "primus inter pares" concept, which means that leaders regard themselves as coordinators, as coaches, and consider themselves as equals. Such leaders should establish a creative atmosphere or space in which project creativity is more likely to flourish. The second leadership style is voluntary expert leadership, which means that during the project the leadership changes in accordance with the project conditions and the communication process. This split leadership prevents the dominance of a single human being and ensures a peer structure.

It is not avoidable that during the communication process conflicts emerge. Even more, a creative project needs productive conflict which fosters different perspectives. In general, task conflict can have a positive influence on project creativity, and relationship conflict is detrimental to group performance (Jehn 1997). After Sgt. Pepper, for example, The Beatles never reached this level of project creativity again. One reason for this was that relationship conflicts increased dramatically. Concerning Braque and Picasso, they reached their peak of creativity in 1911 and afterwards they often worked on their own because the relationship conflicts increased between 1911 and 1914.

Another working style feature with a positive effect on project creativity is friendly competition that pushes the participants to high performance, for example, Lennon and McCartney who were a songwriter team but also solo writers. A song composed by one of them encouraged the other to compose a better one. The same behaviour can be observed in Picasso's and Braque's paintings. Even Herzog and de Meuron, who have a collaborative corporate culture, see competition as a necessary component for creativity:

> Being in a group of seven produces more interesting competition for me and Pierre. It is egotistic, but simultaneously altruistic (Herzog in an interview with Chevrier 2006: 27).

More or less, you can notice a productive and balanced mixture between homogeneity and heterogeneity, yet the project-relevant dimensions in each case may be different. Common motives are, for example, cultural or social background (see Liverpool for the Beatles), intellectual roots (Cézanne for Picasso and Braque), or corporate culture (in the case of Herzog and de Meuron). Heterogeneity is often expressed by the different skills of the participants. The paradox "harmony in opposition" serves as a guideline for the project composition: It should have a variety of talents and perspectives, yet it should be sufficiently similar so that the participants can understand each other and coordinate with one another.

Concluding Remarks

Creative projects cannot act in a sociocultural vacuum. It is relevant for creativity that the context allows creative projects to emerge. Generally speaking, an open-minded and input-orientated culture and structure are helpful to guarantee autonomy and support. The objective for an organization could be as follows: to create spaces, playgrounds, or hot houses (Kunstler 2004) for open communication and an open mind as well as to increase the likelihood of unplanned conversations.

> At Herzog & de Meuron work is punctuated by frequent intervals of compulsory pleasure, relaxation and amusement. At ten o'clock and four o'clock every day, the whole company assembles in the cafeteria for half an hour or so of unorganized conversation and refreshment (Sabbagh 2000: 37).

Project creativity is an essential business resource. The question is how to make creativity an integral part of daily work and what kind of creativity training should be implemented in the corporate culture. Nowadays and in future, a collaborative culture to enhance creativity is necessary for managing business. Project creativity will replace traditional business models such as top-down management or hierarchies. Allowing the space for self-organizing creative projects to occur seems to be difficult for many organizations because the outcome cannot be controlled by the management. In many cases, project creativity emerges from the bottom up. Thus, organizations have to rethink their daily business, especially in times when innovation is the master key to success. There is not any other choice but to promote project creativity with all the risk of a potential failure:

> One thing that prevents us from thus giving primary emphasis to the perception of what is new and different is that we are afraid to make mistakes. [...] All learning involves trying something and seeing what happens. If one will

not try anything until he is assured that he will not make a mistake in whatever he does, he will never be able to learn anything new at all. And this is the state in which most people are (Bohm 1998: 4).

References

Amabile, T.M. (1996): Creativity in Context. Boulder: Westview.

Belmo (1996): The Making of The Beatles' Sgt. Pepper's Lonely Hearts Club Band. Burlington: Collector's Guide.

Bennis, W.G./Biederman, P.W. (1997): Organizing Genius: The Secrets of Creative Collaboration. Cambridge: Perseus.

Bohm, D. (1998): On Creativity, Edited by Lee Nichol. London: Routledge.

Buijs J./Smulders F./van der Meer H. (2009): Towards a More Realistic Creative Problem Solving Approach, In: Creativity and Innovation Management 18 (4), pp. 286-298.

Chadwick, W./de Courtivron, I. (1996): Significant Others: Creativity and Intimate Partnership. London: Thames & Hudson.

Chevrier, J.-F. (2006): Ornament, Structure, Space: A Conversation with Jacques Herzog. In: El Croquis 129/130, pp. 22-40.

Clydesdale, G. (2006): Creativity and Competition: The Beatles. In: Creativity Research Journal 18 (2), pp. 129-139.

Cox, N. (2000): Cubism. London: Phaidon.

Csikszentmihalyi, M. (1990): The Domain of Creativity. In: Runco M.A./Albert R.S. (eds.) (1990): Theories of Creativity. Newbury Park: Sage, pp. 190-212.

Csikszentmihalyi, M. (1996): Creativity: Flow and the Psychology of Discovery and Invention. New York: Harper Collins.

Davies, H. (1968): The Beatles: The Authorized Biography. New York: McGraw-Hill.

Davies, M.F. (1996): Social Interaction. In: Hare, A.P./Blumberg, H.H./Davies, M.F./Kent, M.V. (eds.) (1996): Small Groups: An Introduction. Westport: Praeger, pp. 115-134.

Florida, R. (2002): The Rise of the Creative Class: And How It's Transforming Work, Leisure, Community and Everyday Life. New York, Basic Books.

Gassmann, O. (2001): Multicultural Teams: Increasing Creativity and Innovation by Diversity. In: Creativity and Innovation Management 10 (2), pp. 88-95.

Gilot, F./Lake, C. (1965): Life with Picasso. London: Thomas Nelson and Sons.

Grasskamp, W. (2004): Das Cover von Sgt. Pepper: Eine Momentaufnahme der Popkultur. Berlin: Wagenbach.

Gruber, H.E. (1988): The Evolving Systems Approach to Creative Work. In: Creativity Research Journal 1 (1), pp. 27-51.

Gruber, H.E./Wallace, D.B. (1999): The Case Study Method and Evolving Systems Approach for Understanding Unique Creative People at Work. In: Sternberg, R.J. (ed.) (1999): Handbook of Creativity. Cambridge: Cambridge University Press, pp. 93-115.

Harrington, D.M. (1990): The Ecology of Human Creativity: A Psychological Perspective. In: Runco, M.A./Albert, R.S. (eds.) (1990): Theories of Creativity. Newbury Park: Sage, pp. 143-169.

Henry, J. (2004): Creative Collaboration in Organizational Settings. In: Miell, D./Littleton, K. (eds.) (2004): Collaborative Creativity: Contemporary Perspectives. London: Free Association Books, pp. 158-174.

Herzog/de Meuron (2003): Prada Aoyama Tokyo. Milan: Progetto Prada Arte.

Jehn, K.A. (1997): A Qualitative Analysis of Conflict Types and Dimensions in Organizational Groups. In: Administrative Science Quarterly 42 (3), pp. 530-557.

John-Steiner, V. (2000): Creative Collaboration. New York: Oxford University Press.

Kelley, T. (2001): The Art of Innovation: Lessons in Creativity from IDEO, America's Leading Design Firm. New York: Doubleday.

Kunstler, B. (2004): The Hothouse Effect: Intensify Creativity in Your Organization Using Secrets from History's Most Innovative Communities. New York: Amacom.

Kurtzberg, T.R./Amabile, T.M. (2000/01): From Guilford to Creative Synergy: Opening the Black Box of Team - Level Creativity. Creativity Research Journal 13 (3/4), pp. 285-294.

Kylén, S.F./Shani, A.B. (Rami) (2002): Triggering Creativity in Teams: An Exploratory Investigation. In: Creativity and Innovation Management 11 (1), pp. 17-30.

Leadbeater, C. (2008): We-Think: Mass Innovation, not Mass Production. London: Profile Books.

Leonard, D./Swap, W. (1999): When Sparks Fly: Igniting Creativity in Groups. Boston: Harvard Business School Press.

Lewisohn, M. (1990): The Beatles Recording Sessions: The Official Abbey Road Studio Session Notes 1962-1970. New York: Harmony.

Magyari-Beck, I. (1990): An Introduction to the Framework of Creatology. In: Journal of Creative Behavior 24 (3), pp. 151-160.

Martin, G. (1994): Summer of Love: The Making of Sgt. Pepper. London: Macmillan.

Mayer, R.E. (1999): Fifty Years of Creativity Research. In Sternberg, R.J. (ed.) (1999): Handbook of Creativity. Cambridge: Cambridge University Press, pp. 449-460.

McCully, M. (1981): A Picasso Anthology: Documents, Criticism, Reminiscences. London: Thames & Hudson.

Milliken, F.J./Bartel, C.A./Kurtzberg, T.R. (2003): Diversity and Creativity in Work Groups: A Dynamic Perspective on the Affective and Cognitive Processes that Link Diversity and Performance. In: Paulus, P.B./Nijstad, B.A. (eds.) (2003): Group Creativity: Innovation through Collaboration. New York: Oxford University Press, pp. 32-62.

Moneo, R. (2004): Theoretical Anxiety and Design Strategies: In the Work of Eight Contemporary Architects. Cambridge: MIT Press.

Montuori, A./Purser, R.E. (1999): Social Creativity: Introduction. In: Montuori, A./Purser, R.E. (eds.) (1999): Social Creativity: Volume 1. Cresskill: Hampton Press, pp. 1-45.

Moore, A.F. (1997): The Beatles: Sgt. Pepper's Lonely Hearts Club Band. Cambridge: Cambridge University Press.

Moran, S./John-Steiner, V. (2003): Creativity in the Making: Vygotsky's Contemporary Contribution to the Dialectic of Development and Creativity. In Sawyer, R.K./John-Steiner, V./Moran, S./Sternberg, R.J./Feldman, D.H./Nakamura, J./Csikszentmihalyi, M. (eds.) (2003): Creativity and Development. New York: Oxford University Press, pp. 61-90.

Murakami, T./Nishiwaki, T. (1991): Strategy for Creation. Cambridge: Woodhead.

Nemiro, J.E. (2004): Creativity in Virtual Teams: Key Components for Success. San Francisco: Pfeiffer.

Nijstad, B.A./Paulus, P.B. (2003): Group Creativity: Common Themes and Future Directions. In Paulus, P.B./Nijstad, B.A. (eds.) (2003): Group Creativity: Innovation through Collaboration. New York: Oxford University Press, pp. 326-339.

Osborn, A.F. (1963): Applied Imagination: Principles and Procedures of Creative Problem-Solving. New York: Scribner's.

Paulus, P.B./Larey, T.S./Dzindolet, M.T. (2001): Creativity in Groups and Teams. In Turner, M.E. (ed.) (2001): Groups at Work: Theory and Research. Mahwah: Lawrence Erlbaum Associates, pp. 319-338.

Puccio, G.J. (1999): Teams. In Runco, M.A./Pritzker, S.R. (eds.) (1999): Encyclopedia of Creativity: Volume 2 I-Z, Indexes. San Diego: Academic Press, pp. 639-649.

Richardson, J. (1996): A Life of Picasso: Volume II 1907-1917. New York: Random House.

Rickards, T./Moger, S. (1999): Handbook for Creative Team Leaders. Aldershot: Gower.

Rubenson, D.L./Runco, M.A. (1995): The Psychoeconomic View of Creative Work in Groups and Organizations. In: Creativity and Innovation Management 4 (4), pp. 232-241.

Rubin, W. (1989): Picasso and Braque: Pioneering Cubism. New York: The Museum of Modern Art.

Sabbagh, K. (2000): Power into Art. London: Penguin Press.

Sawyer, R.K. (2007): Group Genius: The Creative Power of Collaboration. New York: Basic Books.

Sawyer, R.K. (2003): Group Creativity: Music, Theater, Collaboration. Mahwah: Lawrence Erlbaum Associates.

Schrage, M. (1995): No More Teams!: Mastering the Dynamics of Creative Collaboration. New York: Doubleday.

Sonnenburg, S. (2007): Creative Complexes: A Theoretical Framework for Collaborative Creativity. In: Jöstingmeier, B./Boeddrich, H.-J. (eds.) (2007): Cross-Cultural Innovation: New Thoughts, Empirical Research, Practical Reports. München: Oldenbourg Wissenschaftsverlag, pp. 149-165.

Sonnenburg, S. (2004): Creativity in Communication: A Theoretical Framework for Collaborative Product Creation. In: Creativity and Innovation Management 13 (4), pp. 254-262.

Stein, M.I. (1975): Stimulating Creativity Volume 2: Group Procedures. New York: Academic Press.

Sternberg, R.J./Kaufman, J.C./Pretz, J.E. (2002): The Creativity Conundrum: A Propulsion Model of Kinds of Creative Contribution. New York: Psychology Press.

Sternberg, R.J./Lubart, T.I. (1991): An Investment Theory of Creativity and Its Development. Human Development 34 (1), pp. 1-31.

Torrance, E.P. (1972): Group Dynamics and Creative Functioning. In Taylor, C.W. (ed.) (1972): Climate for Creativity: Report of the Seventh National Research Conference on Creativity. New York: Pergamon, pp. 75-96.

Van Gundy A.B. (1984): Managing Group Creativity: A Modular Approach to Problem Solving. New York: Amacom.

West M.A. (1997): Developing Creativity in Organizations. Leicester: BPS Books.

Woodman, R.W./Sawyer, J.E./Griffin, R.W. (1993): Toward a Theory of Organizational Creativity. In: Academy of Management Review 18 (2), pp. 293-321.

From Storytelling to Story Creation by the Use of Systemic Meetings – The Swedish Case

Umair Khalid Khan and Hans Sarv

Introduction

The shift from the information society to the knowledge society has identified knowledge as a primary resource for individual and economic growth (Drucker 1992). Intangibles assets replace tangible assets as a key resource and the notion of skilled labour is replaced by the notion of knowledge workers (Drucker 1993) as steps to gain strategic advantage in the knowledge society. The knowledge based view of the firm is becoming more imperative for business survival.

Intellectual capital only resides in the people's minds, the key to which is stories (Denning 2004). The tacit nature of large parts of knowledge makes retrieval, storage and spread difficult, but stories provide the medium to work also this side of knowledge. The SECI model of knowledge creation (Nonaka et al. 2001) defines socialization (S) as the trigger for knowledge generation and knowledge creation. Nonaka refers to socialization as taking place in a Ba, a place where people meet to discuss things. It could be a physical Ba in a form of formal or informal meetings or a virtual Ba, in a form of online communities of practice.

A new form of leadership arises, which is comprised not to lead but to facilitate the people in that particular community and engage their emotions (McKee 2003). The key to this leadership is a focus not only on knowledge creation but also on story creation. When people meet, they assemble the bits and pieces of their past experiences, achievements and mistakes in their life stories, and they do it as a form to share their knowledge. A way to surface and transfer the tacit knowledge embedded in the lives of the people is telling, interpreting and recognizing stories, as a way to create better stories in life. The tacit-tacit dimension of the knowledge which could not be unfolded and coded by the ICT tools can be expressed by daily life stories.

This paper connects to Nonaka's (Nonaka and Takeuchi 1995) theory on *knowledge creation* and suggests *story creation* as a mindset by which communities of innovation can get mobilized on shared missions or aspirations. It is also based on well over ten years of experiences from using *systemic meetings* as tools for story creation in innovation communities of different sorts.

The systemic meetings build on the steps of *story recognition* in daily practices, and *storytelling* followed by *story interpretation* in literal (face to face) as well as virtual, i.e. social media and web based, meetings. It is accompanied by theory based metaphoric language which helps develop story creating strategies and practices in innovation communities.

Our basic reasoning

Most of us have good pictures of the *products* of much reputed companies, such as for example Ford, IKEA and McDonalds. And we probably also have some pictures of the companies' lines of production, or *processes*. When it comes to Ford we may have seen the Chaplin picture Modern Times, or read about the Scientific Management approach. When it comes to IKEA we may associate to high volume production in low wage countries, or their flat packages, or their 6-sided assemble-it-yourself wrench. And when it comes to McDonald we may recall pictures of youngsters rushing at a counter and back stage in a minute detail production line.

This paper takes a third focus, the focus of *stories*, or evolving patterns and values of events connected to product usage, in consumer lives. Processes create products and products create stories. And, as stated by (Spinosa et al. 1997: 3):

> The main contributions of Henry Ford and his motor company, Ingvar Kamprad and his IKEA, and Ray Kroc and his McDonalds are not inexpensive cars, furniture and meals but rather that all three of them, through their companies, changed our everyday *habits as regards travelling, living and eating. They for certain constructed* new realities!

In industry, a product focus has been natural all from its origin in crafting. It has been enhanced through the growth of distant trade. If you are going to sell something to strangers you have to specify what you are selling. A process focus is more recent in industry. But process thinking of different makes has been used extensively during the last few years to speed things up and make products more cost-effective.

In public services process focus and process thinking has also gained wide spread acceptance, for the same reasons as in industry, but also for the sake of public credibility. Product thinking is not that widely used though, probably because there is little direct selling involved in public services, other than for example in the selling of process solution to other public services.

The common denominator between the focus of product and process is that both are built on specifications, planning and control. They have both been fostered by the part of systems thinking that presumes steer ability.

In the ongoing move from a product/process to a story society; and we will come back to the base for seeing such a move, another part of systems thinking is entering the scene, that which is sometimes referred to as systemic thinking. In systemic thinking the emergent patterns of real life events, as perceived by people forming those events, is the governing mind set for people developing products and processes. Products and processes are no longer seen only as matters for specifications, planning and control, but also in the lights of real life events, and the stories that those events tell people, and create in people's minds.

So far we have seen the story society primarily as a story *telling* society. The story society is still in the hands of the story tellers. We see the story tellers in media, in entertainment, in advertising – and in management. But there is also a growing pattern of story *recognition* as an equally important way to improve life. Just like authors and screen writers have always been basing their story telling on story recognition in real life, a recognition of what is really happening among people, also companies in industry and organizations in public services start base their product and process developments on story recognition, on a recognition of what is really happing among people when using products or adhering to process specifications.

The link between storytelling and story recognition is story *creation*. Authors and screen writers want to create stories in the minds of people. Stories-told which mean something to the audience, that they can recognize out of their own life experiences, will create stories in the minds of the audience. The stories created in the minds of authors and screen writers, later to be read or watched as told to the audience, are not the same stories that are created in the minds of the audience. Mind stories that are created in people are individual.

There is also another link between storytelling and story recognition, the link of story *interpretation*. This link is used in for example *dialogue seminars* (Göranzon 2009). Essayistic texts of authors are used for a dialogue based interpretation, based on the dialogue participants' recognition of their own working life experiences.

The interpretative link is also used in *systemic meetings*. The interpretative dialogue in systemic meetings is based not on stories told by authors, but on stories recognized by the meeting participants in their own working lives. The authors may enter the picture in providing a language, or metaphors, or story excerpts that can help the dialogue participants interpret their experiences. But in the systemic meeting the initiating story is a story that is told by one of the participants, a story that has been recognized by the story teller in his or her personal working life. The point is that personal (working of private) life experiences are worth recognizing, by managers as well as product and process developers. They signal improvement opportunities both in the process organizing of businesses or services and in the products offerings to customers.

Story interpretation through dialogue is the above surface version of story creation. They both link story recognition to storytelling but in overt and covert ways, respectively. They both work the interface between order and complexity, an interface that is in focus not just in complexity theory, but also in the philosophies of phenomenology and pragmatism, as well as by linguists, ethnologists and others.

The concept of story creation

The concept of story creation is strongly related to the concept of knowledge management. Japanese professor Ikujiro Nonaka (Nonaka 2007) in referring to successful Japanese companies such as Honda, Canon, Matsushita, NEC, Sharp, and Kao, sees a pattern of *knowledge creation*:

> These companies have become famous for their ability to respond quickly to customers, create new markets, rapidly develop new products, and dominate emergent technologies. The secret of their success is their unique approach to managing the creation of new knowledge.

The focus of knowledge management has changed over time (Maria 2008). The first phase of knowledge management focused on the *outcomes* of knowledge creation, on knowledge as an asset subject to gathering, storing in databases, and making available through information systems. In the second phase, knowledge management focused on the knowledge creating *processes* (Nonaka 2007; Nonaka and Konno 1998; Nonaka et al. 2001; Von Krogh and Grand 2000; Von Krogh 1998), or the ways knowledge was created in companies. In the late 1990s, the focus turned to the *sources and enabling conditions* of knowledge creation (Nonaka and Konno 1998). (Nonaka et al. 2000) connected the knowledge creation process (as modelled by the SECI model) to the place where knowledge was created, to the concept of *ba* as a space for knowledge creation.

In the more recent phases of knowledge management the focus has shifted from knowledge creation within a firm to inter-firm collaborations, towards networks and communities of practice (Lave and Wenger 1991; Wenger et al. 2002; Wenger and Snyder 2000), and also towards the micro processes of knowledge creation in human interactions (e.g. Griffin 2002; Stacey 2004,

2005a, b; Shaw and Stacey 2006). We also see a stronger focus on the relationships between the concept of knowledge management and the concepts of organizational learning and communities of practice (Peltonen and Lämsä 2004).

Narratives play a vital role in communities of practice and in organizational learning. Tsoukas and Chia (2002) argue that narrative knowledge is just as important as prepositional knowledge, if not more so, when it comes to the life in organizations. Focusing attention on narrative and storytelling immediately brings the relational aspect of knowledge to the fore because narratives and stories are socially constructed between people rather than being simply located in individual minds.

Several other authors also stress the importance of narratives and storytelling (Boje 1991; Boje 1995), as well as conversation in organizations (Brown and Duguid 1991; Brown 2005; Lave and Wenger 1991). With this view knowledge is created in the stories a community of practitioners tell each other. Looked at in this way, knowledge is embedded in the ordinary everyday conversation between people. It is primarily localized and contextual, distributed through an organization rather than centralized in data banks. It is embedded in the stories people tell each other about their experience, stories that interactively create their experience.

The step to include also the consumer in this picture of storytelling and sharing of experiences is not farfetched. The stories consumers tell each others on product usage experiences have a vital role in determining the success of the products that communities of practice, linked in business networks, bring out on the market.

Stories that people tell each others in everyday (worker or consumer) lives are not just about knowledge but also about value. The term *story creation* links knowledge creation to value creation through something that we can understand and talk about. Product usage can be seen as a consumption of knowledge producing value to the user of the product.

This view brings us to *systemic theory* and to the theory and practice of *systemic meetings* as a way to interpret the meaning of stories created in the everyday lives of consumers to different levels in the system producing the products. For example: how is supply chain responsiveness to what is happening in consumers' everyday lives created, to the evolving patterns and values of events connected to product usage in consumer lives, as told by consumer stories?

A model of story creation

Story *telling* is frequently used as a means to make complex change intentions understandable and accepted in a community (Denning 2004). It is then used as a top down management tool. Edited stories that communicate a certain idea for organizational change are brought to the people that the management wants to join in on the change. But storytelling, as described in the literature on communities of practice, can also be spontaneous, used for sense making, problem detection and idea generation between practitioners. And it is also used in much the same way in consumer communities.

Spontaneous story telling in communities of practice and communities of consumers reveal much of how processes and products are factually working, at least how this factual working is perceived by the practitioners or consumers. They can therefore be worth listening to among people who design those processes and products, or are in other ways involved in developing and organizing the business. Story telling can also qualify for bottom up attention.

The common denominator between edited and spontaneous stories is that they both are essayistic. They account for real life events, or series of events. In this way they are more holistic than even a complete list of power point arguments. They construct realities rather than reduce them through modelling. They pay respect to what is factually happening in real life. They don't stay within the frame of modelled intentions. They grasp the complexities of real life events.

For companies that want to create value in consumer lives listening to the stories told in consumer communities makes it possible for companies to understand the consumer perceived value of the real life events that are created or co-created by their products. It doesn't have to be stories, as in stories told by one people to another. It can just the same be observing the consumers using the product, or getting interested in it, or buying it, or unpacking it, or assembling it, or getting rid of it. It can be tracing the footprints left from discovering, using and leaving internet services etc.

Oral stories need to be *interpreted* in order for the listener to understand their link to the factual real life events that the listener – if being a company that produces products that are involved in the real life events – can attempt to recreate in some way or other. If observing, or tracing, directly the real life events the stories inherent in them have not yet reached the level of storytelling. The potential stories now need to be *recognized,* i.e. identified and paid tribute to the ways a potential story teller would do. Consumers recognize the stories embedded in real life events before telling them. All product-related events or series of events are not recognized by the consumer as stories that are worth telling. Learning how to see the product-related events through the eyes and minds of the consumer involves also story recognition. The term story telling could also be understood as telling there is a story imbedded in or potentially emanating from the real life events.

The term story creation could also be understood as real life event creation. But the prefix "story", as opposed to the prefix "real life event" sees the story as the linkage between the real life event and the people awareness of it, and the people evaluation of it. Seen this way story creation can be seen as the goal not only of motion picture companies but also of all other types of companies that want get consumer attention and consumer perceived values from their products.

We see the concept of story *creation* as a dynamic link between story *recognition*, story*telling* and story *interpretation*:

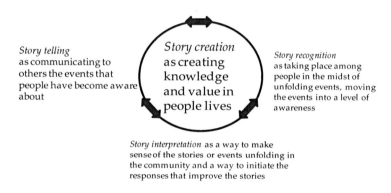

Story telling
as communicating to
others the events that
people have become aware
about

Story creation
as creating
knowledge
and value in
people lives

Story recognition
as taking place among
people in the midst of
unfolding events, moving
the events into a level of
awareness

Story interpretation as a way to make
sense of the stories or events unfolding in
the community and a way to initiate the
responses that improve the stories

We appreciate the value of the services that we produce or consume based on the story surfaced events that they create in our daily lives. Let us now turn to some examples on this and to the role of systemic meetings in the story creating process.

The health care application

As patients in health care we appreciate the value of health care services based on what the story surfaced events that they *create* in our lives, and in our encounters with health care. Likewise as doctors and nurses offering health care services we appreciate the value of what the services do to patients and ourselves based on the stories that surface around them. Patients, doctors and nurses *rec-*

ognize stories more or less consciously. By story recognition they gain the ability to *tell* the stories to others, for their story *interpretation*.

Story interpretation is an important tool for many doctors and nurses in health care, as part of the diagnostic process. It can be both deductive, based on patient storytelling, and inductive, based on patient observations. Both ways, and they can work together interactively, storytelling and story recognition become a base for initiating the service responses that health care can produce. Some doctors and nurses would also use story telling in order to communicate the intentions behind the services and help patients visualize or interpret what they can do to their lives, to help them recognize new events or stories.

This two way circulation of knowledge and value apprehensions is a base for story creation across several levels in for example a health care system. On the individual micro level it is the base of creating better stories in patient lives, better emerging series of events. But story interpretation can also be used for systemic macro development purposes. If health care managers, politicians, researchers etc participate in the story interpretation they can be part of a macro level response. They can develop their own services to the community, they can communicate the intentions of their services by storytelling, they can be part of a macro and micro systemic story creation, helping patients on the one hand and doctors and nurses on the other hand recognize better and better stories in their lives and in their working lives respectively.

Systemic story interpretation is multidisciplinary and multilevel. The same patient or doctor/nurse story can be interpreted many ways, out of many different knowledge bases and from many system level perspectives. Also the knowledge on innovation management and knowledge ecologies can be used to interpret the stories. This can be done in a story interpretative and story creating way, as part of developing the innovation community and the knowledge ecology in the community.

What kinds of multidisciplinary and multilevel responses to the unfolding patient and doctor stories are created in the system? We frequently see such responses when something extraordinary happens in the system, and when this is recognized by media. We probably also can find traces of such responses both on the micro and macro levels, derived from daily interactions between community stakeholders, although those responses would in most cases be off the record and hard to track. They derive from complex reflection, action and learning processes.

On the record developments typically follow a more partitioned track. They would be project or program based. Each discipline or function and each level would typically follow their own track. The project or program tracks would involve other disciplines, functions and levels, but on a partitioned basis.

Partitioned projects or programs can be based on recognition and interpretation of real life stories, but more likely on the development of disciplinary knowledge, functional objectives and level emanating strategies. They would typically be top down and proactive, following a linear logic, rather than top down/bottom up responsive, following the spiral logic of learning.

How do we know this? Our base for the statements is hundreds of *systemic meetings* in many parts of Swedish health care, as well as in other types of organizations and systems.

Let us turn now to the systemic meeting and let us use as an example, as during the presentation at the Innovation in Mind conference, the story of Electrolux as an example.

Systemic meetings as a tool for story creation

Complex organizational phenomena are multidimensional, so people reflecting together see different sub-phenomena, and they learn about others' views by listening to them in the dialogue. In systemic meetings the complex phenomena are accounted for through *story telling* by one of the meeting participants, but not through the type of edited story telling that we would find in most of the story telling literature, but rather through spontaneous storytelling, relating ordinary daily events that the story teller has been part of. The story telling is based on the story tellers' *story recognition*, and it proceeds by story we call the process of naming the complex phenomena found in the recognized story by the other meeting participant's *story interpretation.*

After the (uninterrupted) initial story telling (step 1) the systemic meeting continues with a collegial interpretation of the story, before moving on to participants with "system setting" roles, i.e. participants that would not normally take part in the types of events, or series of events, that the story unfolds. The collegial interpretation is made in a number of steps: as step 2 following upon the uninterrupted story telling questions clarifying what was factually happening in the related series of events, then (step 3) naming the patterns found in the story thus recognized, then (step 4) naming the choices and next (step 5) generating ideas on what could be done to create better series of events in the works of the story teller and her colleagues, to "create better stories" (stories in the sense of factual series of events). Finally (step 6) the story teller is given the opportunity to react and comment on the story interpretations made by here colleagues, and the creational ideas generated from them.

Through these six steps a *secondary story* has then been revealed to the system setters, the story of system actors recognizing, telling, interpreting, and creating stories in the type of work that they do. This secondary story is not told to the system setters, it is experienced by them, and by the system actors. Note that we – again – refer to stories as accounts for real life series of events. This secondary story is unfolding in the room of the systemic meeting. The system setters have not as yet taken part in it. But it is the type of "story" (or series of events) that they *would* normally take part in if it is paralleled to what is taking place in the organization, or the system, on a regular basis. Or *could*; we will now explore this distinction.

This paralleling in this second part of the systemic meeting is in a way a reversed type of paralleling, compared to the paralleling made by the system actors in the initial part of the meeting. They take a real life event into imaginary room interpretation, whereas the system setters in the second part of the meeting are invited to take the imaginary room event into real life interpretation. Do the system setters *want* the system actors to engage in this type of story recognition – story interpretation – story creation in real life, *and* do they want to be part of it? This is the basic question of the systemic meeting.

The interpretations, choices and actions made by the systemic sectors, and the system actors in concert with each other, present a tertiary story, as story that can also be recognized, interpreted and acted upon. In communicating the intent and process of the systemic meeting we sometimes refer to the primary story as taking place in the "stream" (of daily events) in the organizations´ or the systems´ production of value on the market. The secondary story then takes place on the "shore" of the stream, as the system actors go up from the stream turning from a producing mode to a reflecting and correctional acting mode, followed by the system setters joining them on the shore in order to perhaps support and join in on the real life correctional actions. The tertiary story then is seen from the "mountain" overlooking both the stream and the shore. It is created by the concerted action evolving in real life, as incurred by the systemic meetings taking place in the organization (or the system), or stemming from other sources, perhaps based on other types of "systemic" meetings (meetings with knowledge in the systems, encounters with real life series of events in the system etc).

We as authors to this article engage in mountainous type of story recognition, story interpretation, storytelling and story creation. We do it by introducing systemic meetings in organizations and multi organizational settings, taking people to a tertiary story reflection mode based on their own primary, secondary and tertiary story experiences. We also do it in lectures talking about our systemic meetings, and the three levels reflections incurred by them, but also talking about our own systemic thinking based interpretations of the unfolding stories in real life, as told by for example media and research reports.

These ways we have developed a language for systemic reflection. The reflection can be consumption-systemic, production-systemic and innovation-systemic, and it can be so out of the same real life story. Take for example the case of the Swedish white goods producer Electrolux, a case that has been reported in research reports as well as by media and in speeches.

Films of consumers in their homes, showing them using Electrolux appliances under each individuals or family's own specific conditions are providing a story (recognition) base for consumption-systemic reflection, i.e. reflection on the use of the product in the daily life (or "stream") of the individual or the family. But having not only product design staff watch the films, but also manufacturing staff, sales staff, logistics staff and others staffs in the production system the reflections to some extent also become production-systemic. The richness of experiences in the complex daily life stories recognized by the films makes it possible for the various types of staffs to connect the product usage streams to their own streams or processes, like for example how product information is provided to consumers and how the customer service desk is working. From there on the repairs and logistics streams can enter the picture, and then the manufacturing streams etc.

It all depends on what types of problem or opportunity recognition that is provided by the specific film. With a big assortment of films this production-systemic reflection can cover most every part of the production system. The production-systemic reflection then also provides a base for innovation-systemic reflection in that the reflections on factual production stream practices may incur changes in these practices; or changes in the product designs that in the minds and hands of the consumers result in certain daily life practices. The primary stories told by the films have now provided a base not only for extended primary stories but also for secondary stories on changes and innovation processes emanating from the product and production systemic reflections. This way also the tertiary story evolves, based on the type of story recognition and story interpretation and story creation that evolves based on the primary and secondary story evolvements.

Not all product and process changes or innovations at Electrolux are based on story recognition. Many of them stem from technical advances, new solutions offered by vendors, product strategy choices, benchmarking projects, projects applying logistics knowledge etc. But the mountainous position makes it possible to overlook, recognize, name, talk about, interpret and perhaps also alter the ways change and innovation are made in Electrolux. It makes it possible to tell the story of innovation-systemic changes at Electrolux.

The mountainous position may reveal patterns like people assembling far from the shore in groups with narrow tasks resulting eventually in a wide array of partitioned product and process changes each of them trying to make a positive imprint on real life practices. It can reveal a pattern of an agenda based and agenda divided innovation system, each group with their own agenda. It can reveal a pattern of technology push to the plants and the markets. It can reveal a pattern of a reliance of measures of the effects product and process improvements, and of measurement based calculations. It can reveal a pattern of centralized product and process control based on those measures and reports, or perhaps a pattern of product range divided product and process control. Again, the richness of real life events in the Electrolux stream and on the Electrolux shore gives room for many types of pattern recognition and pattern interpretations. It is all in the eyes of the beholders, and the types of glasses or hats they are wearing.

Experiences from the use of systemic meetings

If you wear a hat of systemic thinking, and glasses that are grinded by theories such as complexity theories and learning theories, you may see a slow change of patterns factually taking place on the shore and also the potential of a more determinate intentional pattern change. You may also invite people to reflect on the stories evolving on the shore, helping them recognize and interpret the stories, helping them create new stories, dramatized by such a determinate intentional pattern change. This is what we try to do, and it creates the base of the type of action research that we report in this paper. Again we have developed a language that facilitates this secondary story recognition-interpretation-telling-creation. By inviting people of many sorts to the mountain we have thus created a number of tertiary stories. This paper reports on some of those tertiary stories. It also presents some of the language, and it applies the language to some cases.

Terms like story recognition, story interpretation and story creation are not that much used, at least not in the context presented here. Neither are the terms primary, secondary and tertiary stories. The experience of systemic meetings, or something like it, may be required to fully appreciate the terms. Just like in all other types of developments of terms used for personal reflections through dialogues with others a matching process is required. You have to be able to match the term with a personal experience in order to see the point of using it, and then perhaps start using it yourself. The metaphoric term "the stream and the shore" (in Swedish "forsen och stranden") has gained such popular acceptance and use in many organizations using systemic meetings. Other parts of our language are more sparsely spread, used mainly in mountainous excursions of various sorts, some of them reported here.

The stream and the shore metaphor implies turning from a state of action to a state of reflection. Most people have no difficulty to see their personal need of a "shore" as a retreat from their busy "streams" of daily actions. The turn of state has personal implications to many people. The reflection-action turn back to the stream, using the shore reflections to change personal habits is likewise well nourished by personal experiences, or at least ambitions. Most people see the point of using reflection, and reflection based action pattern corrections, as part of their personal development and as part of improving their lives in general. Most people also can see the logic of doing so also in their working lives, and then not only for personal reasons, but also for the benefit of their organizations and its customers. But many other bits and pieces have to be assembled in their minds to form a new puzzle, a new mind set regarding how innovation and change is taking place in their organizations, and in the networks of their organizations. Then other parts of the language also have to be acquired, matched by personal experiences.

Systemic meetings may provide such experiences. Many organizations use systemic meetings not just for reflections on daily occurrences, but also for corrective action. Systemic meetings are then used as tools for continuous improvements. Some organizations use them primarily for a generation of improvement ideas, followed by a usage of other tools for closing the improvement cycle, for example tools based on the PDCA-logic (Ainalem et al 2008). In both cases systemic meetings form a shore practice, a practice of secondary shore story creation, resulting also in primary stream story creation. Some would also visit the mountain for their own secondary story creation, thus creating also tertiary stories.

Tertiary stories were created in among others the following Swedish cases:

- By a network from the Communal Coordination Alliances on Rehabilitation, Illness, Unemployment and Social welfare, reflecting through systemic meetings during 2010 on the production and innovation practices in the four areas and their overlaps;
- By leaders of stakeholders in a communal area outside the city of Borås reflecting during 2008-2010 on the innovation practices in the area, as demonstrated by systemic meetings, and on the possibilities to strengthen these practices through systemic meetings and other ways of triple helix cooperation in the area;
- By students in two consecutive years of a one year Logistics Masters program of the university of Borås reflecting during 2008-2010 on the innovation practices of companies, authorities and university departments in

the "Sjuhäradsbygden area" (seven communes in and around Borås) as demonstrated by systemic meetings in the three types of stakeholders, as well as in the Logistics Masters program;

- By a group of systemic meeting facilitators initiated by the Council of Stockholm Regional Health Care, reflecting during 2004-2008 on the production and innovation practices in Stockholm health care, as demonstrated by systemic meetings in 10 health care departments;
- By students in two consecutive years of a one year health care leadership program at the University of Ersta Sköndal for leaders in Swedish health care, reflecting during 2006-2008 on the production and innovation practices in Swedish health care as demonstrated by systemic meetings in the program;
- By the management board of the Food Innovation Network of the Scania food cluster, reflecting during 2006-2007 on the innovation practices stemming from cluster cooperation supported by in part by a 10 year fund from Vinnova and the Regional Council of Scania, as demonstrated by systemic meetings between and interviews with key stakeholders in the cluster;
- By systemic meeting facilitators in Scania health care, supported by the development centre of the Regional Council of Scania, reflecting during 2004-2006 on the innovation practices initiated by systemic meetings in Scania health care
- By students in four consecutive years of a one year change management program for leaders in Swedish national authorities and agencies, reflecting during 1994-1999 on the innovation practices of Swedish national public services as demonstrated systemic meetings in the program;
- By bus drivers, public transport researchers, public transport organisers and bus manufacturers reflecting during 1992 on the innovation practices of public transport organisers, as demonstrated by systemic meetings during a one year period.

Although the concept of story creation was not yet developed in the early days of systemic meetings all the above "mountain" reflections (and numerous others) followed the same story creation logic:

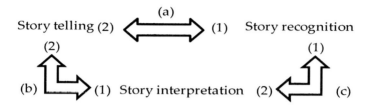

In telling her story (b1) the story teller would rely on her recognition (a2) on real life events, as would the story interpreters (c2), in recognizing and interpreting patterns and choices in the story, but also in asking questions to the story teller (b2), trying to clarify the story tellers recognition of the events. Story creation would then occur through the story tellers (a1) as well as the story interpreters (c1) increased awareness of patterns and choices at stake in real life events, based on their increased story interpretative skills, also involving increased story recognition and storytelling skills.

Already the bus driver mountain experience gave an example on this:

The story telling in this case was based on the bus drivers recognizing and taking notes of daily occurrences in and around the buses, then telling their stories to colleagues for their interpretation in front of a panel of public transport organizers, bus manufacturers and public transport researchers. In the beginning of about 8 meetings (later to be called "systemic"), the notes, the stories and the interpretations were focusing on bus drivers' problems with the buses, the interaction with the passengers, the traffic, the bus line routes and frequencies etc. But as the meetings went on, both the stories and the interpretations saw these types of problems more and more as passenger problems. The bus drivers witnessed about a development amongst themselves of a more passenger friendly attitude during this year of reflections. They became more helpful to mothers with baby carriers, to passengers who didn't know which bus station to get off the bus, which new bus to take etc.

Halting at "the shore" proved its value. Adding to this was also the manifest interest during the year from the public transport organizers and the bus manufacturers to make the bus lines and the buses more responsive to the passenger needs. The stories told by the bus drivers were more and more passenger stories, rather than bus driver stories. And furthermore they became not only stories about the bus travels as such but also stories on the roles of bus travel in passenger lives. The bus drivers started chatting with the passengers, when traffic so permitted and they were in this way able to provide a whole new input to bus line and bus design. The bus drivers were given the opportunity to suggest new bus routes and schedules, as well as to participate (through computerized tools for bus design, under development by bus manufacturers and researchers) in the development of new bus designs. These organized changes were part of the story creation, the "system setting" part.

The mountain reflection on the potential role of this shore arrangement, this arrangement of innovation practices, revealed a major shift from the current innovation practices in the innovation system of bus passengers – bus drivers – public transport organizers – bus manufacturers – public transport researchers. The current innovation practices were mapped through flow charting and other system-analytical tools, but also through mountain reflections on the shore story creation efforts during the project year. A follow up study a few years later showed little impact from the year of innovation system experimentation on the real life innovation system. The shift was judged as too big.

The mountain reflections of the management team of the Food Innovation Network of the Scania food cluster in 2006-2007 had more of an impact, as re-ported elsewhere (Lagnevik et al. 2010). Now "chatting with the passengers", in this case food consumers, had developed through social media.

The shore and mountain reflections in this case were based on food entrepre-neurial story telling. The mountain reflections from a series of 8 "gillen" (Scania dialect for approximately guild, referring back to old Scania traditions of for example eel "gillen" amongst peers in trades and crafts) telling and interpreting stories from 10 different food entrepreneurs provided a clear case to the man-agement team on the logic of story creation. The logic, as practiced by the cluster today, is based on recognition of food consumer stories, and an interpretation of the stories told in the consumer food community. One of several ways used to practice the logic is a social media based network of grocers. This network has the potential to make all the supply and knowledge chains of the Scania food cluster more food consumer responsive, and in the same time more responsive to research.

The first mountainous systemic meeting of the leaders of stakeholders in a communal area outside the city of Borås reflected on the innovation practices of the furniture company HansK in Kinna in the commune of Mark.

Through an intermediary company providing purchasing and logistics services linking Hans K with the Chinese furniture manufacturing market the company is supplying the Swedish furniture retail market with up to date furniture on a profitable basis and without much stock.

HansK's most successful product lines are all developed through story recognition at the homes of their potential end customers, i.e. people buying furniture at retail stores. They use students from the University of Borås for visits to potential end customers' homes, recognizing the challenges of the living rooms, entrance halls, bedrooms etc to be furnished. Through these "excursions" the students are able tell customer stream stories for shore reflections by HansK product, production and logistics designers. These shore reflections have in turn been reflected upon through systemic meetings between students of innovation management at the University of Borås, together with the management of HansK, and also through systemic meetings between leader stakeholders in the commune of Mark. These two sets of mountain reflections have contributed to the creation of new innovation practices, new shore stories, at other companies in the Mark and Borås areas, as reported elsewhere (Sarv and Khan 2010).

Jumping then to the ongoing network from the Communal Coordination Alliances on Rehabilitation, Illness, Unemployment and Social welfare several production and innovation practices have been identified for the purpose' of expanding the network to a learning community on story creation. One such example is provided by the story of INM (Integrated local health care in Malmo, http://www.inm.se) in Malmo, Sweden.

"We call it the in vivo principle" says Richard Bernce, psychiatrist, and one of INM's founding partners. Basically the patient, assisted by a case manager, at every stage of her treatment gets to pick the individual or individuals in her treatment team that she thinks can help her at this particular moment of time. The treating individuals listen together on the patient story, interpret it and come up with the mix of treatments that they can provide. The unfolding story of the patient in her life serves as the base for story creation. The treatment team of INM is systemically enlarged by co-workers in the health-job-economy support provided by the local community.

The systemic set up differs sharply from the traditional referral set up. It is based on parallel action rather than sequential action. It strives to avoid the all too common "illness sink", that is the support seeking individual being trapped in an illness classification, and a predominant view of herself as ill, all too often resulting in long term job sign offs and even early retirements.

To a mountain observer the story recognized at INM is taking place in their stream of daily patient treatments. But to the patient this stream is a shore for story recognition, storytelling, story interpretation and story creation. Basically the group of counsellors meets together with the patient and her case manager on her shore to reflect together on the stories evolving in the patients' life, and for introducing innovations in her stream. But the group of counsellors also meets on a shore of their own to reflect on their own stream; and to introduce innovations in that stream, or – from a patient perspective – they meet on a mountain overlooking both the patient shore and the patient stream. They then see themselves acting on the patient shore and they come up with innovations from doing it. The format of the systemic meeting has been introduced as a way to deal with these mountain reflections.

The view from the mountain

Systemic meetings bring the attention in an innovation system closer to the streams of the end consumers. They assemble people who work closely to those streams with people who work more at a distance, in a hierarchical sense, in a system level sense or in a supply chain sense. They do it literally, by people factually meeting, and they do it figuratively, through the aid of new communication tools:

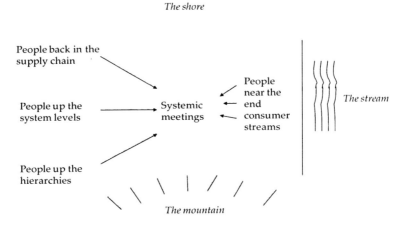

Basically, the idea of systemic thinking and systemic meetings is story interpretation for holistic response to stream challenges from shore contributors. The meetings give the partitioned contributions the common and more holistic frame often lacking when each contributor base their contributions primarily on distance measures and designs of their own outputs in isolation from the outputs of others.

Isolated and partitioned contributions are intentional whereas the holistic frames stemming from shared story interpretation are consequential. Partitioned projects are intentional. They wish to contribute in certain intentional ways. The consequential perspective is limited by those intentions. Shared story interpretation provides a more holistic consequential perspective.

The systemic meeting takes an intermediate perspective. The shore meeting tries to build a bridge between the consequential stream messiness, or complexity, on the one hand, and the intentional shore order on the other. The mountain meeting in turn tries to build a bridge between the consequential shore complexities on the one hand and the intentional mountain order on the other, e.g. the order expressed by theory. Theories on innovation and narration, e.g., can be used both for shore story interpretation and shore storytelling, as in this paper.

The common denominator to the visits on the shore and on the mountain is seeing yourself, or the services that you provide in, in real life series of events, as told by the stories that start the systemic meeting (the shore visit), or observed from participating in the systemic meeting (the mountain visit). In both cases real life complexity is investigated by the aid of language, the language that we are inclined to use in dialogues with others when looking for patterns and choices in real life series of events. In both cases the language is a carrier of knowledge. Doctors and nurses for example may use medical knowledge when characterizing patient story events, but to a higher degree also experienced based knowledge on how their part of health care is working, healthcare as a system portraying the patterns and choices that they recognize from their daily work, also their own patterns and choices.

Basically the setting of the systemic meeting is *inductive*. But through the use of language and knowledge it is also *deductive*. The shared search for patterns and choices can be seen as peddling between the inductive and the deductive state. It is *abductive* in the sense that new language, or new knowledge, that others are using to characterize familiar events may enter your own sphere of language and knowledge (it abducts you in the same time as you abduct it). Through the dialogue with others you learn to see your familiar world in new ways.

The visit to the mountain, overlooking the evolving shore stories, raises more of a problem. Doctors and nurses, if we stay with the health care example, certainly have experiences from participating in improvement, innovation or change processes, processes or their own when it comes to continuous improvements and medical or nursing innovations and – normally – processes directed by other when it comes to major organizational and structural changes. But they are not used to the systemic innovation practice set up by the systemic meeting.

The systemic meeting is constructing a new type of innovation practice, a practice based on shared reflection and concurrent experimentation rather than the type of sequential planning and control practice that is normally used in partitioned improvement, innovation and change projects. Such projects can be incurred by systemic meetings, or reflected upon in systemic meetings. But the systemic meeting centres round the intermediation between complex holistic practice and organized partitioned response. It takes the stand of the complex holistic practice as being *all important*, and the organized partitioned response as being *potentially simple*.

In the planning and control framework the plans for change are subject to elaborate work and the control of change outputs restricted to what can be measured, documented and reported to others. It is collective *we then there*, whereas the systemic reflection-experimental framework is individual *I now here*. The systemic story creation framework is in line with the knowledge creation framework described by Nonaka (Nonaka 2007) in his analysis of the knowledge creating approach and identifies some basic patterns around the theme of "personal insight and personal commitment":

> The centrepiece of the Japanese approach is the recognition that creating new knowledge is not simply a matter of "processing" objective information. Rather, it depends on tapping the tacit and often highly subjective insights, intuitions, and hunches of individual employees and making those insights available for testing and use by the company as a whole. The key to this process is personal commitment, the Employees' sense of identity with the enterprise and its mission.
>
> In the knowledge-creating company, inventing new knowledge is not a specialized activity – the province of the R&D department or marketing or strategic planning. It is a way of behaving, indeed a way of being, in which everyone is a knowledge worker – that is to say, an entrepreneur.

Nonaka takes the example of the Japanese mobile telecommunications company DoCoMo, who developed a product and service capable of mobile video streaming over wired and wireless networks using technology that resulted from the merging and integration of broadband internet technology and third-generation mobile phone technology. The network of companies and communities outside DoCoMo made it possible for this development process to occur at a speed "not yet known to the world". The network was primarily a community of meaning and innovation, not practice, not decision making. According to Nonaka (Nonaka and Toyama 2002), the key characteristic of the process was the synthesizing or the meaning shaping capability of a new grouping of companies and communities, stemming from the free insight journeys and knowledge travels that are easily made in today's global society.

A company that has taken a systemic approach is Seven Eleven Japan (Nonaka et al. 2001) This has made them buy out their American mother company.

> Every new hire at Seven Eleven Japan – irrespective of background and intended ca-
> reers in the company – has to start out with some years at a local Seven Eleven store.
> She is asked to observe closely customer reactions, reflect on them and take initiatives
> for improvements, all on an *I now here* basis. She is asked to do constant *insight jour-
> neying* in the store and turn to knowledge, in the shape of new possible ways to pre-
> pare the coffee, serve the coffee, present the donuts etc. Supporting her in her
> *knowledge travelling* is a field counsellor with eight stores each, constantly travelling
> between her eight stores and constantly consulting (or travelling) the Internet and oth-
> er knowledge sources, not the least the other field counsellors.

Terms like "the stream, the shore and the mountain", *all important/ potentially simple, I now here/ we then there* and insight journeying/knowledge travelling have been invented and used by the authors to support a mountainous reflection based on innovation practices observed in and around systemic meetings, in the contexts described above.

Stacey (2005: 14) supports this type of language creation:

> This step of translating tacit into explicit knowledge is recognized as being problemat-
> ic because it requires expressing the inexpressible. The translation therefore requires
> the figurative language of metaphor and analogy to bring what is below the level of
> awareness into awareness. This is where it becomes important to work and learn in
> teams. How members of those teams relate to each other, how they converse with
> each other and what kind of language they use, all become important matters.

Selecting another way to approach the whole

The systemic meeting is based on the fractal idea of small pieces of nature show-ing patterns of larger pieces of nature. It is based on the idea that it is worth wile to halt on specific series of events, of the types that occur every day in for exam-ple companies. It is based on the idea that accounting for such series of events through spontaneous story telling can help companies and communities improve in a more holistic way than when they take one decision at a time.

If subject to a dialogue based reflection, the stories told by specific series of events may surface important company patterns, the types of patterns that deter-mine how well companies do on their markets, and also the types of patterns that companies give strategic attention, or should give strategic attention. People generating these patterns by their everyday actions may benefit personally from reflecting on the patterns and taking reflection-guided action. Furthermore also companies and other types of organisations can benefit from arranging such reflection-action meetings, such story recognition-telling-interpretation meetings; such systemic meetings.

The basic idea of working the story side, or the side where events unfold into wholes, is that of taking on – wholes. The industrial society has made us great at partitioned undertakings; the knowledge society has made us start working the sum effects of all that knowledge can do the partitioned way.

We have introduced the concepts primary, secondary and tertiary stories. The primary story is that brought in by the story teller to the systemic meeting, from real life. The secondary story is that emerging at the systemic meeting, in working through the primary story. The tertiary story emerges in a community when reflecting together on the primary and secondary stories in the community.

Much can happen as a result of the use of systemic meetings in a community, or very little; it all depends on how the factual innovation system of the community is working. Just like the meeting participants can construct from the primary story subjective views on what is going on in the real life production system, they can construct from the secondary story subjective views on what is going on in the real life innovation system. They are familiar with both systems, either by personal participation in the systems, or by personal participation in similar systems.

If the people in an innovation community don't tell or recognize there is a story in what they come across when meeting with the final beneficiaries of the community, in stores, at service desks, through social media etc, they will not either take part in telling, interpreting and creating stories, other than by chance. Reductionism surveys can say much about the final beneficiaries, and their buying or connecting preferences. But they say the same to everyone and they tend to come up with stereotypes. Stereotype recognition is likely to end up stereotype products or services.

If the people in the innovation system don't identify their own personal roles in recognizing, telling, interpreting and creating stories, or if they don't see that they are involved in such processes at all, they will stick to their partitioned undertakings. They will leave the holistic outcomes to the complex responses that they don't see themselves having any part in. Making an effort to move the innovation system of a company, a value chain, a commune, a region, a hospital, a health care system etc to the story level is a matter of strategic choice.

There are plenty of tools for such a choice today. There are reductionism tools on the process and product levels, facilitating the steps upwards by not having to worry so much about the lower steps. And there are many tools emerging on the story level, like for example computerised innovation community tools, and social media treated as such tools.

But tools are not enough, there also has to be drawings on what to build. And there has to be a personal understanding of what the building of an upper step innovation system really means to the participating members. We hope to contribute to such an understanding, first and foremost through explaining how the systemic meeting can be used, but also through some metaphoric descriptions of the building.

References

Ainalem, I./Hjalmarsson, I./Linnarsson, H. (2008): Ger systemiska möten resultat? Region Skåne: Utvecklingscentrum.

Boje, D. M. (1991): The Storytelling Organization: A Study of Story Performance in an Office-Supply Firm. In: Administrative Science Quarterly 36, pp. 106-126.

Boje, D. M. (1995): Stories of the storytelling organization: a postmodern analysis as "Tamara-Land". In: Academy of Management Journal 38, pp. 997-1035.

Brown, J. S. (2005): Storytelling in Organizations: Why Storytelling Is Transforming 21st Century. In: Organizations and Management. Boston: Elsevier Butterworth–Heinemann.

Brown, J. S./Duguid, P. (1991): Organizational Learning and Communities-of-Practice: Toward a Unified View of Working, Learning, and Innovation. In: Organization Science 2, pp. 40-57.

Denning, S. (2004): Telling Tales. In: Harvard Business Review 82, pp. 122-129.

Drucker, P. (1993): Post-capitalist society. New York, Butterworth Heinemann.

Drucker, P. F. (1992): The New Society of Organizations. In: Harvard Business Review 70, pp. 95-105.

Göranzon, B. (2009): The practical intellect. Stockholm. Santérus.

Lagnevik, M./Sarv, H./Khan, U. K. (2010): Innovation community governance: The case of Skåne Food Innovation Network. In: 9th Wageningen International Conference on Chain and Network Management 2010, Wageningen, Netherlands.

Lave, J./Wenger, E. (1991): Situated learning: legitimate peripheral participation. Cambridge, England; New York: Cambridge University Press.

Maria, J. (2008): Experiencing collaborative knowledge creation processes. In: The Learning Organization 15, pp. 5-25.

McKee, R. (2003): Storytelling that moves people. In: Harvard Business Review 81, pp. 51-55.

Nonaka, I. (2007): The Knowledge-Creating Company. In: Harvard Business Review 85, pp. 162-171.

Nonaka, I./Konno, N. (1998): The Concept of "Ba": Building a Foundation for knowledge creation. In: California Management Review 40, pp. 40-54.

Nonaka, I./Konno, N./Toyama, R. (2001): "Emergence of "Ba": A Conceptual Framework for the Continuous and Self-transcending Process of Knowledge Creation". In: Nonaka, I./Nishiguchi, T. (eds.) (2001): Knowledge emergence: social, technical, and evolutionary dimensions of knowledge creation. Oxford: Oxford University Press. pp. 13- 29.

Nonaka, I./Reinmoeller, P./Senoo, D. (2000): Integrated IT systems to capitalize on market knowledge: In: von Krogh, G./Nonaka, I./Nishiguchi, T. (eds.) (2000): Knowledge Creation: A Source of Value. London: Macmillan, pp. 89-109.

Nonaka, I./Toyama, R. (2002): A firm as a dialectical being: Towards a dynamic theory of a firm. In: Industrial and Corporate change 11, pp. 995-1009.

Nonaka, I./Takeuchi, H. (1995): The knowledge-creating company: how Japanese companies create the dynamics of innovation. New York: Oxford University Press.

Peltonen, T./Lämsä, T. (2004): Communities of Practice and the Social Process of Knowledge Creation: Towards a New Vocabulary for Making Sense of Organizational Learning. In: Problems and Perspectives in Management 4, pp. 249-262.

Sarv, H./Khan U. K. (2010): Intermediation in innovation communities: the case of Centiro. 14th IBIMA conference on Global Business Transformation through Innovation and Knowledge Management. Turkey: Istanbul.

Spinosa, C./Flores, F./Dreyfus, H. L. (1997): Disclosing new worlds: entrepreneurship, democratic action, and the cultivation of solidarity. Cambridge MA: MIT Press.

Stacey, R. D. (2005): Complex Responsive Processes in Organizations Learning and knowledge creation. Taylor & Francis e-Library.

Tsoukas, H./Chia, R. (2002): On organizational Becoming: Rethinking Organizational Change. Organization Science Vol. 13, No. 5, pp. 567-582.

Von Krogh, G. (1998): Care in Knowledge Creation. In: California Management Review 40, pp. 133-153.

Von Krogh, G./Grand, S. (2000): Justification in knowledge creation: dominant logic in management discourses. In: von Krogh, G./Nonaka, I./Nishiguchi, T. (eds) (2000): Knowledge Creation: A Source of Value London: Macmillan, pp. 13-29.

Wenger, E./Mcdermott, R. A./Snyder, W. (2002): Cultivating communities of practice: a guide to managing knowledge. Boston MA, Harvard Business School Press.

Wenger, E. C./Snyder, W. M. (2000): Communities of Practice: The Organizational Frontier. In: Harvard Business Review 78, pp. 139-145.

Outlook

Riding Dead Horses[1]

Andreas Zeuch

About two years ago I was invited as keynote speaker at a congress in Germany. One of the other speakers was a German ex-astronaut holding a talk "From Vision to Mission". He presented his thrilling story of becoming an astronaut, including dozens of spectacular pix such as parabolic flights in the so-called vomit comet, in which zero gravity was trained. No question, it was great entertainment. And then he came to his core statement:"What I want to say is that you have to plan for every eventuality in your company". Believe it or not, nobody, absolutely nobody raised his arm and asked:"Ah excuse me, and if this is so, why have NASA Astronauts died in several missions?" A reminder: The Challenger Space Shuttle crashed in 1986 and the Columbia crashed in 2003. Discovery was affected by a lot of malfunctions before starting, and building the Endeavour Shuttle to replace Challenger became necessary after the crash but was never planned, generating new costs of about two billion dollars.

The NASA is a great symbol for elaborate project management concerning most complex projects and hence an impressive example of the leading paradigm of economics: prediction and control. The most high-impact roll-out of business and economics is the roll-out of this paradigm to the whole of society: to education, health care, politics and so on. Everything has to be measured and evaluated in a certain standardized way; every part of our society is supposed to be predictable and controllable. Ironically we notice painfully: In cold winters the Eurostar still gets stuck in the Eurotunnel, and in hot summers the German ICE mutates into a heat trap. In our worldwide trans-cultural war on uncertainty we overlook the obvious:

We can't control the future, and not even the present.

Innovation has always been not only a matter of great intellects, but also of luck, chance and useful errors.

Last but not least innovation is an inbred part of the human nature in general: We all are born creative, we just have to look at our children playing, talking, interacting, and discovering the world.

---

[1] This lecture is based on my last book "Feel it! Soviel Intuition verträgt Ihr Unternehmen", published by Wiley in 2010.

You might not believe in our creative roots and resources, perhaps because you don't estimate kids' games to be creative or don't experience children regularly, so I've got an interesting story for you.

Once, some years ago, a female obese patient wasn't able to lose weight. She tried everything but her subconscious was sabotaging her efforts and nothing worked. Because of this and some other indications she was a candidate for so called bariatric surgery to stop her insatiable hunger mechanically, allowing only the intake of small amounts of solid food. A few weeks after her surgery she had an appointment in the clinic to check her improvements: There were none! She hadn't lost a single ounce of fat. She had even gained weight. The physicians spoke to her, trying to find out the reason for this incredible development. Finally they were told that she was putting three XXL Glasses of chocolate cream into the microwave every morning and then drinking them. Creativity blazes its trail, even in pathology, if there is no possibility to be creative in a healthy way. It is creative and solution-focused, reframing to interpret this behavior as creative rather than proof of a mental illness. No irony, sarcasm or cynicism intended.

To develop sustainably innovative companies, we have to ensure that all employees are enabled to access their natural creativity at work and have the will to make use of it. And we should be open to chance, errors and passion and react appropriately to the element of uncertainty. How can we make this happen?

It is common knowledge that there is no sense in trying to ride and spur a dead horse. But this is exactly what we try to do every day. Most innovations discussed and / or realized in companies today are on the level of products, processes, business models and strategies. We systematically ignore our most powerful and effective leverage: innovation of the organizational model and management itself. We are still under the spell of two basic "old-school" ideas: first, the effectivity and efficiency of dividing thinking, on one hand, from working functions, on the other hand, as proposed by Taylor's 100-year-old "Scientific Management". That's where management comes from. Second, the homo oeconomicus and the superiority of rationality over emotions and intuition.

Therefore the paradigm of predictability and control still underlies our organizational structures and cultures, as illustrated by astronauts planning every eventuality. Ironically the term "innovation management" is another example of this paradigm, demanding systematic planning, steering and control of innovation in organizations. Effectively every innovation we create and realize within the framework of "old-school" management is doomed to remain cosmetic surgery. After a successful operation we will look a bit (or even a lot) more like we always dreamed: slimmer and sporting a sexier shape. But the mindset is still the same and the fat will return in nasty bumps on other parts of our body. The scalpel has to cut through our skin again and again.

Hence it's much more effective to change the mindset, the paradigm and the basic principles of creating and steering companies themselves. To be thorough and extensive, innovation must occur on the level of the organizational model and management. The paradigmatic assumption of predictability and control and its operative principles should be transformed into the opposite: beginner's mind – instead of specialization; self-organization – instead of hierarchy and control; possibility space instead of planning and steering; error kindness – instead of standardization and, last not least, trust – instead of extrinsic motivation.

The five principles

Beginner's mind – the paradox of open expertise

In 1979 the Australian pathologist Robin Warren, who had no expertise in gastroenterology, discovered a special kind of bacteria in the samples of gastric mucosa collected from his patients[2]. Warren and his colleague Barry Marshall, a general practitioner, postulated a connection between gastric ulcers and these bacteria, since it could be found in almost all patients suffering from gastric ulcerations. The expert opinion on the cause of this disease up to that point had been an association with spiced foods, alcohol and stress. For it was common knowledge that bacteria was not able to survive in the acidic climate of the human stomach. So Marshall and Warren set out to cultivate the bacteria in vitro in order to conduct further experiments.

After cultivating the bacteria successfully – which is another interesting story – they were not able to evoke gastric ulcers in animals. Because of that, Marshall decided to experiment on himself. He ingested a dose of the solution containing the bacteria in question – against his wife's vivid protest. About one week later he presented all the symptoms of an active gastric ulcer. Marshall suffered massive discomfort and was hardly able to eat. Luckily he had come up with an antibiotic therapy beforehand that had already used to cure his patients, even though his successes had not been recognized by his scientific peers. He treated himself and recovered quickly.

---

[2] This case study is described in the following Internet resources (excerpt):
http://www.nobelprize.org/nobel_prizes/medicine/laureates/2005/press.html
http://www.aerztezeitung.de/medizin/krankheiten/magen_darm/article/374525/ob-gastritis-ulkus-magenlymphom-krebs-magenkeim-helicobacter-pylori-mischt-ueberall.html
http://www.pta-forum.de/fileadmin/pta-forum-html/051238.htm

Presenting these results Marshall and Warren expected to be finally taken seriously. But as we have known since Copernicus, experts are extremely resistant to new findings. Not to say, we are as stubborn as mules. Presenting their results at a congress they were shouted down and finally called crackpots. Trying to publish their work in the renowned medical journals "Lancet" and the "New England Journal of Medicine", they were turned down by the publishers and denied entry into the peer review system! Many years later, in 2005, the pseudo-rational experts came to their senses: Marshall and Warren were awarded the Nobel Prize for medicine due to their discovery of "Helicobacter pylori", which causes gastritis and gastric ulcers. By the way, the bacteria's secret was to cover itself in slime to survive in the acidic gastric environment. The changes in therapeutic management were revolutionary: Before their discovery patients underwent extensive surgical procedures with harsh consequences for their digestive tract. Today the brief application of antibiotics is sufficient.

It's not only the scientific domain that is deteriorating to expertocracy. Our firms, society and democratic apparatus are also affected. We don't hire engineers but electro-engineers, aeronautical engineers, mechanical engineers, software engineers and so on. We're highly specialized. We have to be. The amount of knowledge in every domain has become so extensive that we are unable to highlight every area of our profession. Surely focusing has its advantages. We turn into experts that are capable of immersing ourselves more and more deeply in our specialized fields with increasing knowledge and experience, enabling us to develop a profound professional intuition. This is a value to hold up. But we are still ignoring the dark sides. We've turned into geeks and are unable to approach a task from a position other than the expert position. Just remember the gastroenterologists in the case of Marshall and Warren.

It surfaces in companies when the usual interaction difficulties occur: We stay well within our own departments and don't perceive process chains as entities. Not realizing that value creation happens along the way regardless of formally divided responsibilities. What the others are doing is beyond my understanding and not my cup of tea anyway.

Surely these difficulties don't have their root in expertise only. Due to the increased Tayloristic division of labor into management and execution, there is an increased feedback loop in our educational system, already demanding further specialization during the qualification process. This again feeds the spiral of the division of labor. This vicious circle in its exclusivity costs us innovational power and entrepreneurial success and assets.

What we need is what I call open expertise: We have to develop our expertise as hitherto, but we have to let go of our epistemic arrogance as experts. We also should simultaneously develop the capability of looking at our challenges with a beginner's mind. We should be able to switch both positions instantaneously.

Remember the beginner's mind and open expertise next time somebody new in your working environment suggests something different to what is normal or totally beyond the usual thinking.

Self-organization – exorcise the headquarters' arrogance

Would you call a sales increase of 5,300 percent in 21 years a success? I would say so. From being a single product manufacturer of vegetable oil centrifuges, this firm has experienced a remarkable transformation since 1950. Probably the most important part of this transformation happened during a market-shattering crisis in the 80s and 90s when Brazil's economy threatened to break down due to an inflation rate of up to 25% per month. In 1990 prices grew by as much as 1000%. This hyperinflation could only be stopped by a currency reform in 1993.

Thus it is no surprise that the company I am talking about was on the verge of breaking down like hundreds other businesses had done. The owner and CEO tried every well-known management trick to rescue his company – all the science-based stuff about managing and leading productively. Nothing worked. With his back to the wall he made a decision that changed everything for him and his employees. He and his top-management team met the whole workforce and decided to incorporate every employee in all further decisions. Purchases were made in agreement with the workforce, the income of the workforce and top management was dramatically reduced, and the employees received a higher share of profits. This way they survived the Brazilian economy crisis. And much more: They even emerged invigorated. This success encouraged the CEO to follow the chosen path more rigorously. Today there is no human resource department anymore, but the workforce is responsible for employing new colleagues. They decide on their own, when, where and how long they work and even how much they earn. They decide on new locations, new products and their prices, and have free access to all information. That is entrepreneurial self-organization at its best. The company I have been talking about is Semco and its owner and leader is Ricardo Semler.[3]

Mostly, when my colleagues and I present such examples, a lot of people argue in the same way: "That's another country, culture, branch, size, you can't compare it to our company. Our situation is completely different". Well, I will

---

[3] This case study can be found in: Ramo, J.C. (2009): the Age of the Unthinkable. Little, Brown and Company, New York. Cf.
http://www.semco.com.br/en/content.asp?content=3&contentID=605

give you another example from another country, culture, branch and company size.

Ulf Lunge and his brother Lars have achieved something seemingly impossible: They produce high-end running shoes in the high-wage location Germany. The production is nearly permanently sold out; customers are thrilled by the great quality of Lunge running shoes made in Germany. I talked to Ulf Lunge about entrepreneurial intuition, uncertainty, planning and self organization for my recent book "Feel it!" on intuition in business.

He explained his and his brother's conviction about the importance of the extensive empowerment of their employees. Based on their long-time experience, both believe that it doesn't make any sense that the executive board alone makes the decisions, especially on vital questions. They not only allow, but call on their employees to participate in important decisions. Ulf and Lars Lunge have gained insight into their own boundaries, on the one hand, and the power and possibilities of shared decision-making and self-organization, on the other hand.

Remember self-organization next time you walk along a crowded sidewalk wondering why there are so few collisions.

Error kindness – turning taboo into a chance

The 25th of April 2005 was a sunny spring day in Itami, Japan. At 9.16 a.m. the local train left the station with an almost one-minute delay because the young train operator Ryujiru Takami had to steer the train back after having missed the regular stop. Leaving the station, Takami entered a turn marked with a speed limit of 43 miles per hour at 72 miles, trying to make up for his time loss. Takami tried to break, but he couldn't control the train anymore. It tipped and moved on the left-side wheels only for over 100 yards before five wagons derailed and crashed into apartment houses near the railway. As a result of the accident, 106 of the 580 passengers died and 460 were injured, some of them severely. Why did it happen?

Japanese trains are on time. Since 1964 the high-speed train Shinkansen, for example, has an average delay of 18 seconds - for a distance of 310 miles! This precision is expected by customers in Japan today. In order to fulfill this expectation, JR West's Railways, Takami's employer, took fierce action against their workforce. In so-called"additional trainings"operators and conductors were interrogated, sworn at, had to write senselessly extensive reports. Additionally they were made to weed pest plants and had to salute all passing train operators at a station as humiliation. Employees associated with repeated delays were pressed to resign. Some employees committed suicide subsequently to these additional trainings. The operator Ryujiru Takami had already taken part in such a training lasting 13 days. One of the chiefs of the labor union at that time, Osamu Yomono, said:"I am pretty sure that he didn't want to experience such a handling ever again. So he desperately tried to catch up on the delay to escape this terrible punishment. That's why he drove so fast".[4] This example goes to show: Being afraid of committing mistakes just makes them more likely to happen.

Zero tolerance of mistakes also makes it impossible to see and seize the chances inherent in mistakes. We turn a blind eye to the innovative power of error. Every mistake committed menaces our plans and questions the planning, which we put energy into before. As a consequence we're in search of the culprit in order to eliminate the source of error. This way we make it impossible to encounter the error in a creative and mindful way. How we could use the error and what could come from it is not within our mental frame, but we get totally worked up about correcting the plan variance in order to keep up with our set scheme. Zero tolerance of mistakes therefore is a Procrustes' bed: What doesn't fit is chopped off or stretched forcefully. But we should bear in mind that many extremely successful products and developments were made possible by mistakes.

Remember errors as a chance next time you stick a Post-it somewhere or pop an antibiotic pill such as Penicillin.

Possibility space – transforming chance, errors and passion into added value

You all know Gore-Tex. I am pretty sure. Presumably most of you possess an outdoor jacket, trekking or running shoes made waterproof and yet breathable by the fiber. But did you know that W. L. Gore, the developer and producer of Gore-Tex is also successful in a sub-branch of musical instruments? And how it came to illustrate what our consulting group refers to as possibility space so well? One of Gore's employees was a passionate cyclist at the time this story started. He came up with an idea of how the Teflon-based Gore-Tex technology could be used to improve bicycles. If he managed to cover the metal Bowden wires that work the brakes in Teflon, this would make the application of grease to friction points unnecessary. The idea was good, but didn't work. But the development crew came up with a totally different field of application. Guitar strings. Up to that point, metal strings consisted of wound steel that annoyingly

[4] This case study is described in the following Internet resources (excerpt):
http://www.guardian.co.uk/world/2005/apr/29/japan.justinmccurry
http://www.usajobonline.com/Press-Union-chief-blames-bullying-rail-firm-for-Japanese-train-crash-17027.htm
http://www.ctv.ca/servlet/ArticleNews/story/CTVNews/20050428/driver_japan_wrec k_050428?s_name=l&no_ads=

only sounded fresh and brilliant for a short time. After a while the sound dulled because the overtones vanished due to material wear. The reason: Corrosion attacked the metal surface and small particles gathered in between the windings and affected the vibration of the string significantly. Treating the strings with a coating technology prevented them from being spoiled by dirt and skin particles. The result was the guitar string"Elixir" that lasted 3-5 times longer than ordinary strings.

Now all this might not seem special to you, apart from the product innovation. Where is the possibility space in that? Quite simple: Within the firm there was never the concept of entering the musical instrument market; nobody in management had the faintest idea about it. The product was born from someone's passion for cycling and him being allowed the opportunity to invest in this passion during his working hours – without the pressure of having to achieve a set goal with a set amount of resources. At W. L. Gore, 10 to 20 percent of working time can be committed to the employees' special interests. On top of that they are supported by easy access to resources, both financially and concerning manpower. No need for tedious application forms and audits as is the case in many – if not most - companies[5].

Possibility space enfolds on three levels: Most of us have one or the other passion that we have not been able to integrate into our working lives to date. They exist restricted to our leisure time. Of course not every passion can or should be part of our job. It's up to us whether we want to work away meaninglessly or if we want to burn for something. Real flow, real happiness can only be encountered if we love our work for its own sake. But we have to open ourselves to this possibility. If we want persisting innovation we have to open space for ourselves.

The second level is organizational culture. Individual possibility space is crushed if we focus on existing conditions only. Advance concerning the innovation of products, processes or business models demands cultural commitment to possibility space. What's the point in offering your personal possibility space to your company if your engagement isn't acknowledged or even punished? To encourage that kind of behavior, appreciation and trust are necessary prerequisites. Possibility space has to be a cultural marker, making a difference in the interaction between all levels. Breaking out of THE REALITY and entering one's individual possibility space should be natural. There, the innovative power of passion can be set free. We need to be blessed by the insight that chance and error can be added value, even though unplanned for the company. Only if we

---

[5]   http://en.wikipedia.org/wiki/W._L._Gore_and_Associates
      http://www.gore.com/en_xx/aboutus/index.html. Cf. Hamel (2007): 124-137.

take up this approach concerning chance and error, can we utilize them with the necessary mindfulness. We have to give gaps between us a chance.

Last but not least we have to go through with it on the structural level. This includes providing time and resources in an appropriate way. If you take the concept of possibility space seriously, your employees need gaps in their working schedules to be filled with their interest and passions, time to develop own ideas and get own projects started. Of course involving others in their ideas has to be possible up to a certain point. Easy access to a certain amount of financial means is necessary to boost small-scale experiments and first steps in development without justifying kowtows to half a dozen hierarchy levels.

Remember possibility space next time you put on your Gore-Tex jacket or shoes.

Trust – using the natural power of cooperation

Since the economy learns from the military, we're constantly indoctrinated by the tale that economy is war. Managers are considered to be tough dogs or even real economic navy SEALs, trained in the hard art of economic close combat to win the war for talents and to prevent themselves from being swallowed, filleted or shredded to pieces. This is one of the biggest bogey man stories I've come across. We should be aware that this scenario is not in the least inescapable. It has risen mainly from metaphors and tales we use to describe the economy and can't withstand critical questioning in the same way as social Darwinism is disproved by current genetics and upcoming epigenetics. Cooperation starts on the genomic level, yet DNA, the foundation of all life forms, can't replicate without aiding molecules. The real root of performance is cooperation. It is simple. No paramilitary chief executive OFFICER survives without his cooperating network. He is not bound to survive if his employees don't tolerate his egomanic escapades. iGod Steve Jobs himself wouldn't have been able to develop, design, produce, advertise, and distribute the iPhone 4WA (working antenna) without his workforce and suppliers. There is no survival without cooperation. Of course there are situations when cooperation fails. In game theory, a tit-for-tat strategy has proven optimal under the condition of repeated game situations as found in day-to-day working life.

We should stop suggesting to ourselves that economy is combat and war, bearing in mind that the world turns into what we expect. The influence of preset expectation is strikingly highlighted by the Rosenthal effect; this originally refers to an experimental situation where teachers attributed high skills to part of their students, even though they were of average intelligence. After six months the presumed genii showed a significant rise in IQ compared to the rest of the class –

just because the teachers in question expected higher achievement and therefore supported them subconsciously, hence boosting the student's self-efficacy[6]. The role of expectation is not voodoo, but bland psychology.

Distrust and control kill (suffocate) the spirit of innovation. In a working environment poisoned by distrust, nobody offers his inbred, natural creativity. If we don't trust our employees to happily offer their creative resources, it will be so. If we tell ourselves that we need to manage, steer and control innovation, it will be so. Psycho-locigally.

Remember trust next time you don't pass on information because you think your people can't handle it or when you don't receive information because your boss thinks that's best for both of you.

Conclusion

If beginner's mind, self-organization, error kindness, possibility space and trust persistently thrive in our companies, that is management innovation. More precisely, innovation of the manner in which we create and steer companies. The natural innovative power of all co-workers would be set free far more effectively than today. To pinpoint it excessively: We just have to turn things upside down. Transform innovation management into management innovation.

My view is not a consultant's opinion only. It's our experience and conviction that the five principles are important for achieving and preserving an innovative climate where ideas bubble up naturally. My colleagues and I have founded a company where we apply these principles with a simple knack: Everybody, no exceptions, everybody who joins us becomes a managing director. Equal rights and duties, no differences made on this level. You may call it unrealistic, ridiculous, crazy, or whatever you want. We call it a visionary "Real Experiment". But please, please remember: It would have sounded unrealistic, ridiculous and crazy not even 100 years ago if somebody had postulated that we would land on the moon someday soon.

---

[6]   http://de.wikipedia.org/wiki/Rosenthal-Effekt
       The contrary effect can be found in the study of pupils who didn't reach the next school grade (Oerter and Montada 1987: 868-871).

References

Hamel, G. (2007): Das Ende des Managements. Berlin: Econ.
Oerter, R./Montada, L. (1987): Entwicklungspsychologie. Landsberg: PVU.
Ramo, J. C. (2009): The Age of the Unthinkable. New York: Little, Brown and Company.
Zeuch, A. (2010): Feel it! Soviel Intuition verträgt Ihr Unternehmen. Weinheim: Wiley.

Internet sources (in order of case studies and examples)

Marshall/Warren
http://www.nobelprize.org/nobel_prizes/medicine/laureates/2005/press.html
http://www.aerztezeitung.de/medizin/krankheiten/magen_darm/article/374525/o
  b-gastritis-ulkus-magenlymphom-krebs-magenkeim-helicobacter-pylori-
  mischt-ueberall.html
http://www.pta-forum.de/fileadmin/pta-forum-html/051238.htm

Semco
Ramo, J.C. (2009): the Age of the Unthinkable. Little, Brown and Company, New York.
http://www.semco.com.br/en/content.asp?content=3&contentID=605

Amagasaki
http://www.guardian.co.uk/world/2005/apr/29/japan.justinmccurry
http://www.usajobonline.com/Press-Union-chief-blames-bullying-rail-firm-for-
  Japanese-train-crash-17027.htm
http://www.ctv.ca/servlet/ArticleNews/story/CTVNews/20050428/driver_japan_
  wreck_050428?s_name=I&no_ads=

W.L.Gore
http://en.wikipedia.org/wiki/W._L._Gore_and_Associates
http://www.gore.com/en_xx/aboutus/index.html

Rosenthal-Effect
http://de.wikipedia.org/wiki/Rosenthal-Effekt

Anticipation: A Bridge between Narration and Innovation

Mihai Nadin

In Memoriam: Steve Jobs

Who's afraid of non-determinism?

Everyone. No one goes to his physician prepared to accept a diagnosis that *might* be right or wrong. You don't send an e-mail that just *might* reach your addressee, or might reach someone else, or might get lost. You don't turn the key in your car's ignition under the assumption that it might not start (or at least not when you need or want it to). Innovation, which literally means *to renew, renewal,* is another human endeavor in which you don't want to take a risk. It might take you where you don't want to be, to situations you would prefer not to go through. For the sake of illustration, let us recall an innovation broadcasted around 1970: the nuclear pacemaker (*New Scientist,* December 1972) with batteries containing metallic plutonium 238 implanted in someone's chest. Nuclear energy was the big innovation. What better hope could a heart patient wish for?

Germans implant 100th nuclear pacemaker, while Britain orders its first...

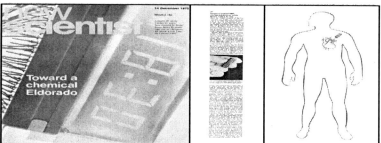

Figure 1: "The advantage of a nuclear pacemaker is its long life time," writes the author of the note in *New Scientist,* ignoring the problem of consequences to the patient.

Then, as now, innovation was romanticized. Although, as research shows, "people are biased against creative ideas" (Mueller, Melwani and Goncalo 2011). If the nuclear pacemaker were the only example, we could still live with innovation, even if, sometimes, the costs attached to it stand in no relation to the outcome. Just for the sake of illustrating this statement, here are some examples of innovations and the narrative associated with them. Grain storage triggers the risk of insect infestation. An insecticide should not alter the characteristics of the stored grain. The narrative is simple: a fumigant – Zyklon B – was developed by Fritz Haber, a distinguished Nobel laureate in chemistry. The rest is the tragic history of millions of Jews murdered in gas chambers. The story is even more provocative: Haber was a Jewish scientist. To speed up the growth of soybeans, Agent Orange was developed. Deployed by the USA during the war in Vietnam, the chemical caused birth defects in over 500,000 people. TNT, the explosive of choice in two world wars, was developed as a yellow dye; Ecstasy for addressing abnormal bleeding. Unfortunately, the number of examples of innovation that humankind could do without is not decreasing. The reason is not only innovation euphoria – cloud computing, nanotechnology, genetic medicine, for example – but also the lack of progress in anticipating the consequences that innovation entails (Nadin 2003). As we shall see, anticipation is different from prediction (which is based on probabilities) and forecasting (based on models that try to account for randomness). The innovation narrative and the narrative of unprecedented consequences are not the same. But they are related. The few examples given above are indicative of the relation.

"Creative destruction" – only a metaphor?

Renew/renewal has a precise reference: there is something (an object O, a process P, an attribute A, etc.) that invites human interest to bring it up to date. Otherwise expressed: the clock of entities subject to innovation has to be reset, brought up to date. One example to make this assertion clear: the horse-drawn carriage (around the 9th century BCE), the engine-driven automobile (from Nicolas Joseph Cugnot, 1769 to Gottlieb Daimler, 1885 or Karl Benz, 1886), the hybrid car (combining combustion engine and battery-powered electricity, built by Victor Wouk in 1972, cf. *hybridCARS* 2006) correspond to moments in time that we define through the clock-based calendar. Each new moment was a resetting to new expectations and requirements. It affected not only the mechanics of moving, but also mobility. Innovation always transcends the immediate object of renewal. It pertains to the life of the people. In the case of the car, the innovation affected culture, urban development, health, economy, manufacturing, politics, and more.

To make current, or to be ahead of time (how much?), is part of the innovation. The word *innovation* (from the Latin *novare*) as such acquires its meaning relatively late: in the 13th century in French-speaking culture; in the 16th century in the German- and English-speaking cultures. Joseph Alois Schumpeter, the famous Harvard University economist who authored a theory of economic development of capitalism, took note of the discontinuity of change resulting from innovation (*Business Cycles*, 1939). In his view of capitalism, there is a "creative destruction" process: market restructuring and the need to understand discontinuity are part of his perspective. Innovation supports the continuous reinvention of capitalism. This applies to every subject that innovation affects: production, distribution, investment, work, leisure, competition, social and political structuring. The major challenge for the capitalist is not managing the market (administering "existing structures"), but rather "making new markets (and destroying them)." The entrepreneur is "the agent of innovation. (cf. *Theory of Economic Development*, especially the German edition of 1935). Disruptions, not continuity, define capitalism. In this respect, innovation transcends the cause-and-effect sequence. Innovation is not a deterministic mechanism, but rather a process of non-deterministic reinvention, with many unpredictable outcomes (bankruptcies as well as success stories). Some were mentioned above. If we jump from nuclear batteries implanted in human bodies to the iPhone and to the innovation of financial derivatives, which led to a world-wide recession (begun in 2007 and not over as of yet), we realize that *creative destruction* (perceived as a disruption) is not just a metaphor. Some markets were destroyed; new markets were created. Some companies went bankrupt; others were saved. Therefore, to understand innovation requires that we also understand that creativity has an implicit destructive component: the new replaces something already in place. The process generates conflict. Intergenerational relations are an example extending throughout the entire history of humankind. Innovations of all kinds (how we care for offspring, education, nourishment, inheritance laws, social changes in the status of youngsters, etc., etc.) have led to many disruptions. For example, the generation of 68 was no longer willing to recognize the legitimacy of parental authority, which carried over to government authority. Their innovation was based on the narrative of challenging the rules.

The narrative

But enough, for the time being, with innovation and the broad meaning of renewal. It is usually idealized, just as each birth is idealized (mothers, better than anyone else, know the risk and pain that new life entails). Nevertheless, the examples brought up are part of what can easily be called the *narrative* associated with innovation. The simplest definition of *narrative* is: a description of a sequence of events as they succeed in time. The word (again, from the Latin *narrare*) means to recount. It suggests that a record of succeeding events in time, a time series, describes what people accomplish and how. Therefore, it adds up to knowledge.

The most intuitive way to organize our own experiences is to take note of how they succeed, one after the other, along the timeline of our own activity. This inspired Gelernter (1992) to generate the *flowing stream*: nothing more than the sequence of every electronic document – mail, photo, draft, URL, notes, etc. – in the order of their reception (or in the order of their generation). It seems a simple idea, but in fact it was the innovation that changed the nature of data management in the broadest sense possible. I would have called it *the narration stream*.

If we have a record of succeeding experiences, we could try to see what these experiences have in common, and what distinguishes them. And we could try to understand them. The most telling narratives are those we experience naturally: the succession of day and night, of seasons; the succession of plant life, of animal behavior in the environment, of celestial bodies (sun, moon, stars, etc.). Innovation cannot change such sequences, although plants that flower in advance of the change in season have been created, as well as fruits that become edible earlier, animals (pets, cattle) that behave in ways that "contradict" nature. In summary: not only the artificial (what we make) is subject to innovation, but also the natural. High-performance sport is an example impossible to avoid: Oscar Leonard Carl Pistorius runs on Cheetah Flex-Foot carbon fiber transitional artificial limbs (made by a company called Ossur), competing with runners who have their natural legs. This would be the inspiring aspect. Performance enhancement through drugs is probably less inspirational (especially in view of the long-lasting consequences). The observer takes note of how humans defy the natural and acquire new means for enhanced performance. It is one thing to confront an animal in nature during its active phases (seeking food, hunting prey), and another while feeding offspring, or during sleep. The same applies to human beings: they welcome visitors, but not necessarily occupiers (in military or business guise). Narration evinces only time-significant connections. It does not report on causality. A tame animal, like the tame human being, can abruptly change its behavior. There is no easily retraceable narration of causality as it pertains to behavior.

And the story?

As fashionable as narrativity (and other attempts to study the narrative) has become, it rarely results in a body of knowledge that makes a real difference in practical endeavors. The main reason for this is the imprecise nature of our understanding of what the act of narration is, and the knowledge that narrations embody. With the exception of Windelband (1915), almost no one has tried to define the distinction between narrative knowledge, corresponding to a historic record of change (*idiographic*), and scientific knowledge (*nomothetic*), corresponding to our attempts to describe how reality works. The idiographic captures patterns of events; the nomothetic focuses on scientific law. Of course, everyone would like to transform the uniqueness of experience captured in the narration into laws, thus opening the avenue towards automating whatever we do. To a certain extent, such attempts have succeeded: all tools are an expression of this preoccupation. In our age of digital descriptions and digital machines (which actually are programs), more progress in this direction is made. A concise formulation of the attempt described above is: to transform the art of doing things into the science and technology of doing things. It remains to be seen if the outcome is always as good as we hope.

Narration and story

For the sake of illustration: "The Queen died, and then the King died." Of course, you can substitute the generic queen and king with whomever you want (people you know, characters in books, your pet dogs). If you so desire, add a precise date for each event. Or take any successive events you kept a record of. This is narration. Temporality defines its condition: something happened after something else.

The Queen died, and then the King died – of a broken heart. Take your example (e.g., Mother died first, father died later) and add whatever the case might be: languished, committed suicide, was poisoned, etc. If your example was different – let's say: She gave birth at 4:45AM; her mother called five minutes later – your story could end with

1. after a nurse called her mother to give her the good news;
2. after she heard her daughter's voice in a dream (or thought she heard her daughter's voice in a dream, or thought she had a dream);
3. before she went to sleep (along the line of "Let me see if she gave birth so that nobody will wake me up");

etc., etc., etc. The list is open. Use your imagination. Write your own stories based on narrations you are familiar with.

Recently (Krulwich 2011), the narration of the death of Richard Feynman's wife made the rounds. The time of death (precise narration) was the time at which the clock in the room where she died stopped. Feynman, no doubt affected by the loss (he was young, she was young, they were in love – so goes the narration), would not allow the coincidence – time of death recorded on the certificate and the time the clock stopped – to obstruct his judgment. He went for the cause (later in life, he helped establish the cause of the *Challenger* space shuttle disaster). That was his story. And in this respect, science is the story into which the narration (of facts, measurements, evaluations, experiments) morphs. The apple falling from the tree, the observations of how this happens (during day or night, sunshine or clouds, noise or quiet, etc.) are the narration. Among the stories, there is one of the ever-hungry traveler (for whom apples fall), another of the reseeding of the tree (can this be the Johnny Appleseed story?), and another for Newton's theory of gravity.

While narration and story – often considered identical – have attracted the attention of many people, their significance as a substratum of life has escaped the attention of science. There is no class in narration for students of life forms and molecular biology, for future physicians and geneticists. Story was given over to writers and, eventually, filmmakers. To paraphrase none other than Abraham Lincoln: We must like stories; we make so many of them. And we like to hear them. (My wife is still working on a book entitled *Stories I Tell My Husband*.) The real surprise, though, is that narration and story play a considerable role in the dynamics of the living. Few people are aware that narration, or even stories, are exchanged at all levels of life (among cells, for example, or among neurons). It is from the embodied narration of life that we get to understand life as a narration, and further generalize to our explanations of reality.

Thesis 1: *Narration is a record of change.*

Change characteristic of the living (from conception to birth, maturity, and death), and change of the physical world (mountains change, stones are "polished" by wind and water, oceans undergo cycles of ebb and flow, etc.) can be recorded. Depending upon the resolution (how fine the grain of our distinctions) of our observations, the various narratives of change constitute a body of knowledge on whose basis science advances and technology is produced. In this sense, narrations are information about change over intervals. Given the complexity of reality, the information is always incomplete (we shall return to this idea). Moreover, the information is not associated with meaning. It only reports on changes, not on the context.

Thesis 2: *Narrations are representations of change.*

Without entering into details, let us take note of the fact that objects $\{o_1, o_2, \ldots\}$, natural or man-made, processes $\{p_1, p_2 \ldots\}$, natural or artificial, attributes $\{a_1, a_2, \ldots\}$, of objects or processes can be described in many ways. They can be named (labeled, as the terminology of cognitive science suggests), measured, depicted in drawings, photographed, videotaped, filmed, turned into sounds, animations, etc. Words can be used (and made up if necessary) to explain what they are. These are all substitutes for something else, i.e., *representations*. Even when the real thing (object, process, attribute) is no longer within our reach, no longer actually present, we deal with its representation as it stands for the real thing. Each representation is partial. To capture everything that defines objects, processes, and attributes as they change in time is impossible, if for no other reason than because time is open to infinity.

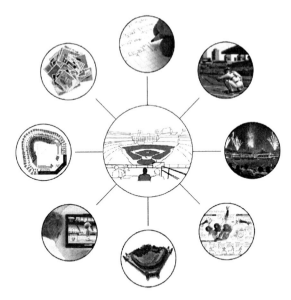

Figure 2: Representations. The aggregate of all representations cannot capture the holistic condition of the reality represented. All representations are subject dependent. All representations are partial.

Narration is a representation corresponding to the perception of reality along the time continuum. The structure of language corresponds to the same perception. It is sequential. The sequentiality of narration corresponds to an understanding of time as a sequence of durations (between successive states of the narrated change).

Interpretation of the narration means no more or less than the attempt to re-constitute the represented from the representation. Succeeding events and their representation are, of course, not the same. Therefore, the "reconstitution" of reality from the representation is not so simple as remaking an image in a puzzle. A person's picture is a representation; the "remaking" of the person is always partial: memories of how the person behaved, moved around, spoke, are part of the interpretation. Reconstitution of the represented from a time series (a scientific method currently in use) can acknowledge the time sequence, confirming it, or challenging it. Indeed, the sequence "Queen dies, King dies after" can easily lead to a story: Queen dies because the King was unfaithful; King dies because Queen poisoned him (or had someone do it), or cursed him. In the story, information is associated with meaning (corresponding to the context). Stories often challenge the sequence: first, second, third, etc. are sometimes reshuffled in the story (third becomes first, or second, etc.). The clock that stopped when Feynman's wife died can easily lead to a story in which the clock stops (first), the sick patient notices it (second) and takes it to mean "My time is up!" (third), and succumbs to death. When I wrote "takes it to mean," I suggested the process of associating information and meaning. The clock of narrations cannot be arbitrarily reset; the clock of stories is independent of the narration clock.

Information and meaning

Thesis 3: *Stories are interpretations of narrations.*

The most convenient explanation of this thesis is that through stories, information is associated with meaning (Nadin 2011). The information regarding the falling apple (or the falling of anything: stones, meteorites, individuals, etc.) reveals the meaning of the physical laws, in particular the law of gravity. But it can, as well, associate the narrative to a story different in its condition from the one expressed in the theory of gravity: poetic, dramatic, religious, metaphysical. Kings fall from power, leaves float in the wind (slow falling), the fall of Rome marked the beginning of the "Dark Ages" (whose meaning is disputed by many); people who fall on account of faith lost need help to get up and get on with life; fallen angels come to earth to redeem themselves; and so on. Some are subject to confirmation through experiment; others, being unique, are not. Recall once again Feynman and the clock that stopped at the time recorded on his wife's death certificate. The narration prompted the physicist, a known atheist, to produce a scientific story: elimination of mystery, poetry, religion, etc. But similar narrations – the clock that stops exactly with the last breath of a dear person, or of some celebrity – populate culture and foster storytelling in many variations. Feynman was entirely given to the story we call *determinism*: there is a cause (e.g., a part of the clock's mechanism fails) and a subsequent effect (e.g., the clock stops) or effects, the meaning of which is expressed in scientific laws. Fighting his emotions – he was, to repeat, very much in love with his wife, as we know from his narration, his autobiography (1985) – Feynman recalled fixing that particular clock more than once. It was not in good shape, therefore it was possible that the nurse, who had to record the time of death, took the clock in her hands, checked the time, returned it to its place, disturbing the fragile mechanism. There is no way to repeat the experiment. This was not a reproducible measurement. Time is not reversible (except in equations, even those describing deterministic processes).

When clocks are more than clocks

What does all this have to do with innovation? The question is justified not only because we are focused on innovation. Imagine, for the sake of argument, a digital clock: no moving parts, nothing to get loose, not even the battery or some contacts. Imagine even a monitor connected to the atomic clock[1]. There is no reason to speculate on Feynman's take if such an interval measuring device had outputted a frozen time identical to that of his wife's death (automatically registered by the various monitoring instruments common to a hospital's intensive care unit). The narration would be more detailed, of course; and the meanings to be associated with the information embodied in the narration would also be different. What changed? Of course, innovation "refreshed," "renewed" the acquisition of information making up the record of events. This, in turn, changed the details of the narration and thus its condition: *from a relatively loose record* (mechanical clocks are not necessarily very precise, and are also difficult to calibrate) *to a tight, integrated record of a higher degree of precision.* We realize that a different narration, which means a different representation, is conducive to a different interpretation; better yet, to a plurality of interpretations. But we also realize that the speed of time plays an important role.

Thesis 4: *The clock of narration and the clock of interpretation are different.*

The clock of narration corresponds to the rhythm of events in the physical world. The clock of interpretation projects into the physical world rhythms characteristic of the change in the living, in particular, rhythms associated with interpretation. When we react to something, the reaction time affects performance. When we imagine things in the future, we have the convenience of controlling the rhythm of time. Indeed, as events unfold in time, the gravity-based machine that measures the interval corresponding to the movement of celestial bodies serves as a reference. This is the meaning of the information delivered by clocks. The living is affected by intervals in the environment of existence; but the living also introduces its own rhythms into reality. Saccadic movements, the foundation of sight, have a rhythm different from the heartbeat and neuronal connections. Birds in flight or the slow fall of leaves are other examples of particular time scales; the heartbeat of animals is extremely varied.

---

[1]   An atomic clock uses an electronic transition frequency in the microwave, optical, or ultraviolet region of the electromagnetic spectrum of atoms as a frequency standard for its timekeeping element.

Time characteristic of life is not reducible to intervals. As a matter of fact, there is no proof that time scales uniformly. In other words, time at universe scale, where we refer to phenomena that happened way in the past (even millions of years ago), and time at the nanoscale, where we refer to very fast interactions, might be different in more ways than order of magnitude. The narration of phenomena from the remote past – let's say star explosions – and the narration of current phenomena of extreme dynamics (such as fermentative metabolism, and earthquakes) are different to the extent that they appear to us as associated with different realities (Lara *et al.* 2009). Being a record of change, each narration is a representation of the dynamics of reality. Each interpretation of a narration is a story: the meaning we associate with the information on record. A faster clock, such as the clock of interpretations, is what it takes to evaluate the possible consequences of the phenomena on record in the narration. In other words, the future itself is nothing but the outcome of a faster clock. As a virtual reality, this future depends on the rate of change expressed by the clock. We refer to possible futures – plural! – because we can build clocks with various speeds: from very slow to extremely fast. Each such clock allows us to investigate the future *not as a probability*, but *as possibilities* (often negating probabilities). This is where innovation takes place.

If the information in the narration is continuously subjected to interpretations from the future, facilitated by the faster clock, its meaning becomes *anticipation*. The Haicheng, China earthquake (February 4, 1975) was anticipated on account of massive human observation of animal behavior. As a consequence, the impact of the earthquake – a physical phenomenon still impossible to avoid –was mitigated by preparatory measures: large segments of the population were evacuated; electricity was interrupted in advance, in order to avoid accidents, water delivery was stopped. As good as this sounds, it gives only a partial description of the story. Anticipatory processes are non-deterministic. The Sichuan, China earthquake (May 12, 2008) was not predicted, although observations (like those in Haicheng) were accumulated. The narration that was meaningfully interpreted in 1975 was not adequate some 30 years later, and the number of victims (not to mention the damage) was huge. If you visit NASA's website (NASA Science, Science News), you can read about new methods for "predicting" earthquakes. One is based on detecting temperature variations of the Earth's surface—which was one among the variables observed in China. The innovation associated with the narrative observed does not automatically become successful. Remember: the goal is to transform the uniqueness of the narration (the idiographic) into laws (nomothetic) generalizing the interpretation. There is no guarantee that this goal can always be met, because the non-deterministic and the deterministic are different in nature. Statistics allow for some generalization, but they do not replace the real.

Fast or slow, clocks are deterministic. They are machines. Interpretations, involving faster clocks, pertain to a reality that is no longer the reality of the phenomena represented by the narration, but of interpretation processes. At the low end of the living – simple forms of life, no cognition, but always a memory substratum – the output of the interpretation process is patterned behavior (the monocell is phototropic; it anticipates the consequences of exposure to light, even if it has no awareness). At the high end, the human being is defined by complexity across its various scales of existence (from the cell level to the whole that defines a unique profile). Narrations are transmitted among cells. These are records of actions validated from one level to another.

New ways of thinking

Interpretations can vary along the continuum from coherent to incoherent. A second example, in addition to that of the earthquakes in China, should help in explaining the idea I am trying to articulate. My intention is to suggest that obsession with a reductionist cause-and-effect course of action, which generalizes expectations associated with the laws of physics (sometimes involving statistics), has to be transcended. We'd better start thinking about alternatives.

The cell is the constitutive "particle" of the living. Cells continuously exchange information. More precisely, they exchange meaningful information, i.e., narrations. Based on this example, which involves many components (physical, chemical, and biological in nature), life unfolds from its inception to death. I learned from an eminent scholar in molecular biology (Professor Harry Rubin, Emeritus, University of California – Berkeley) that cells undergo their own cycle of renewal. By now, this knowledge is relatively unquestioned (see Orford & Scadden 2008 as only one example). Moreover, cancerous cells are almost permanently present in the organism. Scientists have tried very hard to discover the circumstances under which these cells multiply and thus lead to the condition called cancer (of which there are so many variations). This condition has a simple narrative: the mechanical growth of cancerous cells that in the final analysis exhaust life resources. Given the narration, that in the past almost always ended in death, various innovations – e.g., surgery, radiation, alternative healing methods, drug-based treatments—were advanced. Physicians specialized in the domain (oncology); clinics have been built; everyone hopes to find the miracle cure (and get the Nobel Prize). The most prominent innovations are the attempts at surgical removal of the cancerous growth, medication to halt proliferation, establishing a "firewall" (where laser treatment comes into the picture) for containment. All these methods are based on the deterministic model of cause-and-effect associated with grueling chemotherapy (radioactivity comes into play again), itself a major innovation that has helped save many lives. Albeit, no cure for cancer has been discovered or invented. Rubin realized that the question to be asked is not "How do we get rid of something as organic as life itself, without getting rid of life at the same time?" His data, collected over many decades, show that as long as healthy cells surrounding cancerous cells keep the latter in check, no cancer develops. My own hypothesis is that stimulating anticipatory capabilities, characteristic of the living, is probably the answer. Instead of dwelling on the innovation expressed in pills and surgery, let us examine the narration exchanged by cells, and identify under which circumstances healthy cells no longer recognize in advance the dangers associated with the unchecked proliferation of cancerous cells.

Let me explain the alternative thinking I suggest. The narration that leads to cancer is part of the larger narration called *life*. Cells exchange narrations relevant to their continuous reproduction. They interpret narrations received. When the interpretation shifts, their own functioning is affected. The narration becomes the story we call cancer. In terms of anticipation, the question relevant to the cancer story is the following: When and why does the anticipatory function of healthy cells diminish? This, of course, brings the immune system to mind. For those focused on innovation, we know that laser surgery replaced the scalpel. In our days, computer-assisted surgery removes surgeons from the position of total control (and the expected artistry) they once had. Their new role is to monitor and interpret the "narration" of a very precise action that humans cannot perform (degrees of precision in the range not afforded by the human eye, and even less by the hand).

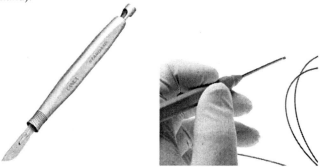

Figure 3: From the scalpel to the bendable laser scalpel

Can machines innovate?

The question could have taken a more provocative form: "Can machines generate narrations?" Followed, unavoidably, by the more drastic question: "Can machines tell stories?" As a matter of fact, some of the fiction sold at airports and bus stations is written by programs. Machines are very good at permutations: take a narration and produce similes. Machine-produced books are variations on a theme within a given structure. It costs less to generate this kind of "fast book" (similar to the technology of fast food production) on a computer than to employ a scribe. (In the past, scribes did exactly the same thing, paid close to nothing in the monasteries where they lived.)

More often than not, on various networks, we exchange messages with artificial intelligence (AI) agents. In search of a wife or husband ("life partner," as the current formula goes), a person searches through matchmaking e-businesses (advertising their services all over the world), and follows the prescribed path. Matchmaking is essentially an exchange of narrations: $life_1$, $life_2$, $life_3$, …$life_i$. Human nature is such that individuals tend to put themselves in a better light. Matchmakers of the past took narrations entrusted to them and made them more enticing (the proposed match is younger, richer, more attractive). Today, a seeking man or woman can end up exchanging narrations with AI procedures, under the assumption that he/she is in touch with other human beings. Automatically, misrepresentations (age, weight, height, earnings) are weighted and a second narration, parallel to the fictitious profile, is automatically generated. Matching becomes an issue of algorithms and procedures. When all is "digitally" ripe, the selection for the man seeking a match, or for the woman seeking life companionship, is made available for interpretation. Real men and women and virtual characters, a mixture that the receiver is not aware of, test each other. Here is where each makes his or her story, by opening a dialog, exchanging information, chatting. More and more possibilities of remote interaction are becoming available in the Web 2.0 world. The innovation of matchmaking – a serious business worth billions of dollars – is the result of many narrations, and even more stories, that have had good and less than good outcomes. Even some of the people involved in the innovation – that is, fully aware of some of the deterministic mechanisms at work – have made their choice in the space of virtual relations (Paumgarten 2011).

Of course, this in itself does not answer the question of automated innovation, not to say automated narration and storytelling. We have seen that the clock of narration corresponds to the rhythm at which objects, processes, and attributes change. An object o_1 (Peter, 38 years old, divorced, father of three, undergoing treatment for alcoholism) becomes o_2 (still Peter, but now 35, single, likes to jog) over a certain interval. For the matchmaking, this change is consequential. The difference in the condition of the two (difference o_1, o_2) is indicative of the depth of change. The AI procedure infers from all the data, true or false, submitted by Peter (or whoever claims to be Peter) to a more realistic narration. It shares this processed narration with candidates who, according to the matchmaking algorithm(s), are deemed appropriate. In simple terms: a machine (the aggregate of procedures and programs) extracts knowledge from the narrations and evaluates the probability of a match.

On the conceptual level, we deal with probable changes of objects, processes, and attributes. A process p_1 becomes the new process p_2 over a certain interval. (Even processes age. Some are preprogrammed to "die" at a certain time; others come to life at a predefined time. The various bots that make our life miserable behave like this.) Attributes A $\{a_1, a_2, a_3, ...\}$ are also expressive of change: changes in skin color, for example, can be interpreted as symptoms by qualified physicians. When everything changes, the narration becomes complicated.

Narrations representing change in the physical world can never be more complicated than the processes for which they stand as a record. Complex systems, such as the human being, or nature as a whole, undergo change at many levels. The record of change is indicative of the complexity of the system, but also of how complex the changes are. The narration of high fever—associated with a cold or the flu – represents some aspects of the functioning of the human thermostat, but also much more than that. The physician always wants to know when the fever started, for how long it has lasted, and if the patients, associates it with something in particular (diet, stress, over-exertion, exposure, unsanitary habits, etc.). Ideally, if he could obtain a continuous record, the physician would be able to make more than the usual reductionist determination: infection, inflammation, cold, influenza, or similar. In complex systems, variables are unfathomably related.

We cannot ignore the fact that all narrations exchanged within the organism are autonomic. Cells do not have secretaries to take note of how the smallest variations in the environment translate into changes that require the finest tuning imaginable. Moreover, there is a lot of anticipation that affects the process. Cognitive science made us aware of the fact that seeing – which we take for granted as long as it is in order – is the result of anticipations that allow us to "ignore" a lot of what makes the world visible. If we could process all the richness of the visual universe, the "price we would pay," i.e., lower performance, would make it impossible to adapt to changing environments. "The brain is futural" (Morton 2011). The observation continues: A lot of memory is proleptic. (Kant used the word *proleptic* to describe anticipation. In other words, memories are used not to dredge through the past but to anticipate. Bill Benzon (in a private e-mail conversation, September 4, 2011)[2] completed the thought: You move through the world. Right? What you see will change as a function of your movement. Vision is computationally expensive. The visual system is primed to anticipate changes in visual input attributable to our own motion.

This is where the question of the innovation machine falls into place. The living "knows" a lot about the world even without having experienced it. Genetic information is continuously transmitted; and there is interaction, in particular the interaction of minds (Nadin 1991). Our minds generate a lot of information – mainly as possibility scenarios. Can machines emulate this non-deterministic functioning? If we expand the understanding of machines so as to integrate the living, the answer is easy to give. Of course, integration of the living and the non-living is not trivial. There are no narrations in the "life" of a stone, in the "life" of water (running or still), of fog, of mountains. This has to be explained. The life of the stone – a metaphor, of course – is the change of the stone over time. However, stones are not born and don't die. They are transformed by the elements (wind, heat, water, etc.), i.e., through physical processes. In this transformation, there is no narration from a stone's atom or molecule to another. Energy exchange is all there is. The same holds true for mountains, water, air, etc. But there is the narration that the living generates of events related to how stones, water, fog, and mountains change over time. If a machine could report on change in the world, it could as well generate narrations. There are observation stations (on the moon, at the North Pole, in Antarctica, on California's fault lines) that generate records of change made of large streams of data. And there are machines that process such data records based on instructions reflecting our understanding of phenomena. They generate information from the data. Eventually, they issue warnings (based on previously acquired knowledge).

---

[2] "Given that our eyes move as we move, it follows that the visual world will change in a way that is precisely matched to our path of motion. As we move straight ahead small distant objects will become larger and larger, thereby taking up more and more of our visual field, until they reach their maximum apparent size and then disappear off the margin of the visual field.

Similarly, if we move our head to the right, say, to track a running horse, stationary objects will move to the left in the visual field while the horse itself will be relatively stable in the center. Since organizing a sharp visual image takes precious fractions of a second, the brain primes the visual system for these movements by sending preafferent signals anticipating the visual effects of our movement (Freeman 1999a, 1999b, 2000; cf. Gibson 1979, 206 ff., 227 ff.)."

What kind of narrations do machines generate?

We have already seen that narrations are time records of change. However, change can as well be the outcome of deterministic processes (the narration associated with gravity explains falling down) or non-deterministic processes (the triggering of cancer cell growth). Given their different condition, it is justified to examine whether machines can generate narrations of both types of change.

Thesis 5: *Machines can narrate deterministic processes.*

Enough has been written about the "9/11" narration of the terrorist acts to make a rehash of the tragic events unnecessary. (The Japanese *kamikaze* of WWII were precursors to the same narration of suicidal acts of destruction.) The aggregate of records of flights, real-time video, random taping, photographs, cell phone calls, and much more actually make up the narration. Those who plotted the criminal act designed it for maximum impact not only in terms of destruction and loss of human life, but also in terms of media impact. This narration has been analyzed to a high level of detail by official commissions and various agencies (dealing with emergency response, construction codes, fire extinguishing, medical care, trauma handling, and so many other related aspects). A huge effort was undertaken from the perspective of avoiding any future terrorist incident (small or large scale). These are all interpretations, that is, stories in which the clock of real-time events is superseded by the "story clock," which is a collection of clocks (some faster than the others).

The reason I bring up this example is because of another story with one outcome as its goal: to change the narration. This is the story of the *Truthers*, who hijacked the narration and keep trying to rewrite it. (There are "truthers" for almost everything that ever happened.) Please take note of the following: the record of an event, the description of an event, and an event's interpretation can remain close or can differ in an extreme manner. The basis for the infinite interpretation is the lack of correspondence between the clock of events and the clock of the story. Within the organism, it is not unusual that narrations are misinterpreted. (High fever is but one example.) However, the coherence of life makes the requirement of establishing a connection between the record (narration) and its interpretation necessary. Persons with six fingers (or with seven toes), or born with missing parts exemplify what happens when the record is faulty, or interpretations go wild. Pistorius, the "Blade Runner" was born with congenital absence of the fibula. This is the narration. When he was eleven months old, his legs were amputated half way between his knees and ankles. This is the interpreted narration: the absence of the fibula made the amputation necessary. The artificial limbs (carbon fiber, Flexfoot, etc.) are the innovation. The meaning is not arbitrary. The Truthers are deniers of the narration, or given to speculative plot interpretation. For whatever reason – and there are theories (i.e., stories) about such reasons – they rewrite the information in order to match the meaning they decide the event should have. Mythomaniacs of all kind populate the world and exercise their right to be heard. There is no innovation to be expected from such narrations; it is always fruitless (even if at times they attract funds from legitimate or illegitimate sources).

If misinterpretation had no practical consequences, the effort to address the issue would be, at best, of academic relevance (or irrelevance). But it all leads to our focus on innovation. The fact that airplanes, meant to transport human beings, were given the function of rockets to hit buildings brings up the need for prevention. So far, prevention translates into expensive (and often absurd) checking of who will have access to a flight (and the politics associated with prevention). Passengers who do not appear trustworthy (whatever that means) are kept at bay or at least discouraged from seeking a place on airplanes. (And everyone else is required to give up convenience, and sometimes more, for the sake of security.) Of course, nobody wants to have suicidal criminals on airplanes – neither for flying into buildings nor for blowing up the plane in mid-air. So much harm is possible, in so many forms (even plastic knives, which replaced metal ones from the coach cabins, can be used in a criminal manner). The required innovation has not yet been considered (to the best of my knowledge): a program that would not allow an airplane to become a weapon[3].

At this juncture, let's return to Schumpeter and the "creative disruption" model that, in his view, encourages the entrepreneur to be innovative. It sounds more than cynical to consider the events of 9/11 as a creative disruption. But I would be less than candid if I were not to see in the broad picture a narrative quite consonant with that of capitalism. For that matter, wars are often interpreted as "engines" of change. (And there are some people who consider that wars play a "creative" role: just think about drones, new weaponry, new strategies, new policies, etc.) So much science and technology are involved, along with so many individuals; so much time resetting takes place. The destruction caused by wars – and nobody should rush to justify them – is followed by what capitalism

---

[3]   Nadin, Mihai, in an e-mail (March 20, 2003) to DARPA, stated: "If the possible action description is represented in a possibility/probability database, it becomes a realistic expectation that neural networks could model all kinds of possible events and attract attention to conditions under which these could take place. Moreover, we could add to the specifications of an airplane, such as piloting program with built-in limitations on certain operations that would prevent planes from flying into vertical structures or taking the plane to the nearest airport if the pilot is disabled.

likes most: new needs, new markets, increased consumption. The narration of war and innovation is probably stronger than that of providing aid to people in need of food, medicine, shelter, and clothing.

Through its condition as a record, narration is an-ethical, that is, free of ethics. Stories are testimonials to the ethics of interpretation. They embody values characteristic of those who tell them. Innovation, as a change in the record that constitutes the narration, is not unlike the story synchronized to the ethics of innovators. The nuclear battery of 40 years ago, the Chernobyl disaster, and the tragedy of an earthquake and a tsunami that destroyed a large section of Japan have in common not the technical innovation (or lack thereof), but an ethics of compromise that overwrites respect for the human being. Anticipation, as a bridge between the an-ethical narration and the inevitable ethical condition (or lack of it) of every innovation, is expressed in what are called consequences of our ideas and acts (Bode 2002).

The innovation machine

For those connected to the Internet (and who is not?), the experience of "creative destruction" and the associated disruptions" is a daily event. As a matter of fact, everyone using digital machines, i.e., programs, has the same experience. Updates come in as we watch a movie (the benefits of online cinema), calculate our taxes, play a game. Usually, so we are told, performance will improve and, most important, since we are subjected to more threats, risks related to security are addressed. Imagine what would happen if electricity distribution or water delivery, not to say sewage treatment, would be updated in "real time" at the frequency at which browsers, readers, players, and cell phone apps are updated. The former are "hard" machines: electricity is distributed within large networks involving high voltage lines, transformers, circuit breakers; in regard to water and sewage, we see what happens when pipes break or flow control mechanisms (valves) need to be repaired. There is literally a mess. Our machines are more and more "soft" and, presumably, intelligent. The fact that each update involves programming (probably done in India and tested in China) does not fully account for the innovation it represents. As a matter of fact, there is no living supervisor who selects you, or someone else, as the receiver of the "creative destruction", i.e. disruption message. Programs check on programs, and everyone checks on all of us (while we debate privacy and related issues characteristic of the past), and the market is kept alive and active.

Updates are usually free (actually, paid for in advance when we acquire the product). But the appearance is misleading. The innovation cycle of the digital age is shorter and shorter. This is part of the unavoidable narrative of the post-industrial age. Within this model, human-based innovation becomes too expensive. Thus, for every aspect of innovation that can be automated, machines are conceived that, like the matchmaking procedures, generate "matches" to the most recent hacker attacks, to "phishing" expeditions, to hijacked browsers, to all the bots supposed to take over our machines and work in the background for the benefit of those who seek instant gratification for their "creative" talents.

Thesis 6: *An innovation machine has at least two clocks.*

An innovation machine consists of a narration (subject to renewal) – objects, processes, attributes – generated in real time (subject to the clock C_n), and a model of itself unfolding in faster than real time (subject to the clock C_m).

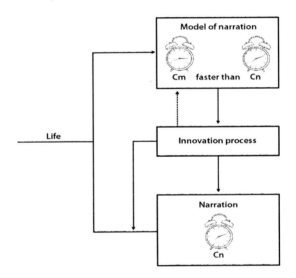

Figure 4: An innovation machine. Model of itself unfolding in faster than real time. The clocks C_n and C_m correspond to the time of narration and to the time of the model.

Narration: Pistorius is born with congenital absence of the fibula – real time.

Model: In the absence of the fibula, legs are amputated – real time.

Innovation: Given the narration, the model (interpretation, i.e., story), a blade-based replacement of legs and feet is desired (the Ossur product) – faster than the real time of the narration.

To further explain, let's take a look at the narration we can call the toaster: To keep bread fresh for a longer time, exposing it to fire (heat) proves useful. Over time, many attempts have been made to do exactly that: bread slices are attached to a simple contrivance and brought close to fire. As electricity became available, heated elements proved more appropriate to the goal. The narration changed: to obtain the feeling of fresh bread (warm from the oven), to obtain the taste of crisp crust; to come up with new dishes. All these narrations are associated with innovations. The real-time process is toasting (at various intensities). The faster-than-real-time is the generation of new expectations.

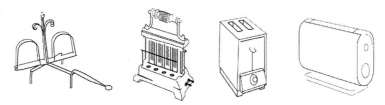

Figure 5: From the fireplace toaster to the Porsche toaster: changed narration, changed design.

The designer's mind, addressing new expectations, works faster than the toaster. The toaster's clock corresponds to the physical process: introduce the slice of bread, adjust to the desired degree of toasting (light, medium, dark), press down the handle. The clock of the design process corresponds to imaging, associations, formulating alternatives, etc. For digital products, the model of the process and the model of the machine itself are also digital. The two clocks are related. The faster the prediction component, the higher the possibility of generating alternative ideas. Therefore, an innovation machine needs an evaluation procedure.

One clock keeps track of the machine's output – let's say word processing, computer graphics, database, e-mail, among other examples. Under the aegis of this clock, performance is recorded as a narration. Interference in the functioning – such as accidental power supply failure, hardware errors; or intentional interference from outside, intelligent agents, hackers, etc. – becomes part of the narration. In order to evaluate the output, the machine needs a projection, into the future, of what it should actually be (desired performance). To compare the real output to an ideal output implies that the second clock has to be also the clock of the process evaluation. In all fairness, updates for security improvement reasons are not the only innovations disseminated in real life over the networks. Quite often, new algorithms are implemented with the aim of optimizing processes. From various parts of the world, better design of processes and improved performance programs found their way to the users. Renewing objects, processes, and attributes in ways that are more possible in our days than in the past accelerates the production cycle. Given the fact that proprietary solutions – embodied in competitive products – have to address the broadest possible market, innovation translates the narrative of higher profits into the creative destructions and associated disruptions it brings about. The model of the niche product – a small section of the market – is less profitable than the model of products for the global economy. This, of course, is part of the narration of a universal means, which the digital is.

In the past, innovation meant renewal of a specific aspect of the narration of human activity. Windshield wipers on automobiles[4] are an example of what innovation meant in respect to the characteristics of a product of wide public interest. The narration develops from "window cleaning" to "intermittent wipers." In contrast to windshield wipers, today's downloads on the computer in charge of a car's functioning represent a different approach: the soft aspects of the car's functioning are affected, this means GPS-based functions, cruise control, monitoring of emissions, etc. Each innovation, whether past or present, juxtaposed two models: reality (of the product) and future (how the product should be altered, modified, renewed in view of higher performance, reliability, security, etc.). The two models were connected through evaluation procedures. Each model had its own clock: real-time functioning vs. desired future functioning. Each evaluation results in new narrations.

A logical question, that goes beyond the scope of this text, is whether an innovation machine can innovate itself. It is rather much the same question as whether machines can generate narrations – and the answer was positive in respect to deterministic change. Furthermore, whether a story machine is possible – and the answer was left open. At our current level of understanding what is needed to interpret narrations and to associate meaning with them, it is rather doubtful that deterministic processes can have non-deterministic outcomes. But science is never a limiting endeavor. There is no science in stating the impossible and declaring No! Therefore, the understanding of anticipation as a bridge between narration and innovation is rather an invitation to cross the bridge and to continue exploring human creativity.

PS: Reviewing this article extended to the day Steve Jobs died. I met him in 1983-1984 – doing work on the user interface for Lisa, a computer well ahead of its time (as was the Xerox Star that inspired it). David Hodge made the contract

---

4   Along the timeline: 1903 (Mary Anderson), 1911 (Gladstone Adams and Whitley Bay), 1919 (Willliam M. Folberth), 1963 (Robert Kearns, intermittent wipers), 1970 (Citroën, rain-sensitive intermittent wipers).

with Apple possible, Thomas Ockerse (my colleague at the Rhode Island School of Design) joined me in the project.

The reason for this note on my interaction with Steve Jobs is connected to the subject of this article. Indeed, the so-called iconic interface, which I treated from a semiotic perspective (Nadin 1988), is a clear illustration of the ideas submitted in this text. During my first encounter with Jobs, I argued that interface is a sign (or supersign). Today I will argue that interface is a narration: the re-creation on the computer screen of the office, an environment familiar to those who would make the computer the most important component of their activity. For this narration to be convincing, representations called *iconic*, i.e., representations based on likeness (cf. Peirce on icons as representations), were used. Moreover, I insisted on the networking capabilities of Lisa – which the subsequent Mac machines unfortunately did not have.

Steve Jobs had his problems with my methodology (and his ways of expressing himself were rather direct). He was impatient, theory did not interest him, he wanted to see results. The same happened years later (1987-1988) when he developed NeXT, a high-end workstation, also ahead of its time (and which I was convinced would be a success). I congratulated him on the innovation, and on accepting my suggestion to involve the renowned designer Paul Rand in developing a *language* for the product. This language could stimulate new narrations. One of the NeXT-based narrations is the world-wide web. Tim Berners-Lee, at CERN, used a NeXT machine to write the first browser – which is yet another narration, superseding the office metaphor. Indeed, narrations have a life of their own; they unfold, like the stories in the 1001 Arabian Nights.

I am not sure that I want to turn to writing down memories, but I did not want to miss the occasion to pay my respects to a person dedicated to innovation. After the two famous Steves (Jobs and Wozniak), garages are no longer just for parking cars.

Acknowledgments

This text is the result of a long process. Many experiments (in the area of human-computer interaction) were carried out: in Rochester, during my William A. Kern Institute Professorship in Communication at the Rochester Institute of Technology; in Wuppertal, within my Computational Design Program; as well as at Stanford University and UC- Berkeley (especially a fuzzy-sets based model of interfaces), at the University of Bremen (during a visiting professorship in the Computer Science Department). More recently, this work continued at the University of Texas at Dallas, with support from antE-Institute for Research in Anticipatory

Systems. I owe a word of gratitude to David Hodge, Richard Zakia, Thomas Ockerse, Leif Almendinger, Jeffrey Nickerson, Frieder Nake, and Lutz Dickmann (my assistant at UT Bremen and by a now a PhD candidate in the New Media Program). Kyle Fagan, a student of mine in the Story Lab graduate class at ATEC/UTD, earned not only a good grade but also my respect for his contributions to that class. Finally, Jason Jacobs comes to mind as someone who developed a good interface for his project in the *Inventing the Future* class (Fagan was also part of it). Of course, the poet Fred Turner, my distinguished colleague (Founders Professor) deserves a word of thank for discussions concerning narration and time. Cassandra Emswiler is the artist who made my visuals into what the reader sees on these pages. Last but not least is my gratitude to the Hanse Institute for Advanced Research (Delmenhorst, Germany) which is hosting me for the 2011-2012 academic year, and especially to my colleagues Dr. Otthein Herzog and Dr. Christian Freksa, with whom I work on my current research.

References

___ (2006): Victor Wouk and The Great Hybrid Car Cover-up of 1974. See: http://www.hybridcars.com/history/the-great-hybrid-car-cover-up-of-74.html.

Berman, B. (Ed.) (2006): Victor Wouk and The Great Hybrid Car Cover-up of 1974. See: http://www.hybridcars.com/history/the-great-hybrid-car-cover-up-of-74.html.

Bode, O. (2002): Die ITA der Gesellschaft. In: Development and Perspectives, 2, pp. 35-68.

Feynman, R. (1985): Surely You're Joking Mr. Feynman. Adventures of a Curious Character. New York: W.W. Norton.

Freeman, W. J. (1999a): Consciousness, Intentionality and Causality. Reclaiming Cognition. Núñez, R./Freeman, W. J. (Eds.)(1999a): Thoverton: Imprint Academic, pp. 143-172.

Freeman, W. J. (1999b): How Brains Make Up Their Minds. London: Weidenfeld and Nicholson.

Freeman, W. J. (2000): Perception of time and causation through the kinesthesia of intentional action. Cognitive Processing 1, pp. 18-34.

Gelernter, D. H. (1992): Mirror Worlds: or the Day Software Puts the Universe in a Shoebox, 1st ed. New York: Oxford University Press.

Gibson, J.J. (1979): The Ecological Approach to Visual Perception. Boston: Houghton Mifflin.

Krulwich, R. (2011): A deathbed story I would never tell. Krulwich Wonders (an NPR Science blog). Sept. 6, 2011, 11:00 AM.

Lara, A.R./Taymaz-Nikerel, H./Mashego, R.R./Gulik, W.M. van/Heijnen, J.J./Ramirez, O.T./Winden, W.A. van (2009): Fast dynamic response of the fermentative metabolism of Escherichia coli to aerobic and anaerobic glucose pulses. In: Biotechnology and Bioengineering, 104:6, 15 December, pp. 1153-1161.

Morton, T.(2011): Comment of August 30.retrieved on September 20, 2011 from:http://ecologywithoutnature.blogspot.com/2011/08/anticipation.html

Mueller, J. S./Melwani, S./Goncalo, J. A. (2011): The bias against creativity: Why people desire but reject creative ideas. In: Psychological Science. Online: http://www.ilr.cornell.edu/directory/jag97/downloads/creativity_bias_final_8 -31-11.pdf.

Nadin, M. (1988): Interface design: a semiotic paradigm. In: Semiotica 69: 3/4, pp. 269-302. Online: http://www.nadin.ws/wp-content/uploads/2007/ 02/interfac.pdf

Nadin, M. (2003): Can Institutions Anticipate? Technologieabschätzung. Theorie und Praxis (Technology Assessment – Theory and Practice), Nr. 3/4, November, pp. 144-148.

Nadin, M. (2011): Information and Semiotic Processes. The Semiotics of Computation (review article). In: Pearson, C. (guest ed.)/ Brier, S. et al. (eds.) (2011): Cybernetics and Human Knowing. In: A journal of second-order cybernetics, autopoiesis and cyber-semiotics 18 (1-2), pp. 153-175.

Nadin, Mihai (1991): Mind—Anticipation and Chaos. Stuttgart: Belser Verlag. Online: http://www.oikos.org/naminds1.htm.

Orford, K. W./Scadden, D.T. (2008): Deconstructing stem cell self-renewal: genetic insights into cell-cycle regulation. In: Nature Reviews: Genetics 9, February, pp. 115-128. Online: http://www.nature.com/nrg/journal/v9/n2/abs/nrg2269.html.

Paumgarten, N. (2011): Looking for Someone. Sex, love, and loneliness on the Internet. The New Yorker, July 4. Online: http://www.newyorker.com/reporting/2011/07/04/110704fa_fact_paumgarten #ixzz1ZoFocYR7.

Windelband, W. (1915): Geschichte und Naturwissenschaft, Präludien. Aufsätze und Reden zur Philosophie und ihrer Geschichte. Tübingen: J. C. B. Mohr, pp. 136-160. History and Natural Science. Speech of the Rector of the University of Straßburg.

About the Authors

Lutz Becker

Dr. Lutz Becker is Professor of Management and Leadership at Karlshochschule International University, Karlsruhe, Germany, teaching and researching in the areas "strategic leadership", "international management", and "change & innovation". He studied media sciences, marketing and business administration and holds a Doctorate in Economics.

Lutz Becker began his professional career in the marketing department of Wilkinson Sword GmbH. He then spent several years with Philips Corporation, working in consulting, product management, and key account management. He was co-founder and board partner of TradeWheels International S.A., Brussels, as well as co-founder and Managing Director of Norman Data Defense Systems GmbH, a leading European provider of data security solutions and smart card applications. In 1995, the Data and Network Security/eCommerce Panel of the Federal Association for Information and Communications Systems (BVB, today: BITKOM) was founded, of which he was Chairman until 2000. In addition, he was a member of the German Internet Media Council ("Internet Medienrat") for several years.

Lutz Becker has published and edited numerous books and magazine articles on technology and management issues. He has been appointed member of the advisory boards of several organizations, including Bergische Institut for Product Development and Innovation Management and Symposion Publishing GmbH, a leading publisher of books and digital media in the field of management and technology.

Suleika Bort

Dr. Suleika Bort is an Assistant Professor of Strategic and International Management at Mannheim University, Germany. Suleika Bort has studied Business Administration in Mannheim, Germany and the United States. She holds a doctoral degree in Organizational Behavior from Mannheim University. Suleika

Bort has already spent some time as a Visiting Scholar at the Scandinavian Consortium for Organizational Research (SCANCOR) at Stanford University, United States and at Kellogg School of Management, Northwestern University, United States. Her current research focuses on social networks and the evolution of social network and institutions. Her work on the diffusion of management concepts has been published in journals including British Journal of Management, Organization Studies and Schmalenbach Business Review.

Leszek Cichobłaziński

Dr. Leszek Cichobłaziński is an Assistant Professor of Human Resources Management and Negotiation at the Management Faculty of the Czestochowa University of Technology, Częstochowa, Poland. His main scholarly interests are in human resources management, motivation in management, the recruitment and selection of personnel, and the evaluation of personnel. His research focuses on the anthropology of organization, organizational semiotics, mediation in collective bargaining as well as on organizational conflict management.

The educational background of Cichobłaziński is in sociology (he has a Degree in Sociology from the Jagiellonian University/Kraków); he holds a Doctorate in Liberal Arts. He has worked as Assistant Professor in the Speech Department at Southern Illinois University, USA, and as a visiting lecturer at the Economics Faculty of Perugia University, Italy.

Leszek Cichobłaziński is a practicing mediator in collective disputes on the list of the Polish Ministry of Work and Social Policy. He is also a member of the International Communicology Institute.

Leszek Cichobłaziński is an author and co-author of numerous scientific papers and books inter alia; his last two books are entitled "People and the Value of an Organization" and "The Role of Capital in Knowledge Based Management", published in 2011.

Barbara Czarniawska

Barbara Czarniawska is Professor of Management Studies at the GRI, School of Business, Economics and Law at the University of Gothenburg, Sweden, as well as Doctor honoris causa at the Stockholm School of Economics, Copenhagen Business School and Helsinki School of Economics. She is a member of the Swedish Royal Academy of Sciences, the Swedish Royal Engineering Academy, the Royal Society of Art and Sciences in Gothenburg and Societas Scientiarum

Finnica. Barbara Czarniawska takes a feminist and constructionist perspective on organization, recently exploring the connections between popular culture, the practice of management, and the organization of news production. She is interested in methodology, especially in techniques of fieldwork and the application of narratology to organization studies.

She writes in Polish, English, Swedish; and Italian; her texts have been translated into Arabic, Chinese, French, Danish, German, and Russian. Recent books in English are: "A Tale of Three Cities" (2002), "Narratives in Social Science Research" (2004), "Actor-Network Theory and Organizing" (edited with Tor Hernes, 2005), "Global Ideas" (edited with Guje Sevón, 2005), "Management Education and Humanities" (edited with Pasquale Gagliardi, 2006), "Shadowing and Other Techniques of Doing Fieldwork in Modern Societies" (2007), "A Theory of Organizing" (2008), and "Organizing in the Face of Risk and Threat" (ed., 2009).

Roland Hergert

Roland Hergert works at the Centre for Environment and Sustainability Research at the University of Oldenburg. He studied business economics in Göttingen, Madrid, and Oldenburg and received his PhD for investigating organizations' perception of sustainability issues and their relevance for business purposes at the University of Oldenburg in collaboration with Volkswagen.

Currently he is developing and coordinating study programmes on the topic of environment and sustainability at the University of Oldenburg. His research focus is on investigating how to integrate environmental and sustainability issues at universities and how to foster processes of transdisciplinary collaboration between scientific disciplines and society.

Umair Khalid Khan

Umair Khalid Khan is Doctoral student at SKEMA Business School, Sophia Antipolis, France, and is associated with the "Knowledge Technology and Organization" (KTO) research group. His main areas of research are regional clusters, management of technology, and innovation and knowledge management.

He holds a Master's degree in Industrial Engineering from the University of Boras, Sweden, and prior to joining SKEMA Business School, he taught innovation, knowledge and change management at the University of Boras, Sweden.

Alfred Kieser

Alfred Kieser is Professor Emeritus of Organizational Behavior at Mannheim University, Mannheim, Germany, and Professor of Management Theory at Zeppelin University, Friedrichshafen, Germany. His research interests include the history of organization, organizational evolution, cross-cultural comparisons of organizations, management fashions, consulting, and organizational learning. He has published articles in journals such as *Administration Science Quarterly, Journal of Management Inquiry, Journal of Management Studies, Organization Science, Organization, Research Policy, Industrial and Corporate Change*, as well as in German journals. He has received honorary Doctoral degrees from the University of Munich and Corvinus University, Budapest, and he is a member of the Heidelberg Academy of Sciences.

Thomas Klug

Thomas Klug is founder and managing partner of the international management consultancy network cogitamus in Germany. cogitamus supports medium-sized and large corporations in the areas of innovation, transformation, leadership, and organization. The focus of cogitamus consultants is largely on dialog with the client, rather than pushing solutions in order to gain better acceptance and results during a more sustainable implementation phase.

Thomas Klug has over 20 years of experience as a consultant (Kienbaum, PA Consulting Group) and as leading manager in the automotive sector (Continental) in Europe, South Africa, and the US. He has worked in diverse functional capacities and as general manager of several international operational units.

He obtained an MBA from the University of Muenster, Germany, and has gained additional competences in change management, learning organizations, and dialog.

Thomas Klug is co-editor of the leadership book "Führung neu verorten – Perspektiven für Unternehmenslenker im 21. Jahrhundert" (Gabler, 2007) (= 'Re-positioning of leadership – perspectives for leaders in the 21st Century'). This book compares leading-edge scientific and managerial approaches in leadership from Europe and the US.

Besides his consultancy work Thomas Klug holds several positions as senior lecturer and researcher at a number of universities/colleges for strategy and international management as well as leadership, learning and change in Germany and Switzerland.

In spite of his classical management career, he sees himself more as an edge walker and non-conventional thinker with a keen instinct for what is possible.

Florian Menz

Florian Menz is Professor of Applied Linguistics and Sociolinguistics at the University of Vienna, Austria. Combining critical discourse analysis with socio-logical systemic approaches, his main research interests include organizational language use, with a focus on business and medical institutions, gender and power-related aspects of interaction, and the interactional representation of pain.

His recent publications are: "Constructing unity and flexibility in uncertain business environments: demands on and challenges for the people inside", in Bylok, Felicijan/ Cichobłaziński, Leszek (eds., 2011), "The Role of Human Capital in Knowledge Based Management", Częstochowa: WWZPCz (pp. 162-171), "'I just can't tell you how much it hurts'. Gender-relevant differences in the description of chest pain", in: Salager-Meyer, Françoise/ Gotti, Maurizio (eds., 2006), "Medical Discourse", Frankfurt: Lang (pp. 135-154, together with Johanna Lalouschek), and "Interruptions, status, and gender in medical interviews: The harder you brake, the longer it takes", in: Discourse & Society 19 (5), 2008: 645-666 (together with Ali Al-Roubaie).

Robb Mitchell

Robb Mitchell is currently a PhD research student at the University of Notting-ham. He was previously based at the University of Southern Denmark where he worked for the SPIRE Centre for Participatory Innovation Research and com-pleted an MSc at the Mads Clausen Institute for Product Innovation. He is also a graduate of the contextual art focused Environmental Art Department at Glasgow School of Art.

He has published research across a range of fields including interaction de-sign, semiotics, design research, computing, educational technology, and organi-zational studies. Successful projects include deploying large-scale mechanical contraptions for provoking cooperation between strangers, a series of collabora-tions with psychologists exploring how personalities can be "swapped" using radio transmitters, extreme interpersonal skills training, facilitating science communication discussion events, and exploring how interactive sculptures and other toolkits can inspire shared sense-making and fresh perspectives on business model and other organizational issues for high-tech industrialists.

Prior to involvement in research, as a curator, producer and event organizer, Robb had co-founding roles in the development of many interdisciplinary creative initiatives including The Chateau, Free Gallery, Machinista Festival of Art & Artificial Intelligence and the Electron Club hack space at the Centre for Contemporary Arts (all in Glasgow). With New Media Scotland he organized the Scottish node of the Upgrade! international network of art & technology gatherings.

Andreas P. Müller

Andreas P. Müller is Dean and Professor at Karlshochschule International University in Karlsruhe, Germany. After a period of five years of entrepreneurial activities in Ecuador, South America, he studied in Mannheim, Germany, where he graduated and finished his Master's degree in Linguistics. While writing his PhD thesis, he held a scholarship from the Institute of German Language (IDS) in Mannheim; his research interest focused on stylistic means in the use of language at the workplace. In his subsequent research activities, his focus moved towards a more anthropological perspective on the conversational interaction of members of organizations. One of his major research projects included comparative analyses of organizational talk in German, Spanish, and French factories. This study was based on participant observation in the factories and on the analysis of previously recorded meetings (published in 2006). At this stage, the intercultural issues of international business came into consideration. In 2006, he joined Karlshochschule International University, as the Head of the Intercultural Management and Communication Program. At the same time he was responsible for the international affairs of Karlshochschule. Among his recent research activities, he seeks a narrative approach towards entrepreneurial innovation, longitudinal research into the acquisition of intercultural competence in order to acquire a deeper understanding of the communicative stylistics in organizational environments. He has published and edited several books and about twenty articles on communication in organizations, the ethnography of organizational talk and the stylistics of verbal interaction at the workplace. His main teaching subjects are intercultural communication, organizational rhetoric, and cross-cultural management.

Michael Müller

Dr. Michael Müller is Professor of Media Analysis and Media Conception at Hochschule der Medien (University of Applied Sciences), Stuttgart. He teaches and researches in the areas of narration, semiotics, communication, and media conception.

Michael Müller studied German literature, philosophy, logics and the theory of science at the University of Munich. He began his professional career as Cultural Manager with Siemens AG and as Editor for on-air-promotion with the German broadcasting company ProSieben/SAT 1. After that, he worked as a consultant and coach for almost twenty years. In 1997 he co-founded the group of consultants "SYSTEM + KOMMUNIKATION" and, together with his partners, he developed a method of storytelling analysis. Since then he has supported companies, organizations, and individuals on the basis of narrative and systemic approaches in the areas of communication and cultural development, reform processes and decision-making.

Michael Müller has published numerous books and articles on the topics of organizational storytelling, semiotics, media, and literature. He is Chairman of the "Institut für narrative Methoden", Heidelberg.

Mihai Nadin

Mihai Nadin's career combines engineering, digital technology, semiotics, cognitive science, and anticipatory systems. He has Doctoral degrees in Electronics and Computer Science and Philosophy, and a Post-Doctoral degree in Logic and the Theory of Science. His book, "Mind – Anticipation and Chaos", sets forth original ideas in cognitive science and education, introducing anticipation to the scientific community. Research in dynamic systems and neuroscience (Stanford University) led him to further elaborate his theory of anticipatory systems. Research at UC–Berkeley led to several articles and the book "Anticipation – The End Is Where We Start From". He established the antÉ – Institute for Research in Anticipatory Systems (2002) as a research and consulting entity (for technical innovation, business, policy development, medical applications, and game-based simulations). It became part of the University of Texas at Dallas (2004), when Dr. Nadin accepted the invitation to become an Ashbel Smith University Professor. His research on the AnticipationScope™ (which he conceived) focuses on capturing anticipatory characteristics of subjects ranging from young athletes to the elderly, with the aim of quantifying significant aspects of human performance. Recent publications include: "Anticipation and Risk – From the inverse problem to reverse computation"; "Play's the Thing. A wager on healthy aging; Anticipation and Dynamics" (which won the publisher's best issue award for 2010). He has recently published an entire issue dedicated to anticipation (*International Journal of General Systems*, 41:1, 2012). In the 2011-2012 academic year, he is pursuing research in anticipatory systems at the Hanse Wissenschaftskolleg. For more information, see www.nadin.ws and www.anteinstitute.org

Anne Reff Pedersen

Anne Reff Pedersen is PhD, Associate Professor at the Department of Organization, Copenhagen Business School. Formerly she was Dean of the Master's in Health Management. Her research focuses on topics in the area of public organizations, health and innovation. She has written several international articles about organizational change and time as well as about identity and coordination in organizations. Her current research project is about health and innovation.

Philippe Rixhon

Philippe Rixhon is the Managing Director of Philippe Rixhon Associates, a research and development company for the performing arts established in 1983. Research includes arts-led arts management, the art of collaboration, copyright in the digital era and evidence-based singing policy making. Developments include music and theatrical productions, a platform for live music, and vibrant arts centres.

He studied philosophy, engineering, management and theatre directing and holds an honorary Doctorate of Arts. Before focusing on the performing arts, Philippe Rixhon spent twenty years managing successful and innovative high-tech projects for major companies in ten countries. He led prestigious teams, and developed groundbreaking systems. With the help of Hewlett-Packard and a grant from the German Ministry of Research and Technology, Philippe Rixhon designed and realised the first complete computer-integrated manufacturing system for mass production, including a rule-based configurator. Later, for Areva and with a grant from the European Commission, he set the fundaments of predictive maintenance and assembled the consortium that delivered it. He has been Vice-President of Zühlke Engineering, the leading Swiss high-tech company, and partner at Accenture, the global provider of management and technology services.

Philippe Rixhon leads collective theatrical creations – playwriting and co-productions – at L'atelier Spectaculaire. Fluent in English, French and German, he publishes and lectures internationally.

Kinuyo Shimizu

Dr. Kinuyo Shimizu is part-time lecturer at Aoyamagakuin Graduate School of Business, Tokyo, teaching "Intercultural Business" and "Presentation Skills".
She studied Intercultural Business and Communication and holds a Doctorate in International Business. She was an adjunct lecturer at Rikkyo University's Language Center for five years.

Stephan Sonnenburg

Dr. Stephan Sonnenburg is professor for creativity and transformative management at the Karlshochschule International University in Karlsruhe, Germany. He is Dean of the Faculty "Management and Performance". Stephan Sonnenburg has broad research interests in the field of creativity, branding and management within which he examines the performative and transformative potential. One of his latest publications together with Sangeeta Singh in the Journal of Interactive Marketing is *Brand Performances in Social Media*.

Hans Sarv

Dr. Hans Sarv was until recently a Senior Professor at the University College of Borås. He previously held a similar position at Linköping University, another Swedish university. He is currently a board member of several organizations, including Volvo Logistics, a subsidiary of the Volvo Group. He also works as a consultant, mainly to Swedish organizations. Originally majoring in business logistics, he now specializes in systemic thinking and systemic methodology as tools to boost innovation capacities in supply chains, health care systems and industrial regions.
After acquiring Master's degrees in Industrial Engineering and Business Economics at Chalmers University of Technology and the Gothenburg Business School, respectively, he took his Licentiate and Doctorate degrees at Chalmers University, both on the Organization of Logistics Systems. He was also a Ford

Foundation Fellow at the Graduate School of Business, Stanford University, for 2 years.

Following a position as Associate Professor at Chalmers University, he had an industrial career as one of the leading directors in the reorganization of the Swedish pharmacy system. He has also worked for the Institute for Future Studies in Sweden. The last 20 years he has combined his consultancy work with teaching and research at Swedish universities. He has authored several Swedish books on the subjects of logistics and change management.

Andreas Zeuch

Dr. Andreas Zeuch is a freelance consultant, trainer, coach, speaker, and author on the topic of "Entrepreneurial Decision Making", "Professional Intuition", and "Effective Decision Culture". He is a leading expert in these matters in Germany. Andreas Zeuch's manner of approaching problems with thoroughly creative concepts as solutions has its firm base in his graduation in music therapy. He obtained his PhD with a dissertation on "Training Professional Intuition", the foundation for his work to date.

His current publication "Feel it! Soviel Intuition verträgt Ihr Unternehmen" has remained among the bestsellers in the category corporate culture on amazon.de since its publication in 2010. Further works also include several books and numerous articles. His activities in new media include his "integral.blog" and the podcast "Abenteuer Intuition" (= 'Adventure Intuition'). In 2011 he co-founded his own publishing company "edition sinnvoll wirtschaften".

CPSIA information can be obtained at www.ICGtesting.com
Printed in the USA
LVOW10s0921060514

384612LV00001B/88/P